100
GREATEST
TRIPS

TRAVEL+
LEISURE

On the deck of
Lapa Rios hotel,
in the Costa Rican
rain forest.

100
GREATEST
TRIPS

SEVENTH EDITION

TRAVEL+
LEISURE
BOOKS

AMERICAN EXPRESS PUBLISHING CORPORATION
NEW YORK

TRAVEL + LEISURE
100 GREATEST TRIPS
SEVENTH EDITION

Editor Jennifer Miranda
Consulting Editors Laura Begley Bloom, Irene Edwards, Peter Jon Lindberg
Art Director Phoebe Flynn Rich
Photo Editor Elizabeth Boyle
Production Associate David Richey
Editorial Assistant Nate Storey
Reporters Kelsi Maree Borland, Gabriella Fuller, Marguerite A. Suozzi
Copy Editors David Gunderson, Mike Iveson, Ed Karam, Sarah Khan, Pablo Morales, Libby Sentz
Researchers Kristina Ensminger, Sebastian Girner, Pearly Huang, Charles Moore, Paola Singer, Rory Tolan

TRAVEL + LEISURE
Editor-in-Chief Nancy Novogrod
Design Director Sandra Garcia
Executive Editor/Content Strategist Jennifer Barr
Managing Editor Laura Teusink
Arts/Research Editor Mario R. Mercado
Copy Chief Kathy Roberson
Photo Editor Whitney Lawson
Production Manager Ayad Sinawi

AMERICAN EXPRESS PUBLISHING CORPORATION
President and Chief Executive Officer Ed Kelly
Chief Marketing Officer and President, Digital Media Mark V. Stanich
CFO, SVP, Corporate Development and Operations Paul B. Francis
VP, General Managers Frank Bland, Keith Strohmeier
VP, Books and Products Marshall Corey
Director, Books Programs Bruce Spanier
Senior Marketing Manager, Branded Books Eric Lucie
Assistant Marketing Manager Stacy Mallis
Director of Fulfillment and Premium Value Philip Black
Manager of Customer Experience and Product Development Betsy Wilson
Director of Finance Thomas Noonan
Associate Business Manager Uma Mahabir
Operations Director Anthony White

Front cover: Nyhavn Canal in Copenhagen, Denmark. Photographed by Marcus Nilsson.

Back cover, from top: Sightseeing at the Duomo, in Milan; the pool at the Ananyana Beach Resort & Spa, on Panglao Island, in the Philippines; steamed spiny lobster at Fatty Crab, in St. John, U.S. Virgin Islands. Photographed by Dave Lauridsen (top), Francisco Guerrero (middle), and Cedric Angeles (bottom).

ISBN 978-1-932624-46-5

Published by American Express Publishing Corporation
1120 Avenue of the Americas
New York, New York 10036

Distributed by Charlesbridge Publishing
85 Main Street, Watertown, Massachusetts 02472

Printed in Canada

A view from
the roof of
the Duomo,
in Milan.

CONTENTS

Opposite: The preferred mode of transportation at c/o The Maidstone, in East Hampton, New York.

An afternoon snack at Harry's Grill, the restaurant in Trieste, Italy's Grand Hotel Duchi d'Aosta.

**KEY TO THE
PRICE ICONS**

HOTELS*
$ Less than $200

$$ $200 to $350

$$$ $350 to $500

$$$$ $500 to $1,000

$$$$$ More than $1,000

RESTAURANTS†
$ Less than $25

$$ $25 to $75

$$$ $75 to $150

$$$$ More than $150

*Starting price for a standard
double at resorts (high season)
and hotels.

†Price for a three-course dinner
for two, excluding drinks.

INTRODUCTION

There are few immutable truths in travel. The world changes as it spins, tossing out our preconceived notions about almost everything around us. However, we at *Travel + Leisure* have a creed, and it is simple: we believe in the power of travel to transform lives and open minds. It not only humanizes and personalizes the remote and foreign; it also teaches us that the authentic, the exotic, and the genuine must be treasured.

In keeping with this sentiment, we bring you the latest installment of *100 Greatest Trips*—our annual compendium of the year's top stories and itineraries, curated by T+L's editors and culled from the thousands of extraordinary destinations we've featured in the magazine and in our five international editions. Organized by continent, country, and region, this seventh edition provides a feast of ideas for every type of journey, along with the expert advice needed to launch you on your way.

Reading the book as a whole brings to light two seemingly opposing trends that continue to hold allure for our readers. The first is that travel is a means of escape from the stress of daily life— no surprise, perhaps, given our hyper-digitized era. These stories include a private-island getaway (the Caribbean's Petit St. Vincent, where you raise a flag to summon staff to your secluded villa); a walk through a centuries-old forest (Japan's Yakushima island, the site of a preternatural landscape of ancient cedars and moss); and even an expedition to the ends of the earth (a luxe trek through the icy wilderness of Antarctica).

The second is that travel is a means not of dropping out but of plugging in—tapping directly into the zeitgeist of a destination of the moment.

To that end, we bring you a report on Brooklyn's bohemian-chic Williamsburg neighborhood; a roundup of the latest resorts in Sri Lanka, which is poised to become the next Indian Ocean hot spot; and a look at the fast-rising skyline of Abu Dhabi, a new cultural hub in the Middle East.

Whichever side of the equation you happen to favor, each entry is rich with the news and insight you've come to expect from *Travel + Leisure* over our more than 40-year history.

As you flip through these pages, thinking about where you might go and imagining yourself there is an appealing diversion. Making your trip a reality is a whole other story. That's why *100 Greatest Trips* functions on a number of levels—as the ultimate armchair-travel read, yes, but also as an invaluable planning tool. Right next to each story, we've noted the resources you need (from hotels and restaurants to what to see and do) to help ease the process. At the back of the book, a directory arranges the stories by category—adventure, arts and culture, shopping, and more—so you can delve deeper into whatever topic suits your mood.

As always, making your travels as interesting and rewarding as they can be is another big component of our mission. We hope this book helps bring the world a little closer to your door.

NANCY NOVOGROD *Editor-in-Chief*

**Opposite:
Strolling along
Ipanema Beach, in
Rio de Janeiro.**

The dining room at Terroni, an Italian restaurant in downtown Toronto.

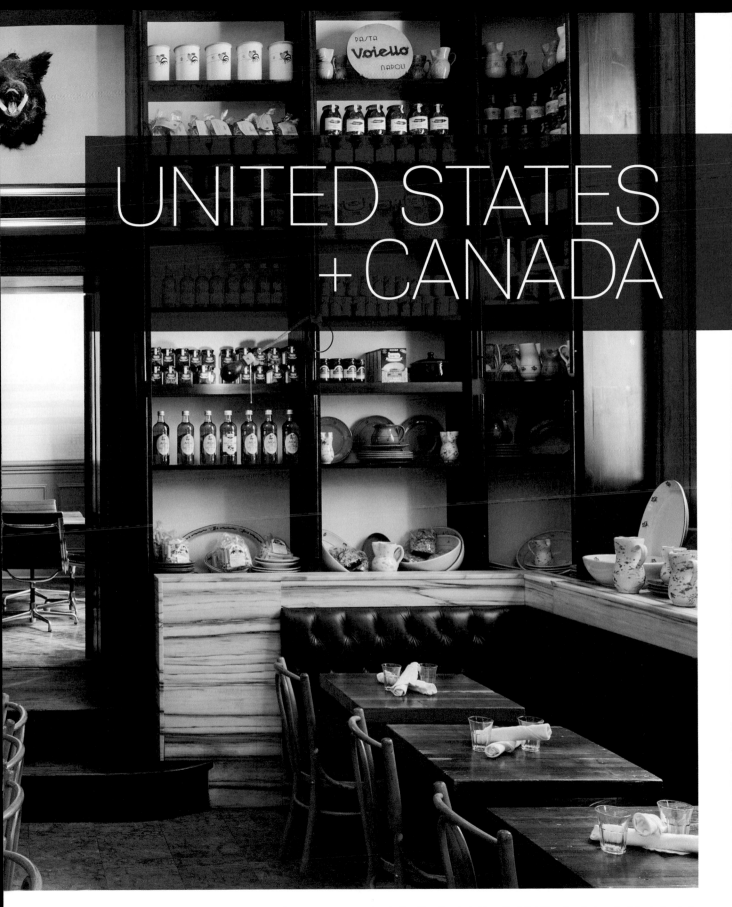

UNITED STATES
+CANADA

UERIDGEMOUNTAINSCHATTANOOGAFLORIDAALABAMA
LMSPRINGSMALIBUEASTERNSIERRASEATTLEOREGON

RHODE ISLAND

Exploring the smallest state's hidden coast

The view from
Ocean House,
in Watch Hill.

E ACH ONE OF THE MILLION OF US who live in little old Rhode Island has our own idea of what makes this place enchanting. For me, it is the coastline that has always cast a spell. The shore is by turns rocky and forbidding, with red granite cliffs tumbling into the Atlantic, or placid and lulling, the cattails of the marshes whispering in the breezes of sheltered inlets.

What Rhode Island lacks in landmass, it more than makes up for in shoreline: 400 miles of it, to be precise. I have spent decades exploring it, but something always catches me by surprise, leaving me thrilled, stunned, or mystified.

I started vacationing here more than 25 years ago. As a child I had visited family friends in the town of Little Compton, but then forgot about the place; just like the gentle fogs that drift across its meadows and ponds, time covered over my memories. When I returned as an adult, arriving on the East Coast after years of living in Texas, I had an instantaneous sense of recognition—the sound of the surf; the smell of mowed grass under a hot sun; the feel of morning fog on my skin. Little Compton is one of those rare childhood places that doesn't look smaller when you return.

Sakonnet, the area in Little Compton where I live, is on a peninsula, the end of the road. Little Compton is one of the last towns on the border of Rhode Island; I like to tell my children that I'm going to the beach to swim to Massachusetts, which is where you end up if you freestyle your way east.

It used to be, a mere five years ago, that there wasn't much to draw the casual visitor to Sakonnet. You had to get on a closely held list to rent a house and commit to at least a month. The beach club and golf club are private, with impossibly long waiting lists for membership. The area is lively in summer, quiet and isolated in winter. Some might say bleak. But that can be romantic.

Summer society is changing. Sakonnet rentals can now be had for a week. The public beach, a

The Green Animals Topiary Garden, in Portsmouth. Above: Kicking back at Ocean House.

beautiful, sandy stretch, is crowded by midday on sunny weekends. There's also a fancy new hotel. The Stone House opened with a veritable bouquet of attitudes—valet parking; hovering and anxious waiters; four different kinds of salt on the table; a menu that was dedicated, with much flowery language, to the farmers and foragers of the area. However, that's calmed down, and so have the room rates. You can easily visit for a few days, wander down to a quiet sliver of beach tucked between the rocks, eat delicious food in the restaurant, and even get spa treatments (gasp!).

Little Compton had a reputation as an artists' colony in the middle of the last century, and I still see bands of plein air painters stationed in cow pastures overlooking the Sakonnet River or on the beach, trying to capture waves crashing against boulders. On the walls of the unassuming Little Compton library hangs a trove of paintings by Molly Luce, who painted scenes from the 1930's on and was once called "the American Breughel" by a New York art critic.

Just 10 minutes up the road lies Tiverton Four Corners, which has been around nearly as long as Plymouth Colony. Painters continue to be drawn to the lambent light here, where the tradition of down-to-earth galleries thrives and a small cluster of shops, among the best in the state, feature charming artisanal work. There's wonderful pastry at Provender and cheese and all the fixings for a picnic across the street at Milk & Honey Bazaar. Gray's is one of the few independent ice cream makers left in a state that used to be full of dairies; it has been operating since 1922.

Next stop is Aquidneck Island. No one can claim to have explored the coast without a stay in Newport, its main city. In high summer, visitors jam the justifiably famous mansions, the "summer cottages" of the nouveaux riches at the turn of the 19th century. If, like Henry James, you find such extravagant heaps "grotesque," you can make short work of Newport. But who can resist a visit to Marble House, where Alva Vanderbilt appeared as the

empress of China at a lavish costume party in her (real) gold ballroom?

Taking the little-known backroads is the only way to stumble upon some of the weirder manifestations of Rhode Island's famousness, including the Green Animals Topiary Garden and the Worm Ladies of Charlestown, who have occasional open houses to teach people how to create a worm bin and make worm tea for fertilizer. Last summer I finally found the infamous hippie hangout the Umbrella Factory Gardens—a series of vintage-clothing stalls set in a 19th-century farmyard—tucked in a bit east of Ninigret National Wildlife Refuge. The garden shop features an astonishing assortment of plants, including (drum roll, please) patchouli, which is a tender thing, but I managed to coax mine to live through the fall, and enjoyed rubbing its leaves and having Proustian moments that involved beaded headbands and fringed boots.

A little farther on is Moonstone Beach, which my sister, who escaped Brown as often as she could,

■ THE AREA IS LIVELY IN SUMMER, QUIET AND ISOLATED IN WINTER. SOME MIGHT SAY BLEAK. BUT THAT CAN BE ROMANTIC.

told me was a nude swath favored by students. Today it is accompanied by signs reminding visitors that this is a family-friendly beach where there is to be no nudity. Still, it's worth the walk.

Onward to Watch Hill, the last coastal town before crossing the border into Connecticut. This grande dame of a village once vied with Newport as the toniest resort in the land, but its turn-of-the-20th-century shingled "cottages" were much less pretentious. More recently it became a rambling, fraying, lost place; the houses were considered white elephants, hard to maintain, constantly battered by wind and salt water.

My son and I used to stay in the ramshackle Ocean House, built in 1868, with its huge stone hearth and communal dining room. The place always felt thrillingly as if it were about to slide into the ocean. Then in 2005, Wall Street financier Chuck Royce spent an astonishing $146 million to tear down the structure and rebuild it, replicating the old exterior and its sunny color. Inside, there is little left of the former place, except for the handsome stone hearth—and the stunning views out over the open ocean.

One night, as I was leaving the hotel's locally minded restaurant, Seasons—where the bread alone is worth the price of admission—it struck me that coastal Rhode Island is a delicious, old-fashioned ice cream sandwich of a place. On either end are the rich, luxurious bits. The fun stuff is in the middle, and you have to catch it fast before it disappears—only to be replaced by something quite similar, in another delicious flavor. But at its heart, the true coastal experience, the one that leaves a trace on the soul, hasn't actually changed that much in 200 years. Its riches remain quietly hidden among coves and crannies, under the scrubby pines and behind the dunes, available to anyone curious enough to slow down and find them.

Adapted from "Rhode Island's Hidden Coast," by Dominique Browning.

GUIDE

STAY
Ocean House
*1 Bluff Ave., Watch Hill;
401/584-7000;
oceanhouseri.com.* **$$$$**

Stone House
*122 Sakonnet Point Rd.,
Little Compton;
401/635-2222;
stonehouse1854.com.* **$$**

EAT
Gray's Ice Cream
*16 East Rd., Tiverton;
401/624-4500;
graysicecream.com.*

Milk & Honey Bazaar
*3838 Main Rd., Tiverton;
401/624-1974;
milkandhoneybazaar.com.*

Provender
*3883 Main Rd., Tiverton;
401/624-8084.*

Seasons
*1 Bluff Ave., Watch Hill;
401/584-7000;
oceanhouseri.com.*
$$$

DO
Green Animals
Topiary Garden
*380 Cory's Lane,
Portsmouth;
401/847-1000;
newportmansions.org.*

Marble House
*596 Bellevue Ave.,
Newport; 401/847-1000;
newportmansions.org.*

Ninigret National
Wildlife Refuge
*50 Bend Rd.,
Charlestown;
401/364-9124;
fws.gov/ninigret.*

Worm Ladies of
Charlestown
*161 E. Beach Rd.,
Charlestown;
401/322-7675;
wormladies.com.*

SHOP
Umbrella Factory
Gardens
*4820 Old Post Rd.,
Charlestown;
401/364-9166.*

BROOKLYN, NEW YORK

Old meets new meets old again in Williamsburg

In Brooklyn's hippest neighborhood, funky shops in onetime tenement buildings continue to reinvent the bohemian landscape, and modern food purveyors with an eye toward tradition draw Manhattan-based gourmands across the East River in droves. But while this decades-long gentrification has been well documented, no one could have predicted Williamsburg's recent rise as a cynosure of style. T+L surveys the scene.

Bakeri
Female bakers dressed in Rosie the Riveter coveralls and kerchiefs churn their own butter at this antiques-filled bakery. Among the tantalizing array of sweets: delicate almond crumb cakes dusted with brown sugar and rich chocolate-peanut cookies flecked with crystals of Maldon sea salt. *150 Wythe Ave.; 718/388-8037; bakeribrooklyn.com.*

Brook Farm General Store
The utilitarian-chic Brook Farm General Store is hidden behind a nondescript façade that belies its sunny interior. Vintage housewares (cast-iron frying pans; maplewood cheese boards) hang next to old-school objets such as English police whistles. You'll also find the husband-and-wife owners' line of kitchen accessories on the shelves. *75 S. Sixth St.; 718/388-8642; brookfarmgeneralstore.com.*

Golden Calf
Shop owner Natalie Vichnevsky has an eye for color and form, and an obvious sense of humor.

(That explains the Mexican ceramic owl pitchers for sale.) There are Chinese antiques and Hungarian *zsolnay* throw pillows, but the best discoveries in Vichnevsky's collection are artist Peter Scibetta's wooden stool

One of Isa's bartenders preparing a cocktail.

mash-ups, with reclaimed-pine seats and birch-log legs. *319 Wythe Ave.; 718/302-8800; goldencalfbrooklyn.com.*

Isa
Follow the folks behind Manhattan's Freemans and Peels restaurants to this airy lunch counter, outfitted in Scandinavian-style furniture built by owner Taavo Somer. Despite the nod to his Estonian roots (*isa* means "father"), the menu is the work of Uruguayan chef Ignacio Mattos, who serves progressive small plates such as salt-cured sardines with orange-juice vinaigrette. *348 Wythe Ave.; 347/689-3594; isa.gg.* **$$$**

Marlow & Daughters
Once home to a neighborhood

barber, the artisan butcher shop has a nose-to-hoof philosophy and specializes in expert cuts of locally raised, grass-fed meat. Chicken and lamb sausages are crafted on site daily; travelers can get orders of the house-made charcuterie to go. *95 Broadway; 718/388-5700; marlowanddaughters.com.*

Marlow & Sons
Credit this canteen in the shadow of the Williamsburg Bridge with kick-starting the neighborhood's food renaissance. The gourmet grocery up front stocks rare cheeses and cured meats, as well as leather totes made from the skins of house-butchered cows and pigs. In the restaurant at the back, simple and succulent dishes qualify as "last meal" material: briny East Coast oysters, rich and creamy pâté, and brick chicken so flavorful you could eat a plate every day and never tire of it. *81 Broadway; 718/384-1441; marlowandsons.com.* **$$$**

Smorgasburg
Every Saturday from April to November, this chockablock food market becomes a hotbed for vendors hawking jams, jerky, and java at open-air stands along the waterfront, and for chefs who've cooked at the likes of Craft and Fatty Crab. Feast on everything from grilled-Gruyère sandwiches laced with champagne-vinegar-pickled onions to *bánh mì*–style chicken dogs. For dessert? Don't miss Kumquat Cupcakery's maple-cinnamon sponge, topped with a swirl of vanilla frosting and an unexpected cube of bacon. *27 N. Sixth St.; brooklynflea.com.*

Rosé and oysters at Marlow & Sons. Left: Brook Farm General Store.

Golden Calf's eclectic housewares. Left: The storefront of Marlow & Daughters.

Kurbit's Cottage
at c/o The
Maidstone, in
East Hampton.
Opposite: At
Vicki's Veggies,
in Amagansett.

THE HAMPTONS, NEW YORK

Savoring Long Island's East End like a local

ON MY FIRST VISIT TO THE Hamptons some 20 years ago, I stayed with friends in a sprawling Southampton rental. We hired a now de-funct taxi service (Mercedes-Benzes, of course) to take us around to overpriced restaurants and red-rope clubs. It was exactly how I'd always pictured Long Island's South Fork—a bit preten-tious for my tastes.

But there was something about this beachy New York destination that spoke to me: the dra-matic dunes; the shingled windmills; and that fa-mous light that has attracted artists as varied as Jackson Pollock and Winslow Homer. So I kept coming back, renting houses with friends and staying at inns from Amagansett to Sag Harbor, East Hampton to Montauk. Eventually, I bought a cottage in Amagansett with my husband (whom I met at a bonfire on Atlantic Beach).

Over the years, I've discovered a very different side to this coastal getaway. My Hamptons is all about low-key seafood shacks, quirky antiques shops, and placid bays that are perfect for beachcombing. Sure, you might run into Paul McCartney at the local café or spot Gwyneth Paltrow's kids selling lemonade at a makeshift stand—but that is just evidence of the Hamptons' many faces.

WHERE TO STAY

The Maidstone Arms, a sprawling Greek Revival inn overlooking the town pond, has been the top hotel in East Hampton for generations. A much welcome overhaul gave it an offbeat new name, c/o The Maidstone, and a Swedish design sensi-bility; most of the 16 rooms and three cottages are inspired by famous Scandinavians (Arne Jacobsen, Hans Christian Andersen, even Edvard Munch). The new guard is led by Amagansett's Inn at Windmill Lane, briefly known as the Reform Club (rumor has it the owners changed the name

because it sounded like a rehab center). The most luxurious hotel in the area, it is worth the splurge: the seven suites have wood-burning fireplaces; each of the three cottages also has its own gym and steam room. On the radar in Shelter Island, La Maison Blanche, named after a hotel in St.-Tropez, channels the south of France with *pétanque* courts, a Gallic brasserie, and an authentic *boulangerie*. There are surprisingly few good places to stay on the water in the Hamptons, but Amagansett's White Sands Resort Hotel is clean and simple, smack on a spectacular Atlantic beach. The ocean views alone make Montauk's hillside Panoramic View Resort & Residences so appealing; the pastel bathrooms and kitchenettes betray its previous life as a 1950's motel.

■ YOU MIGHT RUN INTO PAUL MCCARTNEY AT THE LOCAL CAFÉ OR SPOT GWYNETH PALTROW'S KIDS SELLING LEMONADE.

WHERE TO EAT

The East End is buzzing over chef Tom Colicchio's long-awaited Topping Rose House, in an 1800's Bridgehampton mansion. (There is also an adjoin-ing inn, designed by Alexandra Champalimaud of Hotel Bel-Air fame.) Where to eat when the reservations book is full? Foodies flock to Shelter Island's Vine Street Café for crisp calamari salad and miso salmon served under high, beamed ceilings. It's no wonder that Gabby Karan De Felice's Tutto Il Giorno is so stylish, considering her mother is Donna Karan; the lusty dishes range from *branzino al forno* to house-made pappardelle. In Montauk, two places are adding to the town's new culinary cred: Navy Beach, a former surfer's bar right on the sand with a great menu of ceviches, and the waterfront Crow's Nest, a rustic-chic spot from hipster hotelier Sean MacPherson.

Despite all the changes, the South Fork is still home to fishermen who make a living offshore and to family farms that have been around for

Opposite, clockwise from top left: Corwith Windmill, in Water Mill; inside Shelter Island's La Maison Blanche; evening at the Crow's Nest, in Montauk; *branzino al forno* at Sag Harbor's Tutto Il Giorno.

GUIDE

STAY

c/o The Maidstone
East Hampton;
themaidstone.com. **$$$$**

Inn at Windmill Lane
Amagansett; innat
windmilllane.com. **$$$$**

La Maison Blanche
Shelter Island; maison
blanchehotel.com. **$$**

Panoramic View Resort
Montauk; panoramicview.
com. **$$$**

White Sands Resort Hotel
Amagansett;
whitesandsresort.com. **$**

EAT
Bostwick's Chowder House
277 Pantigo Rd., East
Hampton; bostwicks
chowderhouse.com. **$$**

Canal Café
44 Newtown Rd.,
Hampton Bays;
thecanalcafe.com. **$$$**

Crow's Nest
4 Old West Lake Dr.,
Montauk; crowsnestmtk.
com. **$$$**

Duryea's Lobster Deck
65 Tuthill Rd., Montauk;
duryealobsters.com. **$$$**

Navy Beach
16 Navy Rd., Montauk;
navybeach.com. **$$$**

Nick & Toni's
136 N. Main St., East
Hampton; nickandtonis.
com. **$$$**

Rick's Crabby Cowboy Café
435 E. Lake Dr., Montauk;
crabbycowboy.com. **$$**

Southfork Kitchen
203 Bridgehampton/
Sag Harbor Tpk.,
Bridgehampton; southfork
kitchen.com. **$$$**

Topping Rose House
1 Bridgehampton/
Sag Harbor Tpk.,
Bridgehampton; topping
rosehouse.com. **$$$**

Tutto Il Giorno
6 Bay St., Sag Harbor;
631/725-7009. **$$$**

Vine Street Café
41 S. Ferry Rd.,
Shelter Island;
vinestreetcafe.com. **$$$**

DO
Capri
281 County Rd.,
Southampton; capri
southampton.com.

Channing Daughters Winery
1927 Scuttlehole Rd.,
Bridgehampton;
channingdaughters.com.

Surf Lodge
183 Edgemere St.,
Montauk; 631/668-1562.

Wölffer Estate Vineyard
139 Sagg Rd.,
Sagaponack; wolffer.com.

SHOP
Laurin Copen Antiques
1703 Montauk Hwy.,
Bridgehampton;
laurincopenantiques.com.

Lazypoint
303 Main St.,
Amagansett;
631/604-2870.

Melet Mercantile
102 Industrial Rd.,
Montauk;
631/668-9080.

Sage Street Antiques
114 Division St.,
Sag Harbor;
631/725-4036.

Tomas Maier
411 Montauk Hwy.,
Wainscott;
tomasmaier.com.

Vicki's Veggies
596 Montauk Hwy.,
Amagansett;
631/267-8272.

generations—providing ample resources for chefs such as Joe Isidori at Bridgehampton's Southfork Kitchen. He has gained a following for his unswerving commitment to sustainable seafood, fresh produce, and Long Island wines. The most coveted reservation continues to be East Hampton's 24-year-old Nick & Toni's, which is a who's who: Howard Stern, Lou Reed, and Naomi Watts, just to name a few. Chef Joseph Realmuto sources from the best local purveyors for such dishes as dandelion greens and pork-belly croutons in a white-anchovy vinaigrette.

Still, there's nothing like a platter of fried oysters or steamers by the sea. At Canal Café, tucked into a Hampton Bays marina, you'll get those, plus one of the most generous lobster rolls around. You can't get a better endorsement than chef Bobby Flay, who has been spotted at Bostwick's Chowder House, in East Hampton. Bring a bottle of rosé to Duryea's Lobster Deck, set on a rocky Montauk outcropping and renowned for its well-priced lobster. Just be prepared for a long wait.

■ DESPITE THE CHANGES, THE SOUTH FORK IS STILL HOME TO FISHERMEN WHO MAKE A LIVING OFFSHORE.

WHERE TO SHOP

The surrounding landscape used to be covered with potato fields; now heirloom tomatoes, baby beets, and wine grapes are some of the crops of choice. That means a plethora of places to find the local bounty. Perhaps the most atmospheric is Vicki's Veggies, a bright-red gem in Amagansett for just-harvested corn and incredible pies baked by Vicki herself. Oenophiles can't leave Long Island without a visit to Bridgehampton's Channing Daughters Winery, where vineyards are dotted with the owner's sculpture collection, and Sagaponack's Wölffer Estate Vineyard, which hosts free Friday jazz at sunset, overlooking the vines.

Making a sartorial statement here means standing out from the pack, so it's important to seek out boutiques with an individual point of view. In an Amagansett cottage, Brazilian-born Claudja Bicalho and her Australian husband, Mark Wilson, run Lazypoint, full of sexy-but-sophisticated clothes and jewelry found during their world travels. In a converted Wainscott diner, Tomas Maier (you know him as the creative director of Bottega Veneta) sells some of the most arresting swimwear around.

Thanks to wealthy homeowners who have money to burn (and decorators to help burn it), the Hamptons has its share of wildly overpriced antiques stores. But there are a few reasonable gems, if you know where to look. A top source is Sag Harbor's weekends-only Sage Street Antiques. Get there when it opens: owner Eliza Werner's selection of etched glassware, Art Deco lamps, nautical relics, and white-painted dressers moves fast. You never know what you'll uncover at the refined Sweden-meets–South Fork Laurin Copen Antiques, set in a Bridgehampton farmhouse. On the other end of the spectrum is Melet Mercantile, in an unassuming Montauk garage where Bob Melet—former director of vintage buying at Ralph Lauren—displays used surfboards, 1970's rock concert T-shirts, and other offbeat discoveries.

AFTER DARK

When you're feeling social, a few places are worth the effort. At the Capri, in Southampton, the poolside Bathing Club wakes up when the DJ's start spinning. In Montauk, the pulsing Surf Lodge had come under criticism for its crowds of late-night revelers; the new management promises a more mellow scene, so you can peacefully sip mojitos by the waterfront fire pit. And the season wouldn't be complete without the Fourth of July party at Rick's Crabby Cowboy Café & Marina, in Montauk, a down-and-dirty seafood joint that comes alive one night of the year. Filled with celebs and locals, it's a can't-miss affair that defines summer in the Hamptons.

Adapted from "Insider's Guide to the Hamptons," by Laura Begley Bloom.

Opposite, from left: Fishermen on the coast near Montauk Lighthouse; vintage offerings at Melet Mercantile.

WASHINGTON, D.C.

A homegrown food scene surfaces

New York, Los Angeles, San Francisco... D.C.? For years Washington, D.C., lagged behind the nation's epicurean capitals in both the quantity and quality of its restaurants. But the city's top chefs are closing the gap with unassuming eateries that have crowds buzzing about gourmet burgers, masterly tasting menus, and covert dinner clubs. From historic Foggy Bottom to trendy Dupont Circle, the latest crop also proves that bigger isn't necessarily better.

Sitting at the counter in Toki Underground's casual dining room.

Burger, Tap & Shake

It may be the laid-back kid sister to District Commons, but make no mistake: Jeff Tunks's second Washington Circle restaurant is no slouch. The industrial-chic burger joint offers eight takes on the classic burger—including a chin-drippingly juicy patty crafted from naturally aged chuck and brisket—plus a milk shake of house-made ice cream spiked with a healthy dose of bourbon. It's all served under the watchful eye of America's first president, whose orange-and-yellow visage gazes out on diners from a giant graffiti-style portrait created by local street artist Jazi Rock. *2200 Pennsylvania Ave. NW; 202/587-6258; burgertapshake.com.* **$$**

Little Serow

If you can find this turquoise-hued gem—hidden in an unmarked basement near Dupont Circle—your reward is a deliriously good meal of Isaan dishes (from Thailand's northeastern border with Laos), served family-style with a communal basket of fresh herbs and raw veggies. The rotating menu is posted on the restaurant's website each Monday, so you can research your picks beforehand. Don't miss chef Johnny Monis's hand-minced catfish with sawtooth coriander and crispy shallots, which draws raves from all corners of the Beltway. *1511 17th St. NW; no phone; littleserow.com.* **$$$**

Meatballs

James Beard Award–winning chef Michel Richard made his much anticipated foray into casual dining at this 40-seat spot in the Penn Quarter. In addition to standard beef versions of the titular classic, there are Moroccan lamb, lentil, and crab variations, all fixed with roasted red peppers and your choice of cheese; they arrive at the table piled on top of polenta, pasta, or salad, or stuffed into a hoagie. The standout: a beef grinder, nestled in a garlicky baguette with marinara and mozzarella melted just so. *624 E St. NW; 202/393-1083.* **$**

Seasonal Pantry

It's hard to believe that such an accomplished four-course tasting menu could be found in such a tiny (240-square-foot) restaurant. But here it is: three nights a week, Daniel O'Brien—a culinary MacGyver of sorts—pushes together two wooden tables and creates a 10-seat supper club, where he showcases dishes such as celery custard with sea urchin, oyster, and lemon jelly. The night's specialties are handwritten on notecards that list the ingredients for each course. *1314½ Ninth St. NW; 202/713-9866; seasonalpantry.com.* **$$$**

Toki Underground

Blink and you might miss this top-floor ramen house overlooking the H Street corridor. Inside there are 25 snug bar seats and some whimsical design touches (graffiti-covered walls; colorful plastic dolls in shadow boxes). But 27-year-old Taipei-trained chef Erik Yang is dead serious about his ramen. Our favorite is the traditional bowl, with *tonkotsu* (pork-bone) broth, barbecued pork loin, pickled ginger, and a silky slow-poached egg. *1234 H St. NE; 202/388-3086; tokiunderground.com.* **$$**

Burger, Tap & Shake's "six buck Chuck." Left: Chef Daniel O'Brien in his Seasonal Pantry.

Pork-loin ramen at Toki Underground. Right: Outside Meatballs restaurant.

BLUE RIDGE MOUNTAINS

Two lanes, 469 miles, and countless opportunities to stop and eat

A scenic stretch of the Blue Ridge Parkway.

W HEN I LEFT THE BANK in Charlotte," Diane Flynt said, tromping through her north orchard in clogs, designer jeans, and an immaculate white blouse, "I wanted my final career to be working with the land—I'm an avid gardener, and I like making things." The sun was low, radiating in bursts through the foliage of pippin trees, and we were learning that Flynt has a tendency toward understatement. For her retirement gig, she did indeed end up planting a garden—more than a thousand heirloom apple trees ranging over 25 hilly acres in Dugspur, Virginia. And the things she ended up making from them, once the trees had borne fruit—and after she'd traveled to England for schooling in the blending and fermentation of apple juice—are Foggy Ridge Ciders, four styles of the sort that early settlers drank gallons of, but which has all but disappeared from the nation's dinner tables.

Flynt's hard ciders deserve to be drunk with dinner. Sophisticated and dry, lavishly acidic with understated fruit, they're like a brisk mountaintop breeze with a hint of spring. We first fell for them at Lantern, in Chapel Hill, one of a number of restaurants in North Carolina and Virginia that serve Foggy Ridge. We made a mental note to visit the orchard if we were ever in the Blue Ridge highlands of Virginia.

Then, a week later, a friend in New York told us about a life-changing cheese she'd tasted at Per Se that chef Thomas Keller sources from a small Virginia dairy called Meadow Creek.

The Blue Ridge was clearly summoning us. Small-scale food operations with a keen sense of place and an upstart, indie spirit were breaking out all over, some to national acclaim. And it seemed noteworthy that these hives of local-food culture were clustered along the path carved by one of the largest government-sponsored public works of the 20th century.

Rib eye with tomato hollandaise at Zynodoa restaurant, in Staunton, Virginia. Above: Inside Fairview, North Carolina's Hickory Nut Gap Farm.

The Blue Ridge Parkway is 469 miles of two-lane blacktop running from the Shenandoah National Park in Virginia to the Great Smoky Mountains National Park in North Carolina. It's hard now to fathom how controversial the project was when it was green-lit by FDR's Public Works Administration in 1933. But construction went ahead as planned, with the first section begun in 1935. Something about the triumphant parkway emerging from a period of recession and grand public stimulus seemed apropos. And we were curious to know what it's like to travel—and eat— along the route today.

Our journey began in Staunton, Virginia, just west of Milepost Zero, the Blue Ridge Parkway's trailhead. Staunton has a reputation as a mecca for food lovers. The town celebrity is Joel Salatin, a farmer whose family has been operating Polyface Farm for more than 50 years and who is revered among the locavore set for such witty

polemical farm manuals as *Everything I Want to Do Is Illegal: War Stories from the Local Food Front.*

We asked Salatin if he drew any connections between Blue Ridge culture and the current farm-to-fork movement. He noted, at the core, a peculiar irony: "So often the sustainable-food movement is seen as this urban yuppie thing," he said. "But the gun-toting, canning, freezing mountain people actually exemplified a lot of the specifics that this new Gucci food movement fantasizes about. For the mountain people, it wasn't a fantasy—it was survival, because they didn't have any money!"

At Zynodoa, in downtown Staunton, chef James Harris's take on mountain comfort cooking finds local ingredients playing a French tune; a chicken-liver mousse (the livers from Salatin's farm) is impossibly creamy, served with cornichons and a baguette from Charlottesville's Albemarle Baking Co. Other dishes whistle nouvelle Dixie: Wade's Mill black pepper and cream cheese grits and

Above, from left: Hickory Nut Gap Farm's grass-fed cattle; a suite at the Grand Bohemian hotel, in Asheville, North Carolina.

braised collard greens accompany scallops—trucked in that morning from the Chesapeake—dressed with a red-eye gravy.

"Staunton is amazing," Harris said. "It's like someone dropped a Dickensian village in the middle of Virginia. And I'd put the quality of the produce here up against any other place in America."

What becomes apparent, dining from town to town along the parkway, is just how many different styles of cooking arise from a locavore's devotion. At the Admiral, in Asheville, North Carolina, a cinderblock dive lit by a flickery, old-timey TV against the wall, the kitchen sources its grass-fed beef tenderloin and pork belly from the stellar producer Hickory Nut Gap Farm, its ramps and mushrooms from forager friends. But here, they're the basis of a playful, offbeat—dare we say elegant?—cuisine that pairs seared scallops with

THE BLUE RIDGE WAS SUMMONING US. SMALL-SCALE FOOD OPERATIONS WITH A KEEN SENSE OF PLACE AND AN INDIE SPIRIT WERE BREAKING OUT ALL OVER.

foamed brown butter, smoked Vidalia onions, and navel orange supremes. Cooking local doesn't preclude flashes of *sriracha*, dashi, and the occasional Marcona almond from making appearances. (In true dive-bar spirit, PBR finds its way into mussel broth.)

The spirit of preservation abounds along the Blue Ridge. We found heartening evidence of revival at Knife & Fork, a spare restaurant overlooking the train station and freight lines in Spruce Pine. We were the first to show up for brunch and ordered nearly everything on the menu, which exudes virtue without a hint of sanctimony: nettle soup with fruity olive oil; grilled bread with sautéed ramps, prosciutto, and two gorgeous sunny-side-up eggs with soft yolks the color of orange peel. There was flaky, sweet redfish with tangy grilled rhubarb and a shatteringly crisp fried trout with lemony tartar sauce. Within half an hour every plate was clean, and every table around us was filled.

The chef, Nathan Allen, and his wife, front-of-house manager Wendy Gardner, had worked in Los Angeles at Suzanne Goin's Lucques and AOC restaurants before they decided to move to Gardner's hometown of Burnsville, North Carolina. The plan was to ease their way into the food community, but immediately after setting foot in Burnsville, they saw an available space in Spruce Pine. Three days later, they'd signed a lease, and in four weeks' time, they'd renovated the place, installed the kitchen, and opened Knife & Fork.

"Everybody in L.A. says they want to be farm-to-table, but it wasn't until we moved here that we understood what that meant," Allen told us. "We'll spend forty-five minutes hitting all our growers and getting produce picked that morning. We don't just know our farmers, we know all their kids and dogs too. I think being so closely tied to a food community hasn't been possible since—what—maybe the late eighteen-hundreds?"

Adapted from "Up on the Ridge," by Matt Lee and Ted Lee.

GUIDE

STAY

Grand Bohemian
A decadent hunting-lodge aura reigns over Biltmore Village's most upmarket hotel. *Asheville, N.C.; 828/505-2949; bohemianhotelasheville. com.* **$$**

Hotel Indigo
Within walking distance of downtown Asheville, this outpost of the minimal-chic hotel chain offers spacious rooms with soaring mountain views. *Asheville, N.C.; 800/951-4667; hotelindigo.com.* **$**

Primland
A luxurious eco-resort with a spa, golf, wing shooting, fly-fishing, mountain biking, and horseback riding. *Meadows of Dan, Va.; 276/222-3800; primland.com.* **$$$**

The Storefront
A comfortable one-room B&B in a charming two-story house in downtown Staunton. *Staunton, Va.; 804/218-5656; the-storefront-hotel.com.* **$**

EAT

The Admiral
400 Haywood Rd., Asheville, N.C.; 828/252-2541; theadmiralnc.com. **$$**

Knife & Fork
61 Locust St., Spruce Pine, N.C.; 828/765-1511; knifeandforknc.com. **$$**

Zynodoa
115 E. Beverley St., Staunton, Va.; 540/885-7775; zynodoa.com. **$$$**

SHOP

Foggy Ridge Cider
1328 Pine View Rd., Dugspur, Va., 276/398-2337; foggyridgecider.com.

Hickory Nut Gap Farm
57 Sugar Hollow Rd., Fairview, N.C.; 828/628-1027; hickorynutgapfarm.com.

CHATTANOOGA, TENNESSEE

Checking out the Southern musical milieu

LONG OVERSHADOWED BY NASHVILLE'S grand-ole theatricality, Chattanooga has a rich aural heritage all its own. Blues legend Bessie Smith was born and began creating a name for herself here during the Jazz Age, and big-band conductor Glenn Miller helped make the city famous in the 1940's. Today, an eclectic mix of genres reverberates through the once-gritty backwater's bars and music halls, adding depth to an already storied music scene.

When alt-folk singer M. Ward is touring, he takes the stage at Track 29, a former skating rink that gets its name from the swing classic "Chattanooga Choo Choo." Similarly minded funk and rock bands jam at outdoor festivals like Riverbend, a nine-day celebration that lures some 650,000 visitors each June. Even the Hunter Museum of American Art gets in on the act with a summer series of classical concerts held on the terrace.

Just outside town, however, the vibe has been unmistakably old-school for the last 30 years at the Mountain Opry, where fiddlers and banjo pickers congregate under leafy oaks and wranglers in cowboy boots slap their knees to free bluegrass. The evening's revelry may seem like a beautifully scored dream when you awake the next morning at the Chattanoogan, the city's hotel of choice. Head to the Bluegrass Grill, in a restored 1904 brick building, for cilantro-lime hash browns and an all-day breakfast menu that's sure to recharge you for another night.

The Hunter Museum of American Art, overlooking the Tennessee River.

GUIDE

STAY
The Chattanoogan
1201 Broad St.;
800/619-0018;
chattanooganhotel.com. $

EAT
Bluegrass Grill
55 E. Main St.;
423/752-4020;
bluegrassgrill
chattanooga.com. $

DO
Hunter Museum of
American Art
10 Bluff View;
423/267-0968;
huntermuseum.org.

Mountain Opry
2501 Fairmount Pike,
Signal Mountain;
423/886-3252.

Riverbend Festival
riverbendfestival.com.

Track 29
1400 Market St.;
423/521-2929;
track29.co.

FLORIDA

An East Coast drive-by

Old-world resorts. No-frills fish shacks. The perfect slice of Key lime pie. There's plenty to uncover in Florida's iconic beach towns. Winding from Jacksonville to Key West— with miles of shrubby Atlantic shoreline in between—a low-key road trip along the coast reveals the many faces of the Sunshine State: eclectic crossroads, kooky party capital, and bastion of sleepy Southern charm.

Jacksonville to St. Augustine
(38 miles)

Fly into JAX, then drive south toward the oldest European settlement in America. After 30 minutes along Route 9A, stop for memorable sandwiches and sweet tea at Angie's Subs, a no-fuss storefront popular with surfer types. Back on the road, turn onto scenic Route A1A and continue south for 31 miles until the imposing Castillo de San Marcos comes into view. The 17th-century fort makes a good jumping-off point for a walking tour of the cobblestoned streets of St. Augustine's historic downtown; military re-enactments in the fort's courtyard take you back to the days of Spanish rule. Cool off with the Hyppo's small-batch ice pops (the pineapple-cilantro variety is a favorite) modeled after Mexican *paletas*. After checking in at the Moorish-inflected Casa Monica Hotel, an 1888 property once owned by railroad tycoon Henry Flagler, visit the Floridian for such trusted Southern favorites as shrimp and grits. The restaurant is BYOB, so grab a bottle of biodynamic wine from the bar next door on your way over.

DAY 2

St. Augustine to Palm Beach
(257 miles)

This leg of the journey is a long one. Fortify yourself with breakfast at Casa Maya, a tiny spot serving Yucatecan dishes prepared with organic ingredients (don't miss the "huevos de Popeye," a hearty mix of egg, spinach, and tomato with goat cheese). Hop back on Route A1A, which hairpins along the coast to the Kennedy Space Center, the site of NASA's launch headquarters. The visitors' complex has interactive features such as 3-D IMAX films, astronaut-led chats, and tours to get a closer look at the launchpad in Cape Canaveral. Not really a space nut? Next door is shell-strewn Playalinda Beach, one of the East Coast's most beautiful.

A proliferation of kitschy surf shops and mini-golf courses signals your arrival in Cocoa Beach. The crowds at Jazzy's Mainely Lobster & Seafood Co., a block from the shore, are evidence that you can never have too much fish in Florida. Dive into a lunchtime lobster roll, then get back on A1A for a ride into the sunset. The seven-acre Ritz-Carlton Palm Beach is a welcome sight at the end of your day. The hotel's 42,000-square-foot Eau Spa is a design stunner, thanks to benches positioned next to waterfalls and an open-air relaxation garden. So is the reopened Angle restaurant, with its Regency-meets-supper-club ambience.

DAY 3

Palm Beach to Miami Beach
(63 miles)

Start off in Florida's old-guard enclave, arguably the most rewarding place in the country to score secondhand designer clothes. Two stores not to miss: Palm Beach Vintage, which carries beaded cocktail dresses and accessories, and Groovy Palm Beach, stocked with

Above right: Snacking by the seashore. Opposite: A colorful directional post in Key West.

colorful Lilly Pulitzer and Pucci pieces. Shopping bags in tow, head south one hour on I-95 to artsy Delray Beach. Check out the galleries on Atlantic Avenue and snap up a pair of patchwork madras pants or cotton web belts cut to order at preppy stalwart Trouser Shop.

From there it's about 30 miles to Dania Beach, a small city just outside Fort Lauderdale. Grab lunch at the Islamorada Fish Co., an outpost of the Keys chainlet (housed, appropriately enough, in a Bass Pro Shop). In Miami, shack up at 27-room Quarzo Bal Harbour, a minimalist property that feels less like a hotel than a boutique apartment complex. (It's within walking distance of the exclusive Bal Harbour Shops.) Cap off the day with dinner in Miami Beach at Pubbelly, a welcoming Asian-inspired gastropub that has a distinct hipster vibe.

DAY 4

Miami Beach to Islamorada
(80 miles)

Order a *café con leche* from the walk-up window at David's Café II before venturing to the cutting-edge galleries in Wynwood, Miami's most unexpected cultural hot spot. Take in the art scene aboard a Vespa on a Roam Rides guided tour. The neighborhood's other attraction consists of a clutch of high-design restaurants; the most impressive is Wynwood Kitchen & Bar, where the art-filled

Left, from top: The Self-Centered Garden at the Ritz-Carlton, Palm Beach's Eau Spa; Wynwood Kitchen & Bar, in Miami.

Islamorada to Key West
(81 miles)

For your last day of traveling, fuel up with coconut French toast at the Green Turtle Inn, a revamped 1940's diner. Feeding the tarpon off the dock of watersports center Robbie's of Islamorada is a rite of passage that shouldn't be neglected on your way to Key West, the southernmost town in the continental United States. You could brave the carnival-like atmosphere of Mallory Square, but better to make like Rita Hayworth and toast the day's end in a more civilized fashion at Casa Marina's Sun Sun beach bar. Then walk to Pepe's Café, a quaint little shack that's the oldest restaurant in Key West, for the pleasingly tart Key lime pie. Garnished with whipped cream, it's an appropriately sweet footnote to your trip.

The sea-facing pool and cabana area at Islamorada's Casa Morada.

interiors are as much of a draw as the Latin-inflected menu.

Continue for an hour and a half on Route 1 to Islamorada, the gateway to the easy, breezy Keys. (Still hungry? Just 30 miles from Miami, savor the down-home cooking at Shiver's BBQ, which specializes in hickory-smoked ribs slathered with house-made

sauce.) Angler alert: more world-record fish have been caught in Islamorada than anywhere else on the planet. Charter a sportfishing excursion or rent a boat at Holiday Isle Resort's tiki-festooned marina. Retreat to Casa Morada, a petite, well-styled hotel on the beach.

GUIDE

STAY

Casa Marina, a Waldorf Astoria Resort
Key West; 888/303-5717; casamarinaresort.com. **$**

Casa Monica Hotel
St. Augustine; 888/213-8903; casamonica.com. **$**

Casa Morada
Islamorada; 888/881-3030; casamorada.com. **$$**

Quarzo Bal Harbour
Bal Harbour; 305/222-7922; quarzomiamihotel. com. **$$$**

Ritz-Carlton, Palm Beach
Manalapan; 800/241-3333; ritzcarlton.com. **$$$**

EAT AND DRINK

Angie's Subs
Jacksonville Beach; 904/249-7827. **$**

Casa Maya
St. Augustine; 904/217-3039. **$**

David's Café II
Miami Beach; 305/672-8707; davidscafe.com.

The Floridian
St. Augustine; 904/829-0655; thefloridianstaug.com. **$$**

Green Turtle Inn
Islamorada; 305/664-2006; greenturtlekeys.com. **$**

Islamorada Fish Co.
220 Gulf Stream Way, Dania Beach; 954/927-7737; fishcompany.com. **$$**

The Hyppo
St. Augustine; 904/217-7853; thehyppo.com.

Jazzy's Mainely Lobster & Seafood Co.
Cocoa Beach; 321/613-3993. **$$**

Pepe's Café
Key West; 305/294-7192; pepescafe.net. **$**

Pubbelly
Miami Beach; 305/532-7555; pubbelly.com. **$$$**

Shiver's BBQ
Homestead; 305/248-2272; shiversbbq.com. **$$**

Wynwood Kitchen & Bar
Miami; 305/722-8959; wynwoodkitchenandbar. com. **$$**

SHOP

Groovy Palm Beach
Palm Beach; 561/628-9404.

Palm Beach Vintage
West Palm Beach; 561/718-4075; palmbeachvintage.com.

Trouser Shop
Delray Beach; 561/278-5626; trousershop.com.

FLORENCE, ALABAMA

Old-school but not old-fashioned

On your travels through the picture-perfect towns of Alabama, it's not hard to blink and miss Florence, a Tennessee Valley hamlet with an all-American ambience that borders on nostalgia. But hidden beneath the surface, a hip local scene inspired by the region's historic underpinnings is giving visitors a reason to stop and linger over its down-home treasures.

Billy Reid

For upmarket pieces with a rough-hewn sensibility, pop into fashion designer Billy Reid's flagship. The tailored suits and broken-in button-downs are displayed in a brick-walled showroom outfitted with rustic-chic accoutrements—think deer antlers and antique candelabras. *114 N. Court St.; 256/767-4692; billyreid.com.*

FAME Recording Studios

Florence is one of four cities that make up the Shoals, an area known for its rich rhythm-and-blues legacy; Aretha Franklin, the Rolling Stones, and Bob Dylan all cut records here. To get a better idea of what's been dubbed the Muscle Shoals sound, take a tour of the renowned FAME Recording Studios, birthplace of hits like Wilson Pickett's "Mustang Sally." *603 E. Avalon Ave.; 256/381-0801; fame2.com.*

Marriott Shoals

Base yourself at the Marriott Shoals hotel, on a coveted swath along the Tennessee River, bordered by two Robert Trent Jones–designed championship golf courses; the 200 guest rooms highlight the local pastime with bronzed panels depicting angling scenes. If you're looking for a respite from the Alabama heat, you can indulge in a massage at the hotel's spa or simply sit back by the best pool in town. *10 Hightower Place; 256/246-3600; marriott.com.* **$**

Trowbridge's Ice Cream & Sandwich Bar

Trowbridge's Ice Cream & Sandwich Bar isn't retro in that faux-Mayberry sort of way. This unassuming, eight-stool lunch counter is the real deal: Paul Trowbridge began churning and scooping orange-pineapple ice cream here in 1918, and three generations later his family continues the tradition. Ask for the trademark egg-and-olive sandwich, toasted on the stainless-steel press. Or order a white-bread banana sandwich, with mayo and peanut butter on the side. *316 N. Court St.; 256/764-1503.* **$**

W.C. Handy Home, Museum & Library

The Father of the Blues was born in a modest log cabin in Florence in 1873. At present, it serves as a repository for the composer's original sheet music and personal instruments. Drive by to take it all in, or seek out events each summer, when Handy is honored with a weeklong music festival held throughout the Shoals. *620 W. College St.; 256/760-6434.*

Ye Old General Store

The vibe is equal parts Salvation Army and no-fuss country mart at Ye Olde General Store, the place to find overalls, hats, and other stock from American brands such as Carhartt and Duck Head. *219 N. Seminary St.; 256/764-0601.*

The 1902 Matthews-Davis house, a historic residence in downtown Florence.

A poster at FAME Recording Studios. Right: Trowbridge's Ice Cream & Sandwich Bar.

Designer Billy Reid in his showroom. Left: The Billy Reid flagship store.

OXFORD, MISSISSIPPI

Tailgates and tradition in a tight-knit community

IF YOU'RE SEARCHING FOR the cultural epicenter of the modern South, look no further than Oxford. The venerable college town has an illustrious history, serving as geographic muse for William Faulkner's Yoknapatawpha County novels in the 1930's. It's also home to the University of Mississippi (Ole Miss for short), the backdrop for a key integration battle during the 1960's Civil Rights movement. Currently, the school houses the Center for the Study of Southern Culture, which documents the region's most iconic elements, from barbecue contests to roadside juke joints.

The fun continues off-campus. Thacker Mountain Radio hosts live weekly broadcasts of musical performances and book readings (plus signings by the likes of Ole Miss graduate John Grisham) from Courthouse Square. And the Lyric theater, a onetime livery stable owned by the Faulkner family, plays host to such popular indie acts as Passion Pit and the Lumineers.

Alumni visit often, especially during football season, when the Grove, a 10-acre lawn shaded by magnolias and elms, becomes the setting for the sport's most elaborate tailgate (think cocktail dresses, sterling-silver bourbon flasks, and crystal chandeliers). Even if you don't know the words to the school's "Hotty Toddy" cheer, you'll still be welcomed at the Z, a three-room guesthouse run by a pair of recent grads who dole out pitchers of sweet tea and freshly baked cheddar-buttermilk biscuits on the front porch. That's Southern hospitality at its best.

The lounge at the Z bed-and-breakfast.

GUIDE

STAY
The Z
1405 Pierce Ave.;
713/927-1295;
thez-oxford.com. **$**

DO
The Lyric
1006 Van Buren Ave.;
662/234-5333;
thelyricoxford.com.

University of Mississippi
University Circle;
662/ 915-7211;
olemiss.edu.

NEW ORLEANS

Channeling Saigon on the bayou

Above, from left: Karl Takacs, owner of Phò Tâu Bay; fruit from the Versailles Farmers' Market. Opposite: Toppings for *pho*.

NEW ORLEANS IS A FOODIE town. It is filled with famous restaurants doing the traditional dishes they have done for a hundred years and with restaurants whose chefs have become brand names by spinning variations on those traditions—Paul Prudhomme, Susan Spicer, John Besh, and Emeril Lagasse, among others. The Takacs family and their restaurant, Phò Tâu Bay, are not names that spring to mind, but they rank as one of my big culinary discoveries since I moved to the city in the fall of 2008.

I had been vaguely aware of a community of Vietnamese shrimpers working the Gulf, but it was a surprise to find so much authentic, high-quality Vietnamese food here, though it does make sense—

both cuisines bear a French influence and have signature dishes built around the baguette: the *bánh mì* and the pʋ'boy.

According to Kathleen Carlin, a colleague of mine at Tulane who has written about the community for decades, New Orleans has a significant Vietnamese-American population, like Orange County, California; Arlington, Virginia; and Houston. But it is, compared with those places, the least assimilated, the most self-contained. When large numbers of Vietnamese started arriving in the city in 1975, the economy was hot and the housing market tight. They ended up living in Section 8 housing way outside the city center, in Versailles, and later in Gretna, and other Westbank as well as New Orleans East communities. "Versailles used to be the last thing you passed before you were in the swamps on the way to Mississippi," Carlin told me. "Just in back of beyond."

At Phò Tàu Bay, in Gretna, I had the idea it would be fun to learn to cook Vietnamese food. Its essence is so in line with our current preoccupations, chief among them freshness, lightness, and locally grown ingredients. My family and I go there for dinner on Wednesdays with friends who also have little kids. Phò Tàu Bay's main attraction is the food, but it helps that it is run by a family that always makes our menagerie feel welcome. We order *goi ga* and *goi tom* (chicken and shrimp salads), spring rolls, *pho*. The table is crowded with bowls erupting with herbs, sprouts, lime.

One day I passed the door to the kitchen. It was open. I peered at the various pots and pans, the tubs of fresh produce that make every Vietnamese table into a kind of garden, looking for the *nuoc mam,* which is made from fermented fish. There was a huge vat sitting in the corner: surely it was where the soup stock for the *pho* had been concocted. How do they do it? I wondered. It felt like I was peeking at a magician backstage. Like so many other men in America, it seems, I have discovered cooking and also the transporting effects of culinary adventure; I imagine myself a culinary explorer. But there is a fine line between exploring and trespassing. Someone in the kitchen looked up and saw me. He walked over to the door wearing an expression that I chose to interpret as a polite smile, maybe even a welcoming one, and closed it in my face.

I went up front and asked Karl Takacs Jr., the raven-haired man behind the register, if I could observe the doings in the kitchen. Karl Jr. is in charge of building up the daily pot of *pho* for which the place is famous. He is the third generation in his family to work at Phò Tàu Bay. And he is always very friendly. So I was surprised when he shook his head and said, "Sorry, can't do that."

"Why not?" I said.

> ■ 'THOSE GUYS ARE NOT GOING TO GIVE YOU THEIR *PHO* SECRETS,' EMERIL TELLS ME.

"It's nothing personal. We've got a lot of people asking."

"Who else is asking?"

"Emeril," he said. "He's in here all the time."

"Those guys are not going to give you their secrets!" Emeril Lagasse tells me. "There's something in that pot, or there's something in that vermicelli salad. There is something they're not telling you. I have been trying to wrap my brain around it for at least ten years!"

It was the Groucho principle at work—Phò Tàu Bay's kitchen is the club that will not have us. Not only do we like the food, but it also seemed clear, as we spoke, that we both kind of like the mystery of being shut out of its creation.

Emeril is fixated on the gigantic pot of *pho* at Phò Tàu Bay. He orders it every time. "When you get that taste, the depth, what Karl Sr. and Karl Jr. are doing.... I have tried to get it out of them. I have tried to duplicate it. Is it cinnamon? The way they roast the cardamom?" (It's neither.) "And it's a hole-in-the-wall, as you know. There is nothing fancy in this joint! It confuses people."

Phò Tàu Bay's story, I discover from Emeril and then from the Takacs themselves, is as intricate and shrouded as its food. They once had five restaurants in New Orleans, but after Katrina they were reduced to the original location. This was not the family's first setback, however. Just as the Gulf's climate echoes that of Vietnam, so the Katrina debacle echoed earlier catastrophes. Surviving one disaster, it turns out, can be helpful when you are faced with another.

Karl Takacs Sr. is tall and broad-shouldered, and he moves around the Phò Tàu Bay kitchen with a bit of a limp. He was shipped out as a GI to Vietnam, where he fell in love twice—first with *pho,* which one could argue is Vietnam's national dish, and then with Tuyet, the daughter of the owner of Phò Tàu Bay, which was his preferred

Above: A server with a steaming bowl of *pho* at Dong Phuong Oriental Bakery & Restaurant.

spot in Saigon. He married Tuyet. But then it all crashed and burned with the fall of Saigon. The family moved to the United States, and Tuyet's father and sister taught Karl how to cook. The next iteration was a no-frills restaurant selling *pho* in Gretna in 1982. Thus began the start of another mini-empire, which was then wiped out by Katrina. Now the ex-GI, Tuyet, and their son are the chefs.

There are many other fantastic Vietnamese restaurants in New Orleans—Dong Phuong Oriental Bakery, in New Orleans East, and Tahn Din, in Gretna, notable among them. The Versailles community is a pleasure to roam for its restaurants and markets. But recipes and demonstrations are out of the question. So I try to get snippets of information every time I go to Phò Tâù Bay. Last time, I marched up to the register, at that moment manned by Karl Sr., with a bit of fried shallot in my palm. It's a tiny explosion of flavor and texture, artwork in miniature.

"Tell me the story of how this came to exist," I said.

"You get 'em precut, and you flash-fry them very fast or they burn…" and he went on for a while, pride overwhelming the secrecy.

On a few occasions I have called Karl Jr. on the phone, my shaky attempt at *goi ga* in front of me, for advice. I list the ingredients I have used. Then, as if this were some Vietnamese food-crisis hotline, he suggests a few I have left out.

Another day, bantering with the Takacs, it came out that Karl Jr. had visited Vietnam once.

"What did you think of the *pho*?" I asked.

"I think ours is better," he said. At first, I thought this was blasphemy. Then I realized that, at Phò Tâù Bay, all of the recipes are part of one family's secret oral history. Those recipes are the equivalent of diamonds smuggled from the home country in the lining of a coat, the foundation on which a family's fortunes will rise again.

Adapted from "Saigon on the Bayou," by Thomas Beller.

GUIDE

STAY
Ritz-Carlton New Orleans
The city's top hotel is centrally located in the French Quarter.
921 Canal St.; 800/241-3333 or 504/524-1331; ritzcarlton.com. **$$**

EAT
Dong Phuong Oriental Bakery & Restaurant
14207 Chef Menteur Hwy., New Orleans East; 504/254-0214; dpbanhmi.com. **$**

Phò Tâù Bay
113-C Westbank Expwy., Gretna; 504/368-9846. **$**

Tan Dinh
1705 Lafayette St., Gretna; 504/361-8008. **$$**

BENTONVILLE, ARKANSAS

An unexpected cultural find

The Crystal
Bridges Museum
of American Art.

GUIDE

STAY
21c Museum Hotel
21cmuseumhotels.com.

DO
Crystal Bridges Museum
of American Art
600 Museum Way;
479/418-5700;
crystalbridges.org.

UNTIL NOW, BENTONVILLE, ARKANSAS, has been famous for one (very big) thing: it's the home of Walmart. But another landmark is emerging in this small town, thanks to a multimillion-dollar infusion from Alice Walton, the youngest heir to the retail empire. The Crystal Bridges Museum of American Art is a showcase for her impressive collection, transforming the once sleepy region into a world-class cultural destination. It's also an audacious gamble that a large-scale arts institution can thrive in the Ozarks.

Crystal Bridges is already being touted as a countrified Guggenheim Bilbao—and Walton herself as a latter-day Morgan or Frick, digging deep into her pockets and dreaming big. To hedge her if-you-build-it-they-will-come bet, she hired Israeli architect Moshe Safdie to design the museum, set on 120 wooded acres just outside town; its gently curving pavilions hover dramatically over and around ponds fed by natural springs. Walton's greatest investment, though, may be the collection itself, which covers the full sweep of American art, from Colonial portraitists Gilbert Stuart and John Singleton Copley to 19th-century masters Winslow Homer and Thomas Eakins, with some modern icons (Andy Warhol; Roxy Paine; Jenny Holzer) thrown in for good measure.

This may be enough to attract culture seekers from around the country, if not the world. But there's another enticement. Walton also approached 21c Museum Hotels—which put Louisville, Kentucky, on the art-world map—about opening a property in town. Designed by Deborah Berke, it's due in January 2013.

TEXAS

A wildflower-filled drive through the Lone Star State

The stables at the Inn at Dos Brisas, in Washington, Texas. Opposite: Wildflowers along the roadside.

It was native daughter Lady Bird Johnson who spearheaded the beautification of the nation's highway system in the 1960's, replacing billboards and junkyards in Texas with vast fields of wildflowers. Since then, visitors have flocked to the state's various bluebonnet trails—which fan out from Austin for miles in every direction—and rumors persist each spring that anyone caught picking them will be arrested. (Not true, but if somebody with a shotgun approaches, run first and explain later.) To time your trip accordingly, contact the Texas Department of Transportation's wildflower hotline, then let the blossoms lead the way.

DAY 1

Houston to Brenham to Cat Spring (105 miles)

There's plenty of lowbrow fun to be had in the towns that dot the landscape along the bluebonnet trails in Washington County. Set along Highway 290, Brenham resembles the backdrop for a sprawling MGM western; the tin-ceilinged shops that line Main Street are on the National Register of Historic Places. Stock up on jars of candied jalapeños and "brisket slather" barbecue sauce at Hermann General Store, then swing by the colonnaded Heritage Museum to take in 19th-century knitted garments, crafts, and other domestic goods (think antique gas lanterns and fire engines).

As you continue north on FM 50 (FM stands for roads that were deemed "farm to market"), the wildflowers get some competition from the blooms at the Antique Rose Emporium. Its owner belongs to a group of "rose rustlers" who embark on search-and-rescue missions for forgotten varieties with names like Autumn Damask and Mrs. Sam Houston, many of which are still found in cemeteries and older neighborhoods in the area.

Nearby is the Windy Winery, a producer of 1,500 cases a year from the local bounty. Those with a sweet tooth might prefer the signature Blue Bell milk shakes at the Dairy Bar, a divey diner that serves the best burgers in town. Afterward, a starry Texas night lights the way for the 45-minute drive to BlissWood Bed & Breakfast, a working ranch with centuries-old live oaks and bass-stocked lakes.

DAY 2

Cat Spring to Round Top to Warrenton to Bellville (75 miles)

Pie for breakfast? Yes, ma'am. At Royer's Café, in Round Top, try one of the 15 house-made choices (butterscotch chip; lattice-crust cherry), all topped with ice cream, lest you anger the servers (really, they'll charge extra for deviating from the menu).

Follow the wildflowers on Highway 237 southwest for a few miles. St. Martin's is a tiny wooden building with an incongruously ornate tabernacle

Left, from top: Bud the Pieman, founder of Royer's Round Top Café; Newman Castle, near Bellville.

The pool and terrace on the grounds of Washington's Inn at Dos Brisas.

that claims to be the world's smallest Catholic church.

Near Bellville, 40 minutes away, you'll find an even smaller chapel (plus an iron portcullis, five turrets, and a moat) at the fantastic crenellated Newman's Castle. Call ahead and the owner—you can usually reach Newman in town at his namesake café—will give you a tour of his medieval-style abode, which he designed on napkins in between frying doughnuts and cutting

biscuits. Back over the drawbridge, retire to the slightly more modest Dove Cottage, an intimate French-country guesthouse.

DAY 3

Bellville to Chappell Hill to Washington (35 miles)

Braking for bluebonnets while traveling north along Highway 36, you arrive at the Chappell Hill Lavender Farm. Pile your basket with bushels of handpicked herbs, aromatic bath salts, and

lavender-flavored pasta (an acquired taste). Route 290 brings you to the Chappell Hill Museum for a lesson on the remarkable history of plantation women, whose skills involved stitching linens and the somewhat less ladylike business of butchering and preserving meat.

From there, head north on FM 1155 to Washington, where you've saved the best for last: the Inn at Dos Brisas, with four Mission-style casitas and five haciendas. Guests can scoot around the property—home to meadows, organic farms, an infinity pool, and a horse barn—in self-drive golf carts. Dinners are some of the best in Texas (roasted sablefish with sweet peas and wasabi rhizome; Rohan duckling with foie gras) and are served in a grand dining room dominated by a Loire Valley fireplace from circa 1760; wine lovers will take comfort in the 2,500-bottle-strong wine cellar. The bluebonnets, after all, would never steer you wrong.

GUIDE

MASON CITY, IOWA

An architectural hotbed that's off the beaten path

POCKET-SIZE MASON CITY (population 29,000) is the last place you'd expect to be a high-design mecca. Unless you happen to know that it harbors the only remaining Frank Lloyd Wright–conceived hotel, not to mention a number of other architectural treasures. Stop by the new Mason City Architectural Interpretive Center for a map and an insightful overview, then hit the pavement to see them all for yourself.

The 1908 Stockman House is the sole Prairie School–style Wright residence in Iowa, featuring an open floor plan that blurs the lines between indoors and out—a revolutionary concept at the time. The country's finest collection of Prairie School houses, built by contemporaries such as stone master Walter Burley Griffin, is located in the Rock Glen–Rock Crest Historic District.

After an $18.5 million restoration, Wright's 27-room Historic Park Inn Hotel, the structure that set off the town's design boom in 1910, is taking reservations for the first time in nearly 40 years. In the lobby, the original stained-glass skylight casts a warm glow over tiles from the early 1900's, and common areas are filled with replicas of Wright-designed furniture. The man who changed the way Americans live said his vision was shaped by summers spent on his uncle's rural Wisconsin farm. Fitting, then, that his legacy is thriving in a corn-filled corner of the heartland.

The Frank Lloyd Wright–designed Historic Park Inn Hotel.

GUIDE

STAY
Historic Park Inn Hotel
*7 W. State St.;
800/659-2220;
wrightonthepark.org.* **$**

DO
Mason City Architectural
Interpretive Center
*520 First St. N.E.;
641/423-1923;
mcarchitecture.org.*

COLORADO

Two wintertime classics face off

Separated by some 100 miles, the ski meccas of Aspen and Vail couldn't be more different in spirit: the former is the see-and-be-seen equivalent of a snowbound St.-Tropez; the latter, a family-friendly take on a modern Bavarian village. Both have a surfeit of charm—so the only real question is, which do you choose to call your own?

Where to Stay

ASPEN Discerning skiers are heading to the iconic St. Regis Aspen Resort (*877/787-3447; stregis.com; $$$$*) for its butler service, Remède Spa, and ideal location between the mountain's two main lifts. A redesign gives the hotel a brand-new lobby and library, and the 179 rooms have a touch of Gilded Age opulence (ornamental metalwork; custom leather beds by Ralph Lauren). The 45-room Hotel Aspen (*800/527-7369; hotelaspen.com; $$*) is a hip alternative for travelers who prefer to spend their money on lift tickets or late-night magnums of Veuve Clicquot.

VAIL After several years and a $2 billion investment, Vail's village redevelopment is complete. The Four Seasons Resort Vail (*800/332-3442; fourseasons. com; $$$$*)—with its claw-foot tubs, slopeside ski club, and 75-foot heated outdoor pool—is the crown jewel of this renaissance. Budget-conscious visitors can find deals on rentals and hotels at vailonsale.com.

Après-ski

ASPEN Twentysomething bump-skiers take over the faux-fur-trimmed banquettes at the Kimpton's Sky Hotel

(*800/546-7866; theskyhotel. com*). A quieter scene unfolds as you sip hot toddies on fireside sofas in a lounge at the Little Nell (*888/843-6355; thelittlenell.com*), the area's most fashionable address.

VAIL The Arrabelle at Vail Square, a RockResort, has breathed new life into the Lionshead base area, with everyone from Mexican power brokers to Denver day-trippers convening at the hotel's Tavern on the Square (*970/754-7777; rockresorts. com*). On the menu: elk lettuce wraps, buffalo meatloaf, and a variety of local microbrews.

Where to Eat

ASPEN Upmarket fare such as osso buco makes Cache Cache (*970/925-3835; cachecache. com; $$$*) the choice reservation, though townies are flocking to casual newcomer Justice Snow's (*970/429-8192; justicesnows. com; $$*) for the artisanal drinks and addictive tempura pickles.

VAIL The house-cut steaks and 500-bottle wine list at Elway's (*970/754-7818; elways.com; $$$*) are giving competition to seasonal-American favorites Kelly Liken (*970/479-0175; kellyliken. com; $$*) and Larkspur (*970/754-8050; larkspurvail.com; $$*).

After Dark

ASPEN With a five-page spirits list that includes more than 80

tequilas and mezcals, Jimmy's, an American Restaurant & Bar (*205 S. Mill St.; 970/925-6020; jimmysaspen.com*) is the place for cocktail connoisseurs.

VAIL The Red Lion (*304 Bridge St.; 970/476-7676; theredlion. com*) is the area's standby; come for cans of Colorado-brewed Dale's Pale Ale and cover songs performed by guitarist Phil Long.

Bring It Back

ASPEN Look for delicate gemstone jewelry at the light-filled shop Maja DuBrul (*970/920-1133; majadubrul. com*), run by the granddaughter-in-law of Walter Paepcke, who founded modern-day Aspen.

VAIL Don't leave without stopping at Gorsuch (*970/476-2294; gorsuch.com*), the family-run boutique where coyote-fur boots and turquoise belt buckles set the bar for mountain fashion.

Outside Vail's base lodge.

A snowboarder catching air on Buttermilk Mountain, in Aspen. Left: A lounge at Aspen's Little Nell.

Justice Snow's bar in Aspen. Left: Rosemary-crusted rack of lamb at Elway's, in Vail.

PALM SPRINGS, CALIFORNIA

Chasing desert highs in an iconic weekend getaway

T

HIS IS A TALE OF TWO DESERTS: one as glittering and artificial as a futuristic theme park, the other as spare and elemental as boulders and cactus. It's a roughly 32-mile journey north from Palm Springs, the Midcentury Modern center of Southern California's low desert, to the beautifully barren high-desert communities of Joshua Tree and Pioneertown. Yet the cultural and spiritual distance between the two is almost immeasurable. The high desert is a frontier for artists that looks and feels like the Wild West. Style-obsessed Palm Springs' closest cousin might just be West Hollywood.

Having lived in Los Angeles for 15 years, I'm no stranger to Palm Springs or its surroundings. And yet, each visit feels like a slightly different party with a new host—or perhaps the same old showgirl with a face-lift. The millennium has been kind to the city: a government rebate on room occupancy taxes has encouraged multimillion-dollar hotel renovations; the Coachella music festival brings thousands of young rockers and ravers to the area; the Palm Springs International Film Festival draws Hollywood A-listers; and Modernism Week attracts architecture and design addicts.

Joshua Tree National Forest. Opposite: Sunbathing at the Colony Palms Hotel.

"The recession weeded out the mediocre," Palm Springs painter Eric Nash tells me and fellow artist Russell Bennett over pizzas and salads at Birba, a Modernist café in the trendy Uptown Design District. Uptown, as it is known by the locals, has long lured drive-by design fans: it's a place where interior decorators and vintage-furniture hounds go to score home accessories in such Palm Springs styles as postwar modern, Hollywood Regency, disco-era minimalism, and Philippe Starck contemporary. Now, with two hip hotels, the Colony Palms Hotel and the Alcazar Palm Springs, and new restaurants, including Birba and its sister lunch spot, Cheeky's, the neighborhood has become the city's latest in-crowd hub. Art galleries are also sprouting up amid the vintage stores. Nash, who does moody charcoals of ravens and night skies, and Bennett, an abstract painter, show their work at Stephen Archdeacon Gallery, an airy space with darker-themed works. Nearby, Atomic Age–inspired illustrator-painter Josh Agle (better known as Shag) showcases his art at Shag: The Store, which is filled with cartoonish depictions of the Palm Springs lifestyle: neo–Rat Packers sipping cocktails by grand-piano-shaped pools.

IF PALM SPRINGS IS FOR THE MARTINI-HOISTING SET, THE HIGH DESERT IS ITS ANTITHESIS.

The four-block-long Uptown strip caters to Agle's Shag fantasy with all the Eames and Saarinen you'd need to furnish a modern home. Wandering into Christopher Anthony boutique and the mansion-style Boulevard, however, I find high-ticket 20th-century decorative arts by mid-century architect-designers such as Paul Frankl and prints by Shepard Fairey. Visiting the nearby Stewart Galleries, a treasure trove of paintings and furniture, is like stumbling into your very rich, very tasteful bachelor uncle's attic.

In Palm Springs, everything old is always, eventually, new again. That's certainly true for hotels. After nearly 90 years as a vacation spot, the city endures as a place where visions of the future that were formed in the past now define the present. As a result, Midcentury Modernism is the default design style, but Hollywood Regency, the ornate 1930's MGM-movie-set trend initiated by Kelly Wearstler at the Viceroy in Palm Springs in 2003, has also taken off, reaching giddy heights. At the 1950's Riviera Palm Springs, a $70 million redo—complete with a crystal-studded billiard table and miles of patterned wallpaper—proves that even in Palm Springs, "more is more" is usually over-the-top.

In the Uptown Design District, however, the Colony Palms and the Alcazar have both been reimagined: their original Spanish-colonial aesthetic is one of the last native design styles to get a high-drama makeover. A few years ago, Martyn Lawrence Bullard of Bravo TV's *Million Dollar Decorators* redid the 1930's Colony Palms into a glam-Moroccan oasis featuring a two-story luxury suite named the Palme d'Or Residence. He also created the generally mobbed Purple Palm, the intimate hotel's olive-green-and-violet bistro, which harks back to Hollywood supper clubs. Renovated by Birba owners Tara Lazar and Marco Rossetti, Alcazar is a smaller, less scene-y alternative to the Colony Palms. Room 22 is a white sugar cube with IKEA furniture and quirky paintings, a refreshing change from the *Jetsons*-style design that saturates the rest of the city.

So too is the Horizon Hotel. Designed by Palm Springs Modernist William F. Cody in 1952, the surprisingly minimalist (no restaurant, no spa) Horizon is a haven in the burgeoning East Palm Canyon Drive corridor—once a strip of cheap motels, now the center of cool-hunter hangouts such as the Jonathan Adler–designed Parker Palm Springs and the Ace Hotel, as well as a secret stash of vintage design shops on nearby Perez Road, which has been dubbed Resale Row. It has stood the test of time, defining the architectural ideals of its era and the magnificence of Palm Springs' zoning code, which restricts structures more than two stories high and streetlights in residential areas. Its window-walled rooms frame what might be the best views of the nearly 11,000-foot-high San Jacinto Mountains that the city has to offer, and the hotel's A-series rooms have private outdoor showers; Marilyn Monroe, it is said, caused a commotion by actually using one. (Hollywood lore is the water-cooler currency of Palm Springs, where you can visit Elvis's Honeymoon Hideaway, a 1962 Modernist masterpiece, and take architectural historian Michael Stern's Modern Tour to see Frank Sinatra's Twin Palms villa—yours to rent for $2,600 a night.)

If Palm Springs is for the movie-star-struck, Eames-chair-loving, martini-hoisting set, the high desert is its antithesis, a bohemia for solitary stoner-like contemplation, where the imaginations of artists, designers, and architects can run as untamed as the landscape. Like Palm Springs, the high desert has one main road—Highway 62, which rises up thousands of feet from the low desert floor—but instead of butterfly-roof buildings, it is dotted with folk-art installations and Western saloons. Palm Springs entices the senses; the high desert exalts the natural world and stirs the soul. And yet it too is in the throes of reinvention. In Desert Hot Springs, an early example of Modernist architect John Lautner has been transformed into Hotel Lautner, complete with all the contemporary luxuries, including a newly added spa pool and outdoor showers. Originally built in 1947, the compound was conceived as a prototype for a planned community, with four apartments featuring private step-up garden patios. It is one of the few Lautner buildings that is open to the public.

Travel farther north and the high desert offers new architecture that rivals the post–World War II buildings of Palm Springs and Lautner's desert dream homes. And today, a small group of designers are pioneering structures from straw bales, rusted steel, shipping containers, and agricultural building materials that could sit beside midcentury Palm Springs homes as contemporary examples of futurist design. None are more impressive than two rentable properties by architect Robert Stone,

the all-black Rosa Muerta bunker and the Acido Dorado, a golden Xanadu that seems to burst out of the desert landscape in Joshua Tree.

As well as a home for bold new buildings, the high desert is also a crafty art colony filled with unusual studios and galleries. At the Noah Purifoy Outdoor Desert Art Museum of Assemblage Sculpture, I am amazed by the ingenuity and keen social satire in what first appears to be a junkyard, where entire environments are rendered from the detritus of modern life: a train composed of aged upright vacuum cleaners; a shack with bicycles launching off its roof; sculptural towers of toilets

and bowling balls that seem to defy gravity. To walk through it is to experience recycling as art.

Palm Springs may have swank, low-lit supper clubs, but in the high desert, casual dinner parties are part of the community spirit—social without the snobbery. Eating out is equally simple and considerably tastier than it is in fussier Palm Springs restaurants, if characteristically odd: the only Indian food in Joshua Tree is at Sam's Pizza; chili and barbecue that rivals the best in Texas can be found at Pappy & Harriet's Pioneertown Palace; and I quickly become addicted to the fresh, chewy granola bars and Rock Climbers Revenge banana-date-cashew smoothies at the Natural Sisters Café. Go ahead, snicker at that name—I did—but it's emblematic of the unrepentantly unpretentious high-desert ethos.

I'm also amused by the New Age–sounding Sacred Sands, the two-suite inn that Steve Pratt and Scott Cutler built from straw bales and rusted corrugated metal. Rough on the outside, the two rooms are cool and sexy, with dark, sparkly walls, beds with ironed linens, and light fixtures made from scrap metal, Moroccan lanterns, and a burled wood lamp. There are no televisions, not even in the owners' quarters. "This is a place to disconnect from the static and connect to nature and to ourselves," Pratt says. Which is exactly what I do, drifting off into a sunset siesta as a solid steel fence clangs in the wind. This is the essence of the high desert, the "aah" moment that leads to the "aha" epiphany. Here, there is a frequency—a low internal hum—that is not as easily received as the high-pitched buzz of Palm Springs. That vibration fills my head on a trip to Pioneertown as I walk along Mane Street (the pun is intentional). At the end of the road, a slyly witty stop sign perfectly captures the welcoming spirit and cosmic directive of both deserts, high and low. It reads simply: IT'S YOUR DECISION. I decide to stay another night, to watch the stars and enjoy the big, empty silence. If I want excitement, after all, there's always Palm Springs.

GUIDE

STAY

Ace Hotel & Swim Club
701 E. Palm Canyon Dr., Palm Springs; 760/325-9900; acehotel.com. **$**

Acido Dorado
Joshua Tree; prettyvacant properties.com; two-night minimum. **$$$**

Alcazar Palm Springs
622 Indian Canyon Dr., Palm Springs; 760/318-9850; alcazarpalmsprings. com. **$**

Colony Palms Hotel
572 N. Indian Canyon Dr., Palm Springs; 800/557-2187; colonypalmshotel.com. **$**

Horizon Hotel
1050 E. Palm Canyon Dr., Palm Springs; 800/377-7855; thehorizonhotel.com. **$**

Hotel Lautner
67710 San Antonio St., Desert Hot Springs; 760/832-5288; hotellautner.com. **$$**

Riviera Palm Springs
1600 N. Indian Canyon Dr.,

Palm Springs; 866/588-8311, psriviera.com. **$$**

Sacred Sands
63155 Quail Springs Rd., Joshua Tree; 760/424-6407; sacredsands.com. **$$**

Viceroy Palm Springs
415 S. Belardo Rd., Palm Springs; 760/320-4117; viceroyhotelsandresorts. com. **$**

EAT

Birba
622 N. Palm Canyon Dr., Palm Springs; 760/327-5678; birbaps.com. **$$**

Natural Sisters Café
61695 29 Palms Hwy., Joshua Tree; 760/366-3600. **$**

Pappy & Harriet's Pioneertown Palace
53688 Pioneertown Rd., Pioneertown; 760/365-5956; pappyandharriets.com. **$$**

Purple Palm
572 N. Indian Canyon Dr., Palm Springs; 800/557-2187; colonypalmshotel. com. **$$$**

Sam's Pizza & Indian Food
61380 29 Palms Hwy., Joshua Tree; 760/366-9511 **$$**

DO

Noah Purifoy Outdoor Desert Art Museum of Assemblage Sculpture
Joshua Tree; 213/382-7516.

Stephen Archdeacon Gallery
865 N. Palm Canyon Dr., Palm Springs; 760/673-7520; stephen archdeacongallery.com.

SHOP

Christopher Anthony
800 N. Palm Canyon Dr., Palm Springs; 760/322-0600; christopheranthonyltd. com.

Shag: The Store
725 N. Palm Canyon Dr., Palm Springs; 760/322-3400.

Stewart Galleries
191 S. Indian Canyon Dr., Palm Springs; 760/325-0878.

Adapted from "Desert Highs," by David A. Keeps.

Surf breaking
on Malibu's
Point Dume
beach.

MALIBU, CALIFORNIA

A place where life really is a beach

Everybody has a chronic travel daydream, the escape to fantasize about when conference calls drag on or e-mail gluts the inbox. In the grip of a deadline, I'm a surf-side California dreamer. I can't actually surf, but something about the image of wave riders barefooting it across Malibu's Pacific Coast Highway at dawn, boards tucked under their arms, makes me wish I were Sandra Dee as Gidget frolicking on Surfrider Beach in a bikini or Cheryl Ladd hanging out at Kris Munroe's beach house in *Charlie's Angels*.

Some people argue that the food and fashion scenes in Malibu are unremarkable; it's hard to see beyond the Barbie and *Baywatch* image of the place. But to my mind Malibu—especially its free-spirited barefoot approach to life—is the fountainhead of many of America's most influential style trends. Most fashion editors roll their eyes if you suggest that trends in clothes move from west to east. As a big-city native, I, too, find the reality of Malibu's wave of surfer style easier to ride in a daydream than in reality. But when you think about how casual our culture has become, how we dress less for business than for comfort, it's hard to dispute that American fashion etiquette has been shaped by California's outdoor-life, laid-back style. The long-skirted bohemian look, hoodies, Vans, those weird Vibram FiveFingers shoes, anything neon, hobo bags, trilbies, and vintage graphic T-shirts are all products of the West Coast's skate and surf culture.

My first stop after dropping my bags at the Malibu Beach Inn—a once rundown motel rehabbed by David Geffen—was lunch at Taverna Tony with Ron Herman, the legendary Los Angeles retailer. It was Herman who, along with his uncle Fred Segal, helped shape the Malibu look of sexy, colorful, and casual clothes: jeans, tight T-shirts, and print dresses. Segal bought a dumpy motel on Cross Creek Road back in 1975 and set up shops in the ground-floor rooms, filling them with imported European labels and turning it into a shopping center called the Malibu Country Mart.

In the galaxy of great retail stars, Herman is a supernova. He is also a rebel who knows what he likes and looked *verklempt* at the idea of dining at one of Malibu's more touristy spots. He loves to tell the story of the time three out-of-towners asked him how to get to the town of Malibu. "I told them there is no Malibu," Herman says with a laugh. "It's just a highway and three strip malls."

It's true that if you don't know what to look for or where to go, you could cruise up Pacific Coast Highway from Santa Monica and never notice the back sides of billionaire mansions on Carbon Beach. You could get all the way to Zuma Beach, on the northern end of Malibu, with its postcard-perfect lifeguard stations silhouetted against the sunset, and be wondering, "Are we there yet?"

As many songwriters have pointed out, Malibu is as much a state of mind as it is that 27-mile slice of California coastline that runs from Topanga to Ventura County. Head north and on your left lie the famous point breaks known to surfers around the world. If you look closely off Point Dume, you can see dolphins jumping or, in late spring, gray whales migrating north with their calves. On your right are the cliffs and Santa Monica Mountains terraced with gigantic estates and rehab centers. After heavy rains, the cliffs tend to slide across the highway, further isolating Malibu from the sprawling madness of Los Angeles.

When Segal opened the Country Mart, he made a playground for local kids to romp in while their moms shopped for gypsy blouses and low-slung jeans. "We were dressing people for the beach, but also for the country," adds Herman over a huge California salad. "That's what made Malibu unique and still does—the authenticity of the country life mixed with beach life." The Country Mart is just as popular now as it was back then. You might see Oscar nominees pushing their offspring on swings between lunch at the Italian trattoria, Tra di Noi, and shopping for sun-faded T-shirts at Planet Blue.

Thirty-five years ago, Malibu was a place where families lived earthy and artistic lives up in the canyons. They had horses and farms; they came down to the Country Mart in riding clothes. Artists still live up in those hills, but so do Courteney Cox, Pierce Brosnan, and Kelsey Grammer.

A premium on privacy and independence has prevailed in Malibu since the end of the 19th century, when May Rindge and her husband, Frederick, bought Rancho Malibu and later fought to keep a railroad and public roads from running through it. To this day Malibu has no Main Street or town center. The post office is in a strip mall next to a greasy spoon called the Country Kitchen, where a guy named Morry shoos away paparazzi while serving breakfast burritos by the side of the highway. The trailer park, whose residents refer to their homes as "land yachts," is called Paradise Cove, and the best lobster and fish tacos can be ordered from the same ramshackle restaurant on site.

This nonconformist style tends to minimize the distinctions between high and low. You can come to Malibu just to drop in on a wave, as so many day-tripping surfers do, or you can come to Malibu and drop $47 million on three oceanfront lots. There's an appealing absence of attitude and status anxiety.

"When I was growing up here, people did not wear clothes," says Laurie Lynn Stark, whose husband, Richard, cofounded the Chrome Hearts brand in a Malibu garage. "You went barefoot in a bikini to the market, and that was not weird. T-shirts with cowboy boots and boxer shorts rolled down was not an unusual look."

This spirit of sunstruck dishabille, which seems blended from Malibu's traditional anti-conformity and its mountain and ocean views, can make even the most simply dressed urban fashionista feel conspicuous, as I did in a plain uniform of black pants and jacket. Indeed, if you show up at Nobu in anything fancier than sandals, you'll get the side eye from locals. And when people come back from L.A., they apologize for being so dressed up.

Some Angelenos drift up to Malibu for the outdoor lifestyle or the close-knit community and never go back. Rande Gerber and Cindy Crawford found Malibu to be the ideal place to raise their kids. "I can run my business from my home office and watch my son surf after school," says Gerber, who opened a branch of New York's Café Habana in the Malibu Lumber Yard shopping center in part so that he could have a place to go for dinner with his family and friends.

The first time I visited Malibu, I remember talking with a friend about the vast difference between the casual vibe of his Malibu lifestyle and my stressed-out frenzy back in New York City. In retrospect I didn't "get" Malibu. I couldn't imagine why people would pay millions of dollars to live in rickety houses overhanging the ocean with the Pacific Coast Highway zooming through their living rooms. And the surfer dudes who parked on PCH seemed mad to me. But on my recent visit it was only a matter of hours before I had peeled off black layers of urban gear and suited up in jeans and a T-shirt, captivated by the sight of sun-bleached barefoot surfers crisscrossing parking lots, surfboards in hand, stoked to catch a wave.

Adapted from "Malibu State of Mind," by Kate Betts.

GUIDE

STAY
Casa Malibu Inn on the Beach
Prime views of area real estate from Carbon Beach. *22752 Pacific Coast Hwy.; 800/831-0858.* **$**

Malibu Beach Inn
22878 Pacific Coast Hwy.; 310/456-8004; malibubeachinn.com. **$$$**

EAT
Café Habana Malibu
3939 Cross Creek Rd.; 310/317-0300; habana-malibu.com. **$$$**

Country Kitchen
21239 Pacific Coast Hwy.; 310/456-8708. **$$**

Taverna Tony
23410 Civic Center Way; 310/317-9667; tavernatony.com. **$$**

Tra di Noi
3835 Cross Creek Rd.; 310/456-0169; tradinoimalibu.com. **$$$**

SHOP
Chrome Hearts
3835 Cross Creek Rd.;

310/456-5533; chromehearts.com.

Malibu Country Mart
3835 Cross Creek Rd.; 310/456-7300; malibucountrymart.com.

Planet Blue
3835 Cross Creek Rd.; 310/317-9975; shopplanetblue.com.

Ron Herman
3900 Cross Creek Rd.; 310/317-6705; ronherman.com.

Lunchtime
at Mammoth
Mountain Ski
Area's McCoy
Station.

EASTERN SIERRA, CALIFORNIA

A journey into the Wild West

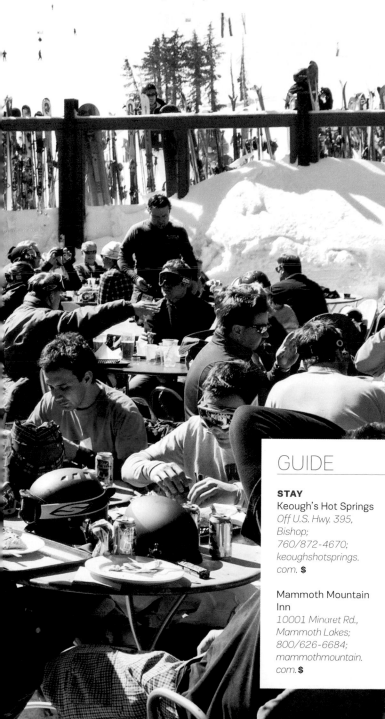

THE EASTERN SIERRA IS HOME to some of the most striking landscape in the country: silvery desert, vast lakes, fairy-tale mountains with a thick frosting of snow. Western movies have long loved this part of California's rugged central corridor. In Lone Pine, bone up on the Hollywood connection at the Museum of Lone Pine Film History, then stop for lunch at the convivial Alabama Hills Café; the berry pies are so fresh that the fruit is still sizzling. At the Eastern California Museum, in Independence, you can learn about the local mining lore. From there it's 35 miles north to Keough's Hot Springs, where the combination of steaming water, icy air, and a winey picnic dinner will send you toppling into the heated tent cabins and groggily, happily to sleep.

Start the next day in Bishop with several bracing shots of java at Black Sheep Espresso Bar, in Spellbinder Books, an excellent independent bookseller. Down the street, the bait and flies at Culver's Sporting Goods speak of summery afternoons on the Sierra's glassine lakes. Mammoth Mountain, however, reveals a more heart-pounding pastime. There are few feelings better than waking up at the Mammoth Mountain Inn to slopes covered in new-fallen powder—just beckoning you to jump right in.

GUIDE

STAY
Keough's Hot Springs
Off U.S. Hwy. 395, Bishop; 760/872-4670; keoughshotsprings. com. **$**

Mammoth Mountain Inn
10001 Minaret Rd., Mammoth Lakes; 800/626-6684; mammothmountain. com. **$**

EAT
Alabama Hills Café & Bakery
111 W. Post St., Lone Pine; 760/876-4675. **$$**

DO
Beverly & Jim Rogers Museum of Lone Pine Film History
701 S. Main St., Lone Pine; 760/876-9103; lonepine filmhistorymuseum.org.

Eastern California Museum
155 N. Grand St., Independence; 760/878-0364; inyocounty.us/ecmuseum.

SHOP
Culver's Sporting Goods
156 S. Main St., Bishop; 760/872-8361.

Spellbinder Books
124 S. Main St., Bishop; 760/873-4511; spellbinderbookstore.com.

A view of downtown Seattle from the deck of the Bainbridge Island ferry.

SEATTLE

The Emerald City—beyond Starbucks and Nirvana

A S THE PLANE BEGINS ITS descent into Seattle's airport, I write in my notebook: "New take on Seattle necessary for article. Avoid all weather clichés and weather by-products. No rain, no melancholy, no coffee, no flannel, no grunge."

It's not going to be easy. As we cut through the melancholy, leaden sky, the new Boeings parked on the tarmac like so many late-model cars, our airplane shakes from the crosswind on approach, pelted by the Northwest's machine-gun fire of rain, the remains of my coffee spilling onto my flannel shirt, and the chorus of Nirvana's "Smells Like Teen Spirit" queuing up in the Wurlitzer of my mind. "Hello, hello, hello, how low." Welcome to Seattle. Always different. Always the same.

I write fiction for a living, so I go to Seattle *a lot*. Perhaps because of homegrown Amazon.com, perhaps in spite of it, Seattle (and its smaller cousin Portland, Oregon) is one of the last places in America where books are still a dominant part of the culture—consumed, discussed, pondered, and critiqued with gusto. But let's hold off on the literary for a moment. Seattle is a frame of mind. Nature surely wasn't on sabbatical when she conjured up this landscape of hills and water. Even the world's most distracted person will find room for serious meditation and introspection here, a place for the mind to power down into a deep regenerative sleep as a fresh drizzle plays against the windowpane. I'm on the life-affirming ferry ride from Seattle to Bainbridge Island, the city's rather quaint steel-and-glass skyline receding behind me, nature rushing in to tickle the eye with aquatic sparkles of sun, the green, hibernating islands strung out across the horizon like outstretched arms. A big, bearded man choking on his loneliness tells me the story of his life, which concludes with the line "I was too stressed out working at the Hilton, so now I just take the ferry back and forth." This seems to me to sum up some greater Pacific Northwestern wisdom. Cue

Boats going through the Ballard Locks. Above: A breakfast spread at Café Presse, in Capitol Hill.

the melancholy—this is not a city that turns its back on sadness. There are many things to do here but after a while, with a sense of resignation, one just may take the ferry back and forth.

These days Seattle is hovering on the edge of greatness. If and when a comprehensive light-rail system is finished, easing the city's Bangkok-grade traffic jams, that "world city" effect may well be achieved. But not everyone may be pleased. More than just about any other place in America, Seattle is a city of fierce neighborhood patriots, all attached to their particular hills like the Romans.

My friend Christopher Frizzelle is one such patriot of a particular hill, in his case Capitol Hill, perched commandingly over downtown, one of the world's great full-service neighborhoods, awash in everything from Seattle-style Indian *thali* to salted-caramel ice cream. Chris works at America's strangest and clearly best alternative newspaper, named, appropriately enough, *The Stranger*. How strange is *The Stranger*? It once ran an article on Seattle's six sexiest trees.

Any visitor could tell you that Seattle is a welcoming, unpretentious city, but it is best to harness the town's quirky (read: insane) residents to expose its nooks and crannies. So for an entire week I handed myself over to Chris and Bethany Jean Clement, *The Stranger*'s managing editor and food critic, and to a small group of Seattle friends. We ate, we drank, we drank and ate, we scrambled all over in a series of increasingly contentious cab rides, we read books, we looked at fish and clouds, and we did some other things that I can't remember.

But did I mention that we read books? Seattle is home to the Elliott Bay Book Company, a legendary fixture of downtown's Pioneer Square that relocated to Capitol Hill. The Book Company has hosted readings by anybody who's anybody, from Seattle resident Sherman Alexie to gadfly Ralph Nader. But the best reading series in Seattle may not involve any writers at all. These are Chris's regular readings held at the historic Sorrento Hotel. No bearded poets mounting the podium here. People simply gather with their books and silently read. Kind of like your college library, except it is held in the Sorrento's gorgeous Fireside Room, replete with plush banquettes, an original fireplace, and, very much unlike your college library, an excellent selection of liquor. The hush, the gentle communion, along with the flicker of intent conversation, permeates the alcoholic glow of the room. These are some of the most attractive people I've seen in Seattle, and their noses are buried in books and booze.

The Seattle Central Library is itself a wonder, one of the first significant buildings in the United States by Dutch architect Rem Koolhaas. After a roll down First Hill from the Sorrento Hotel, I see Koolhaas's library sparkling in the middle of the dull downtown core like a dark crystal. Set within the business district's no-frills street grid, the library's angled sheaths of glass skin conceal a chartreuse dream world of tomes, escalators, and reading spaces, the blue slivers of Elliott Bay peeking between the city's towers. Looking out upon the water with a book in hand, one feels present inside a giant hive mind, a perfect balance of the interior and exterior life that defines Seattle.

The next day, we head to lunch at Café Presse, on Capitol Hill. Every neighborhood in the world should have a replica of the Presse. The décor is minimal Northwestern, and Seattle's cool kids are actually more like cool adults. The Caffé Vita brand café au lait is masterful. The roasted-carrot soup is as creamy as the aforementioned café au lait. Café Presse is effortlessly cosmopolitan. It's one of the few places in the neighborhood where you can watch soccer games and, should the inexplicable urge strike you, score fresh copies of *Le Nouvel Observateur* and *Le Monde Diplomatique*.

For dinner, I join friends in Seattle's current grungy (forgive me) neighborhood of the moment, the industrially deformed, airport-adjacent Georgetown. Here we find ourselves completely cut off from Capitol Hill's fine selection of French

■ EVEN THE WORLD'S MOST DISTRACTED PERSON FINDS ROOM FOR SERIOUS INTROSPECTION HERE.

Opposite: Browsing through the stacks in Capitol Hill's Elliott Bay Book Company.

GUIDE

STAY

Edgewater Hotel
Pine furniture and river-rock fireplaces accent this cozy, lodge-style property on Elliott Bay. *2411 Alaskan Way, Pier 67; 800/624-0670; edgewaterhotel.com.* **$$**

Four Seasons Hotel Seattle
This 147-room hotel near Pike Place Market features bay views and a terraced pool. *99 Union St.; 800/819-5053; fourseasons.com.* **$$**

Hotel 1000
Futuristic hotel that's ideal for business travelers, located within walking distance of Pike Place Market and Pioneer Square. *1000 First Ave.; 877/315-1088; hotel1000seattle.com.* **$$**

Sorrento Hotel
900 Madison St.; 800/426-1265; hotelsorrento.com. **$**

EAT AND DRINK

Café Besalu
5909 24th Ave. N.W.; 206/789-1463; cafebesalu.com. **$**

Café Presse
1117 12th Ave.; 206/709-7674; cafepresseseattle.com. **$$**

Corson Building
5609 Corson Ave. S.; 206/762-3330; thecorsonbuilding. com. **$$$$**

9lb Hammer
6009 Airport Way S.; 206/762-3373; ninepoundhammer.com.

Ocho
2325 Market St. N.W.; 206/784-0699; ochoballard.com. **$$**

DO

Gas Works Park
2101 N. Northlake Way; 206/684-4075; seattle.gov.

Seattle Central Library
1000 Fourth Ave.; 206/386-4636; spl.org.

SHOP

Elliott Bay Book Company
1521 10th Ave.; 206/624-6600; elliottbaybook.com.

newspapers, but beneath a freeway overpass we encounter another unlikely jewel, the charming Corson Building, a restaurant by the owner of Capitol Hill's beloved Sitka & Spruce. This former Italian stonemason's house delights with a lion-faced fireplace, rustic communal tables, and the softest of autumnal candlelight. On our visit we go ape over an elastic, complex geoduck, cured pork loin with almonds still in their furry green skins, buttery morels, and Dungeness crab so fresh and true that this dish alone makes living in the Pacific Northwest worthwhile.

We walk out of the restaurant's vegetable garden, as bucolic as you can get for being under a freeway, and into the diesel-scented night. The freight trains still thunder by the 9lb Hammer bar, which has been drawing vast crowds into its high-ceilinged, dimly lit industrial space, formerly used as cold storage but now suffused with deep, boozy warmth.

The best place to recover from a night out is Gas Works Park, in Wallingford. I sit on the sun-warmed grass and stare at the postindustrial wonderland that once was the Seattle Gas Light Company's gasification plant, its rusted structures abutting the central Lake Union like the skeleton of a particularly dear mammoth. Seaplanes are landing, the skyline glittering, the college kids are getting high. When the sun is out, everything feels possible. Seattle is your Dungeness oyster, a land of unfettered blue and green.

I haven't had a perfect day in an American city in ages, so I feel the need to shout out about this one. It did not take place in any post-Cobain hipster utopia. Instead, Chris and I spend a day in Ballard, which began life as a Scandinavian fishing village about a half-hour's drive northwest of downtown. For breakfast we get into a Soviet-long line at Café Besalu, but the results are well worth it: a seductive cardamom pretzel; an expletive of an asparagus,

Manchego, and ham quiche; an orange-glazed brioche that lands like a warm, moist patch on the tongue. With coffee in our bellies, we feel awake and ready to hit Ballard's aquatic landscape.

The edges of the fishing village are lined with boatyards, and we walk with a caffeinated step along the train tracks that skirt the yards, running into the most authentic hobo camp I've ever seen, seemingly lifted straight out of the WPA era.

We spend an inordinate amount of time hanging out by the Ballard Locks, watching the boats lifted and lowered into place with a kind of innocent fascination. There's a drama to the locks, the spray of greenish water, the taut lines tying the boats together, the boat captains preparing their craft, the anticipation of entry and departure.

My finest Ballard discovery is a Spanish tapas bar named Ocho that is slightly off the tourist strip of Ballard Avenue, attached like a little mole to the side of an Azteca chain restaurant and a divorce lawyer's office. A snug place that feels like it has been there since the Inquisition, it features copper, tin, and gilded mirrors, and about 30 people crammed into heaven. We chug unremarkable Estrella lager to capture the authentic Spanishness, and match it with thick, olive-soaked *jamón serrano*, salty anchovies exuding pepper and brine, a toothpick banderilla holding together chorizo, apple marmalade, and Valdeón blue cheese, then more courses of cold, smooth asparagus gazpacho, flaky lamb meatballs slathered in wine, and a deviled egg with caviar, soft and spicy. Ocho is one of the best, most authentic, and happiest restaurants I have visited in years. The highly evolved New York tapas bar scene feels crude by comparison. Two guys, probably with the combined age of 42, work the kitchen, and $53 pays for a full drunken meal for two. I love Seattle.

■ WHEN THE SUN IS OUT, SEATTLE IS YOUR DUNGENESS OYSTER, A LAND OF UNFETTERED BLUE AND GREEN.

Adapted from "Seattle State of Mind," by Gary Shteyngart.

WILLAMETTE VALLEY, OREGON

An unspoiled wine region ripe for discovery

THE WILLAMETTE VALLEY REVELS in its role as the "anti-Napa." A 45-minute drive southwest of Portland, Oregon, it has no big-name estates or oversize tour buses; vineyards are small and irregularly shaped, threaded between strawberry patches and fields of ryegrass. Despite all that, the wines here are quietly spectacular. And slowly but surely, word is getting out.

The catalyst for this newfound awareness is the LEED-certified Allison Inn & Spa, in Newberg—the first Willamette hotel wherein the term *thread count* came into play. There are fireplaces and fruit- and herb-scented bath salts in the guest rooms, cascading water and kinesis machines in the fitness center, Steven Smith teas in the sun-drenched lobby. With its refined yet low-key hospitality, and a signature restaurant serving seasonal specialties made with the area's bounty, the Allison draws a discerning (and predictably wine-savvy) crowd.

Local grape growers and self-taught enologists aren't typically the sort to court publicity, but ask the concierge about winery visits and you'll get a personalized itinerary. Planted on a prehistoric rock ledge in the Eola-Amity Hills, the vines on the windswept Antica Terra estate produce bottles of uncommon minerality, best shown in their 2010 Pinot Noir. At the Trisaetum winery in Newberg, try the 2010 Ribbon Ridge Vineyard Dry Riesling, all tangy lime and grapefruit. And at Bethel Heights, a family-owned vineyard edged by 100-year-old walnut trees, white-grape lovers swoon over the 2010 Estate Chardonnay. You'd better get there fast.

GUIDE

STAY
Allison Inn & Spa
2525 Allison Lane, Newberg; 503/554-2525; theallison.com. **$$**

TASTE
Antica Terra
979 S.W. Alder St., Dundee; 503/244-1748; anticaterra.com.

Bethel Heights
6060 Bethel Heights Rd. N.W., Salem; 503/581-2262; bethelheights.com.

Trisaetum
18401 Ribbon Ridge Rd., Newberg; 503/538-9898; trisaetum.com.

Bethel Heights winery's lush vineyards.

OAHU, HAWAII

Taking stock of the islands' next food wave

Lani Kai Beach, in Kailua. Opposite: Drinking up at a coconut stand on the North Shore.

T HAS BEEN TWO DECADES SINCE A COTERIE of forward-thinking chefs put Hawaii on the culinary map. Seizing on the then current trend for East-West fusion (think wasabi mashed potatoes), they blended classical techniques with Hawaiian ingredients, mixed in bold Asian flavors, and called their style Hawaii Regional Cuisine. It was a thrilling amalgam, and HRC's star burned brightly for a spell, making celebrity chefs of Alan Wong, Roy Yamaguchi, Sam Choy, and Peter Merriman. But as Pac-Rim fusion's novelty faded, foodies' affections shifted, like those temperamental Kona winds, to more beguiling shores. By the turn of the millennium, the term *fusion* had become a slur.

Which isn't to knock the HRC chefs' chops. Most of the original crew are still doing fine work today—and, for plenty of visitors, their names, dishes, and many restaurants still define Hawaiian dining, fickle food trends be damned.

But something else has happened, as a new generation of food pioneers emerges. They've embraced HRC's creative spirit and applied it to more traditional Hawaiian foods, drawing from the islands' past as much as the globalized future. They've amped up their commitment to sustainability, to local farmers and ranchers and fishermen, and to unsung or forgotten ingredients. They've moved past the gimmicky aspects of fusion to embrace its tenets naturally, intuitively, as only pan-ethnic, polyglot Hawaiians could do.

They're cooking some extraordinary food. And they're making it more accessible, in presentation and price, to Hawaii's workaday population, not just to well-heeled diners and tourists.

That last point is fundamental and explains a lot about where you'll find the new breed. Hawaii's next wave is cresting not in the fine dining rooms of Waikiki, but in an ever growing number of roving food trucks, farmers'-market stands, plate-lunch diners, guerrilla pop-ups, surfers' haunts, barbecue pits, and hyper-creative hot-dog and hamburger joints. Suddenly Hawaii is one of the most exciting places to eat in the country.

The beachhead of the movement is a defiantly casual Honolulu restaurant called Town, run by Oahu-born chef Ed Kenney. With his sleeve tattoos and flair for charcuterie, Kenney would fit right in among the hipster chefs of Brooklyn; Portland, Oregon; and Montreal—except he's clean-shaven, built like a surfer, and as Hawaiian as they come.

Flush against the hillsides of suburban Kaimuki, far from the thrum of Waikiki, Town feels more neighborhood canteen than haute-dining mecca. The interior is a study in slacker chic, with hardwood benches, rough-hewn plank walls, and portraits of island farmers hung with easel clips.

The kitchen is far more ambitious. Take that charcuterie: all of it cured in-house, and all made with Hawaiian pork, from the spicy soppressata to the cumin-spiked terrine. Tart pickled star fruit provides the ideal counterpoint.

Kenney's beef comes from the Big Island's Kuahiwi Ranch, where it's pasture-raised and grain-finished for a pleasing minerality balanced with the depth of fat. A seared flatiron steak is served with local watercress and dense, chewy coins of fried *paiai*, or mashed taro root. *Paiai*—the solid form of Hawaii's beloved poi—has all but vanished from island menus, since small-scale production of it virtually ceased. But a native Hawaiian named Daniel Anthony recently began selling his own organic, hand-pounded brand, to the delight of chefs like Kenney. If anything could stand in for fried potatoes with steak, it's this.

Other curious regional ingredients find their way onto Kenney's plates. A filet of buttery opah (moonfish) is sprinkled with feathery limu seaweed and sided with *pohole* ferns, lending umami and earthiness to the fish. Town especially dazzles with island-farmed greens and herbs, most of them sourced from MA'O Organic Farms, on Oahu's western shore. Even the bartenders get in on the act, muddling arugula, celery, sage, and fresh turmeric into the cocktails.

Indeed, turn up any Saturday at Honolulu's crazy-popular KCC Farmers' Market and you'll be floored by the range of ingredients on offer: tropical rambutan, sea asparagus, wild mushrooms, bitter melon, abalone, goat cheese, duck eggs, sweet Ewa corn, tangerines, taro, Kona coffee beans, locally made Madre Chocolate, Maui lavender, avocados the size of your head. For a traveler accustomed to islands in, say, the Caribbean—where fresh produce is depressingly scarce—the variety and quality of homegrown foods is startling.

Hawaii is blessed with such natural bounty that it's shocking to learn that the state actually imports 85 percent of its food, at a cost of $3.6 billion a year. Dismaying but true: between the high price of local labor, the loss of farmland to rezoning, and the vagaries of the global supply chain, it's cheaper (at least superficially) for Hawaiians to ship food in rather than grow it themselves. This, in one of the most remote places on earth.

At the edge of Kaneohe Bay, an old fishing pier juts into the water. Roped alongside are a few dozen houseboats and rusty-hulled fishing boats. At pier's end stands a ramshackle bait-and-coffee shop that, for 30 years, served basic diner grub to fishermen and surfers. In 2011 two friends—chef Mark Noguchi and restaurateur Russ Inouye—took over the lease. Today, He'eia Pier General Store & Deli is one of the best restaurants in Hawaii, if you could properly call it a restaurant.

■ ON OAHU, YOU CAN EAT EXCEPTIONALLY WELL IN THE LEAST ASSUMING PLACES.

Opposite, clockwise from top left: Sustainably harvested Madre Chocolate; surf's up on Oahu's leeward coast; a salad at Town restaurant, in Honolulu, made with organic vegetables from MA'O Organic Farms; Town's chef de cuisine, Dave Caldiero, left, and owner, Ed Kenney.

Noguchi, 37, was born on Oahu and raised on the Big Island. After training at the Culinary Institute of America, he worked in some of Honolulu's top kitchens, including Town. At He'eia Pier, Noguchi gets back to basics, elevating traditional Hawaiian food without elevating the prices. No dish costs more than $13.

The daily-changing menu reads like a familiar array of plate-lunch staples, but when the food arrives it's on another plane entirely. Noguchi's *ahi katsu* is delicate and flaky, brightened with fresh scallions and spiced with a surprisingly nuanced teriyaki sauce. His *musubi* are light and fluffy and shaped like dainty quenelles, nothing like the leaden, gummy rice balls Hawaiians are accustomed to; in lieu of the regulation Spam, they're paired with a chopped *ahi* salad dressed with *shiso*, Kewpie mayo, vinegar, and torn mint. And the marvelously elemental *luau* stew—tender chunks of slow-cooked pork, onions, and taro leaf—could make a Hawaiian grandmother weep. The milieu is comfort food, but refined and enhanced.

Like Ed Kenney, Noguchi is fond of sourcing odd, overlooked ingredients, such as *akulikuli* (sea purslane), a tidal succulent that he harvests just down the shore. The plant's magenta flowers are used to make leis, but few younger Hawaiians realize that *akulikuli* leaves are actually edible: crisp, full of juice, and deliciously salty. Noguchi uses them in a salad with pickled limu seaweed, Hawaiian chilies, and plump tomatoes.

Oahu has a reputation for overpriced food, one that's certainly justified at the tonier resorts. But you can also eat exceptionally well in the least assuming places, wearing little more than board shorts and flip-flops. (Trust me, you'll fit in better if you do.)

You can, for instance, find a soul-stirring tuna *poke* made by a Korean lady at the back of the Kahuku Superette, a dingy-looking North Shore grocery. You could spend a whole afternoon in the food court of Honolulu's Shirokiya department store, sampling hundreds of humble Japanese

delicacies—from salmon-roe *donburi* to *yakisoba* (fried noodles). You could troll the industrial district near the Honolulu airport to find Mitch's, a hole-in-the-wall fish market that hides one of the city's top sushi bars. You could also make the rounds among Oahu's vaunted food trucks, which have exploded in popularity and number, going from 90 three years ago to more than 250 today. (What, you thought L.A. owned that game?)

Or you could have a great meal at one of the itinerant lunch stands that set up inside farmers' markets. Best among the current crop: the Pig & the Lady, run by a young Vietnamese-American chef named Andrew Le. His *bun bo Hue*—the lusty, spicy noodle soup of his father's hometown—is the finest I've had outside Vietnam; if you look serious about it, he'll drop in a slow-cooked pig's trotter. Japanese tourists swoon over *bo la lot* (grilled beef wrapped in betel leaf) and Hoi An–style *com ga* (chicken rice seasoned with turmeric and topped with shredded banana leaf).

Three nights a week, Le takes over the storefront space at Hank's Haute Dogs, a terrific hot-dog joint run by Henry Adaniya, once the toast of Chicago, and transforms it into a remarkable pop-up restaurant, also called the Pig & the Lady. It's here that the chef really shines, with an ever evolving, five-course tasting menu. A recent dinner started with a knockout punch: Chioggia beets, speck, and raspberries, draped in horseradish crème fraîche and sprinkled with mint. Kaffir lime and Vietnamese lemongrass gave a kick to the salmon cured with Sichuan peppercorns, fennel, and grapefruit. A crispy confit pork belly was plated with pickled onions and black rice purée, topped with a soft quail egg, then drizzled in a *sriracha* vinaigrette.

So hold on a minute. Aren't some of Le's dishes—with their East-West flavor collisions—pretty much what we used to call "fusion"?

Well...yes. We just don't use that word anymore. Yet for many Americans, fusion-by-any-other-name is precisely how we eat now. Young chefs are again turning east (and west, north, and south) for inspiration, and embracing the remix, the hybrid, the mash-up: the Korean taco, the sunchoke-and-beef-cheek *shu mai*.

And so Hawaii finds itself once again in sync with the times. But as Noguchi is quick to point out, trendiness has nothing to do with it. "This is how Hawaiians have been eating all their lives," the chef says. "My entire larder is ingredients I grew up with." So-called fusion cooking—be it refined Hawaii Regional Cuisine or a down-and-dirty *loco moco*—never went away here. How could it? From the earliest Marquesan settlers onward, the islands have been defined by far-flung influences, resulting in a remarkable demographic diversity: Polynesian, Filipino, Japanese, Portuguese, Chinese, Malay, British, Vietnamese, and on and on.

"Hawaii has always been a melting pot of ethnicities, cultures, and cuisines, as much as New York or Miami, if not more so," Noguchi says. "Look at us: we *are* fusion. Here it's not just a concept or some fleeting trend—it's a way of life."

Adapted from "Hawaii's Next Wave," by Peter Jon Lindberg.

GUIDE

STAY

Kahala Hotel & Resort
Fresh from a major renovation, with thoughtful in-room details. *5000 Kahala Ave., Honolulu; 800/367-2525; kahalaresort.com.* **$$$**

EAT

Hank's Haute Dogs
324 Coral St., Honolulu; 808/532-4265; hankshautedogs.com. **$**

He'eia Pier General Store & Deli
46-499 Kamehameha Hwy., Kaneohe, Oahu; 808/235-2192. **$$**

Kahuku Superette
56-505 Kamehameha Hwy., Kahuku, Oahu; 808/293-9878. **$**

Mitch's Fish Market & Sushi Bar
524 Ohohia St., Honolulu; 808/837-7774; mitchsusi.com. **$$**

The Pig & the Lady
Check out thepigand thelady.com for dates and reservations for the pop-up restaurant. Also visit their stand at the KCC Farmers' Market.

Shirokiya Food Halls
Ala Moana Shopping Center, 1450 Ala Moana Blvd., Honolulu; shirokiya.com.

Town
3435 Waialae Ave., Honolulu; 808/735-5900; townkaimuki.com. **$$$**

SHOP

KCC Farmers' Market
4303 Diamond Head Rd., Honolulu; Saturdays, 7:30–11 a.m.

Madre Chocolate
20A Kainehe St., Kailua, Oahu; 808/377-6440; madrechocolate.com.

MA'O Organic Farms
Look for their stand at the KCC Farmers' Market. *maoorganic farms.org.*

Architect Daniel Libeskind's modern addition to the Royal Ontario Museum.

TORONTO

Canada's largest city lights up

SAFE, CLEAN, BLAND: these were the adjectives traditionally applied to Canada's financial and media center. Lately, however, Toronto has undergone a remarkable sea change, gaining a newfound swagger and an edgy style.

The city's transformation can be traced, in part, through its evolving skyline. In the past decade, global starchitects have reimagined downtown: there is Will Alsop's Sharp Centre for Design, Daniel Libeskind's Michael Lee-Chin Crystal (an addition to the Royal Ontario Museum), and Frank Gehry's expansion of the Art Gallery of Ontario. Then there are the high-rises; among them are the new flagship Four Seasons Hotel, a massive Shangri-La Hotel, and properties from Ritz-Carlton and Trump.

While downtown grows more international, creative classes have established outposts all their own. Queen West is the apotheosis of this energy, a neighborhood that feels like a playground for street-style photographers—not surprising given the expanding collection of fashion boutiques such as Nomad and Klaxon Howl. To the north, chef-owned Frank's Kitchen has a menu that reads like a caricature of what you'd think Canadians might eat (rare elk loin, an even rarer venison tartare). Another option: Terroni features authentic regional Italian specialties (think ricotta-stuffed zucchini blossoms) that have found an unlikely home in this emerging capital of cool.

GUIDE

STAY
Four Seasons Hotel
*60 Yorkville Ave.;
800/819-5053;
fourseasons.com.* **$$$**

Ritz-Carlton
*181 Wellington St. W.;
800/542-8680;
ritzcarlton.com.* **$$$$**

Shangri-La Hotel
188 University Ave.;
*866/565-5050;
shangri-la.com.* **$$$$**

Trump International
Hotel & Tower
*325 Bay St.; 800/311-
5192; trumphotel
collection.com.* **$$$$**

EAT
Frank's Kitchen
*588 College St.;
416/516-5861.* **$$$**

Terroni
*720 Queen St. W.;
416/504-0320.* **$$**

DO
Art Gallery of Ontario
*317 Dundas St. W.;
ago.net.*

Royal Ontario Museum
*100 Bloor St. W.;
rom.on.ca.*

Sharp Centre for
Design
*100 McCaul St.;
ocadu.ca.*

SHOP
Klaxon Howl
*706 Queen St. W.;
klaxonhowl.com.*

Nomad
*819 Queen St. W.;
nomadshop.net.*

CANADA

Secret island retreats north of the border

Caribbean isles they're not—the water is chilly and the beaches are rocky—but outdoor enthusiasts will find plenty of places to love in Canada's lesser-known archipelagos. Ideal for hiking, biking, and kayaking, each has the air of a semi-forgotten place where Mother Nature calls all the shots.

Langara Island, British Columbia

Sea lions crowd rock-strewn inlets, and ravens soar over moss-covered cedars on 8,000-acre Langara, the northernmost spot in the Haida Gwaii chain. The island is reachable via a two-hour flight from Vancouver, but you'd never know it was even that close, given the unspoiled landscape. Get familiar with migrating orcas and humpback whales as you seek out salmon and halibut with the West Coast Fishing Club (*888/432-6666; westcoastfishingclub.com; four days from $5,930 per person, all-inclusive*), an outfitter that arranges multiday guided fishing tours that end at a hilltop timber lodge known as the Clubhouse. Bookish types can take a lesson in Canadian history on neighboring Graham Island, where the Haida Indian cultural center displays 100-year-old dugout canoes and burial caves. Come sunset, retire to the hotel's Solarium restaurant for chef Kim Bedford's locally sourced Pacific Northwest specialties such as prawns served with anise-liqueur *espuma*.

North and South Pender Islands, British Columbia

On the Southern Gulf Islands of North and South Pender—two islets united by a one-lane bridge—temperate rain forests abut a scalloped coastline that was once a stomping ground for Prohibition-era rumrunners. For panoramas of the jagged shore, stay at Poets Cove Resort & Spa (*9801 Spalding Rd., South Pender Island; 888/512-7638; poetscove.com; $$*), a 46-room resort with soaking tubs and fireplaces and a 96-slip marina. Before taking to the sea on a chartered boat, however, stock up on snacks and treat yourself to just-baked cinnamon buns and focaccia at the Sunday-morning farmers' market, eight miles away on the north isle.

Cape Breton Island, Nova Scotia

Thanks to a culture that mixes Scottish, Acadian, Irish, African, and native Mi'kmaq influences, Cape Breton, just off Nova Scotia, has a rich musical heritage. Celtic-style fiddling is played in parish halls and casual venues such as the Thursday-night ceilidh (*kay-lee*)—a dance gathering that also incorporates bagpipes, whistles, mandolins, and singing—at Rollie's Wharf, in the main port of North Sydney.

Hotels take advantage of the island's rustic physical allure: at Castle Moffett (*902/756-9070; castlemoffett.com; $*)—a turreted inn on 200 acres overlooking the Bras d'Or Lakes—rooms have cozy fireplaces and four-posters. If you're looking for adventure, the best hiking trails are found in Cape Breton Highlands National Park (*16648 Cabot Trail Rd., Chéticamp; 902/224-2306*). Sunbathers have their pick of beaches: Black Brook is flanked by a spectacular headland; Ingonish is home to a freshwater lake; and Lifeguard Beach, on the Gulf of St. Lawrence, is protected by breakwaters that allow for its sun-warmed shallows.

Îles de la Madeleine, Quebec

Were it not for the gusty winds that sweep along the beaches of Îles de la Madeleine, in the Gulf of St. Lawrence, 130 miles by plane from mainland Quebec, this dozen-island string may have remained isolated forever. But now a growing community of sailors book far in advance for one of the 10 renovated rooms at the gray-brick convent turned hotel Domaine du Vieux Couvent (*Havre-aux-Maisons; 418/969-2233; domaineduvieuxcouvent.com; $*). Windsurfers should sign up for an afternoon trip with Aerosport (*866/986-6677; aerosport.ca*), the most seasoned local outfitter. For an experience that's even farther off the beaten path, take a 50-minute ferry ride to L'Île-d'Entrée, a favorite fishing haven off the coast.

Above: A lounge at the West Coast Fishing Club, on Langara Island. Opposite: Cruising past the island's lighthouse.

CARIBBEANCRUISEVIEQUESST.JOHNVIRGINGORDAA
ST.VINCENTANDTHEGRENADINESCARIBBEANCRUISEVI

CARIBBEAN

LLAANTIGUADOMINICAST.BART'SST.LUCIAST.MARTIN
SST.JOHNVIRGINGORDAANGUILLAANTIGUADOMINICA

CARIBBEAN CRUISE

A leisurely sail through the islands

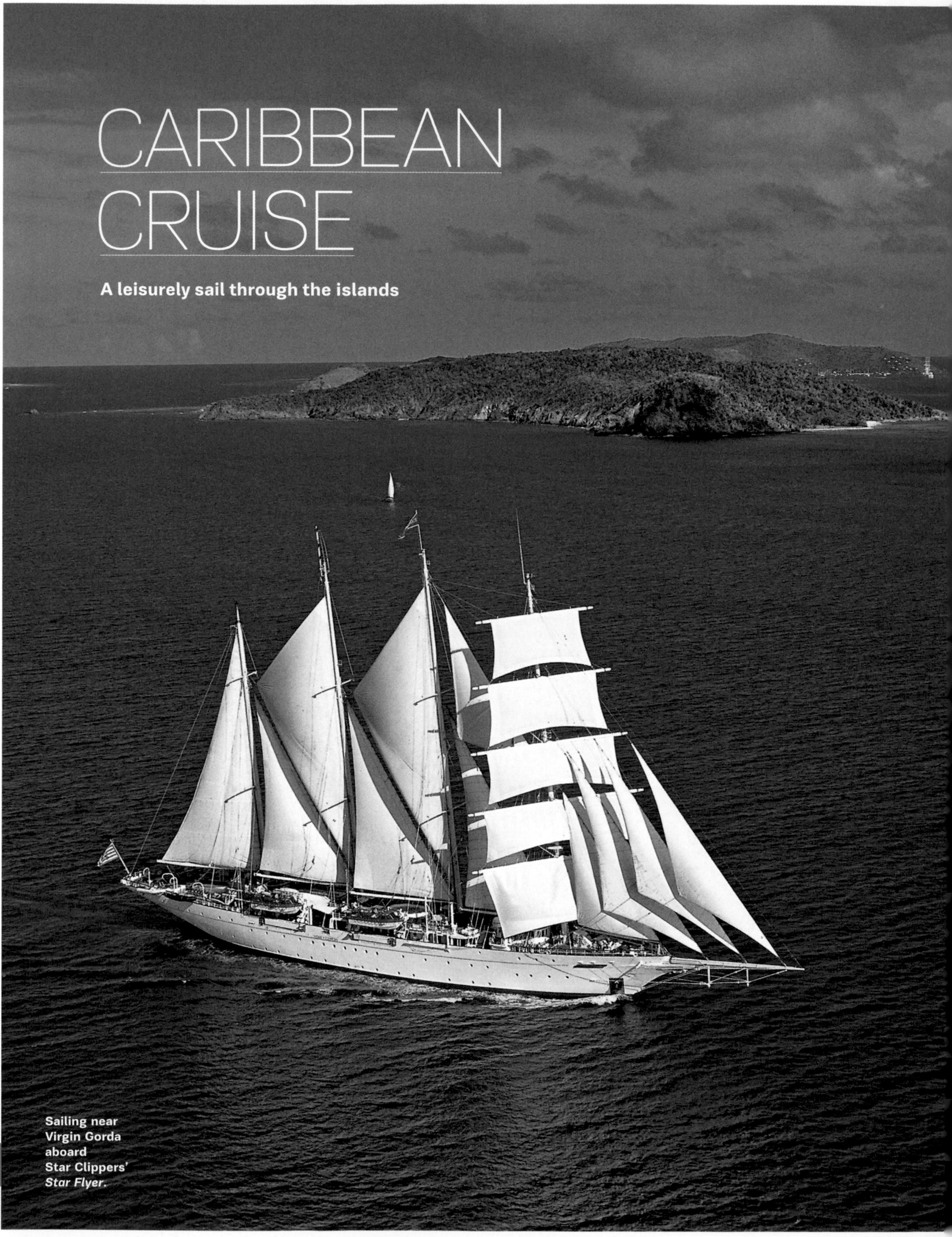

Sailing near
Virgin Gorda
aboard
Star Clippers'
Star Flyer.

Motoring on
St. Kitts. Below:
Hoisting sails
on the *Star Flyer.*

THE FIRST INDICATION THAT this is nowhere near your typical Caribbean cruise: the climb up a rope ladder to a perch known as the Crow's Nest, a necessary part of regular crew operations that's offered here as a passenger perk. Your second: the lullaby swing that serves as a kind of nautical hammock, slung from the ship's bowsprit, a bill-like structure that stretches out over the indigo sea.

I am aboard the *Star Flyer,* a 1996 replica of a 19th-century vessel and one of three owned by the Star Clippers Line. There is no waterslide, no formal night, and no children's program; only one of our port calls involves a gauntlet of jewelry stores. But perhaps the biggest tip-off is that in our seven days at sea, we'll sail—literally, thanks to the 16 sheets atop our four-masted clipper—more than 300 miles, from St. Maarten through the Virgins, on to St. Kitts and St. Bart's.

That's fine with the 170 passengers, who have developed an effortless camaraderie. "It doesn't get much better than this," sighs Ammie, my new Swedish friend. "I like being on the boat—the movement, the sense that we're going somewhere. We're not stagnant."

Just where we're going ceased to matter days ago. In a nod to Robert Louis Stevenson, the cruise line has dubbed this the Treasure Islands itinerary; Norman Island, one of our beach stops, is said to have inspired his classic tale of pre–Johnny Depp pirates and an X-marks-the-spot map. But the true journey, it seems, is the timeless dance of sail and sea and the winds that sweep us across the waves.

Sail-away is a ritual established our first evening as we depart from the dock at St. Maarten. Wine glasses in hand, passengers settle on the top deck. As the sails rise against a full moon, Vangelis's theme from *1492: Conquest of Paradise* sounds from the speakers, and the moment is heart-swelling.

Days take on an easy rhythm: breakfast and a briefing (in three languages, no less) by our

twentysomething Danish cruise director, Philip. A few hours of sailing to our next island, where we take tenders (small dinghies) to the beach. Back on board, the white-haired Captain Klaus blows a wistful tune on his bagpipes to mark daylight's end.

About half of the passengers are Europeans. Some, like Ellen and Rich from Long Island, are veteran sailors who have booked with Star Clippers more than a dozen times in the Caribbean and Europe. "You actually sail," the couple responds when asked the reason for their devotion.

This is rarer than you might think. Many cruise sailing ships hoist the canvas for show; on others, crew members push a button to raise sails above vessels that are more floating hotel than schooner.

Some never raise the sails at all. What Star Clippers offers is true sailing, with ropes as thick as your arm, braided through blocks and around winches (granted, they're electric), neatly coiled by sturdy crew hands and looped on stanchions—plus schedules subject to headwinds.

■ THOUGH THE SHIP HAS A DIESEL ENGINE THAT SUPPLIES THE POWER, THE 16 SQUARE-RIGGED SAILS PROVIDE THE MAGIC.

Above all, this is sailing with comforts. Cabins feature cushy beds topped with duvets, snug private bathrooms, and in-cabin televisions with DVD players. Two plunge pools and an air-conditioned library known as the Icebox provide refuge from the heat. Dinner is a genteel meal plucked from an ever changing six-course menu. Rack of lamb, veal parmigiana, vegetable curry? No one can eat it all.

To handle the social end of things, the maitre d' seats guests as deftly as any matchmaker, mixing tables of unfamiliar groups who speak the same language. The first night we're seated with like-aged couples who soon become pals: June and Bill from Ireland (his grandfather worked in the yard that built the *Titanic*); Adrian and Alexandra from Wales; Chris and Sue from Suffolk and London.

Intimate experiences not readily shared back home become fodder for easy discussion. Job anxieties, alternative-energy studies, beloved

books—no topic is off-limits. Conversations are continued during the morning warm-up on deck or on a kayak trip through an isolated cove. And, of course, en route to the next little island.

On Anguilla, we slip to shore via tender, then wander up the beach to Johnno's, a tin-topped bar adorned with posters of Coltrane, Ella, and Miles. A makeshift band tunes up; a local singer pours out a moody rendition of "Misty." The guy on the clarinet turns out to be Larry, a fellow sailor.

Virgin Gorda brings one of the trip's few organized excursions, to the eerie beach boulder field known as the Baths. On Jost van Dyke is what may be the most beautiful of the beaches; by afternoon it's also the most vibrant, thanks to the Pain Killers that flow nonstop from the Soggy Dollar.

Our arrival in St. Kitts comes nearly five hours later than scheduled, thanks to fierce headwinds. To fill the time, the sports staff—a trio of Scandinavians who look like they've stepped out of an Abercrombie & Fitch catalogue—arrange a deck-golf tournament, a spirited contest involving a wooden mallet, a flat puck, and chalk-drawn sea monsters guarding the "holes." It's a goofy pastime, much like the crew fashion show (hunky divemaster Martin is a standout in a terry sundress).

There's a retro quality to all this. Then again, it's yearning for a vintage experience that has brought us on this cruise. Though the ship is equipped with a diesel engine that supplies the power to take us to port, the 16 square-rigged sails provide the magic.

The winds lead us to St. Bart's, where most of our group simply soak up the stylish insouciance of Gustavia, trying to resist a $2,000 camel-and-red purse at Prada, smiling at the officious French bulldog guarding Vuitton.

But despite its savoir faire, St. Bart's can't compete with our sail-away home. Though there's time enough to have dinner ashore, everyone grabs an early tender to the clipper. Our cruise lasts just a few brief hours more before it heads back to St. Maarten and flies into the past.

Written by Jane Wooldridge.

GUIDE

Star Clippers
*305/442-0550;
starclippers.com;
seven nights from
$2,075 per person.*

W Retreat &
Spa's vibrant
Living Room
lobby.

VIEQUES, PUERTO RICO

A style haven revealed

THE LUSH AND UNASSUMING islet of Vieques—the site of a former U.S. military base just eight miles east of Puerto Rico—has quietly established itself as a capital of cool, thanks to chic hotels luring travelers with an eye for sophisticated design.

In the town of Pilon, Hix Island House—architect John Hix's prescient green-luxury concept—has been making waves since the late 1990's. The *wabi-sabi,* bunker-like concrete complex relies on solar power to heat shower water, which then runs off to irrigate the surrounding flora; the 19 guest rooms (outfitted with Frette linens and Donna Gorman–designed fabrics) are naturally cooled by trade winds. Taking the eco-friendly model even further, the new six-room Casa Solaris guesthouse is totally off the electrical grid.

On a far larger scale, though no less thoughtfully conceived, is the 157-room W Retreat & Spa, Vieques's first full-service resort. As at Hix Island House, the spirit of indoor/outdoor living is embraced to great effect; at this 30-acre hideaway it's enlivened with Spanish designer Patricia Urquiola's trademark splashy prints and moody pastels. There's also dark tropical wood, multicolored woven loungers, and contemporary furniture by Moroso and B&B Italia—making the lobby, pool, and sunken fire pit area are the hottest places to see and be seen.

GUIDE

STAY
Hix Island House
Pilon; hixislandhouse.com. **$**

W Retreat & Spa
Isabel Segunda; wvieques.com. **$$$**

ST. JOHN

America's smallest Virgin Island makes a splash

Stingray-shaped St. John has all the things you look for in a Caribbean getaway: sugar-sand beaches; brilliantly clear skies; sparkling bays with sweet names like Waterlemon and Cinnamon. There's also a low-key culinary scene that is opening up the least developed of the U.S. Virgin Islands to a new breed of in-the-know pleasure seekers. And yet, the landscape remains as unspoiled as ever.

An aerial view of the Eco Serendib Villa & Spa.

Eco Serendib Villa & Spa

The eight-suite Eco Serendib—perched on top of Point Rendezvous and overlooking St. John's southwestern shore—checks all the right boxes in the epicurean fantasy genre. The retreat will grow your choice of organic vegetables in its on-site garden before you arrive, then have chefs prepare them for meals and cooking demonstrations held in a granite kitchen that looks out on Fish Bay. In keeping with the sustainability focus, the property artfully balances style (a Chihuly-esque blown-glass sculpture) and substance: the owners have installed solar panels and rainwater-harvesting systems, as well as partnered with Virgin Islands National Park to prevent beach erosion by replanting scores of native sea grape and orange manjack trees.
Point Rendezvous; 215/830-8300; ecoserendib.com. **$$$$$**

Fatty Crab

The first offshore outpost of Zak Pelaccio's acclaimed New York City dining spot puts an Asian spin on classic Caribbean ingredients (think peekytoe-crab ramen, mahimahi sliders, and green mango and papaya salad). Don't miss the restaurant's Smoke Out Sundays, a messy and downright delicious barbecue feast with chili-jam brisket and pork ribs.
Cruz Bay; 340/775-9951. **$$**

La Plancha del Mar

This two-year-old Spanish- and French-influenced restaurant specializes in meats cooked over a traditional iron grill (thus the *plancha* in the name). But that's not the only food group that gets the star treatment here. A dish of cornmeal-crusted calamari starts dinner off right, while a shellfish paella proves there's plenty to savor for those with less meaty tastes. On summer Saturdays, a movie night features an evolving prix fixe menu; diners cleanse their palates with passion-fruit sangria.
Cruz Bay; 340/777-7333; laplanchadelmar.com. **$$**

Le Château de Bordeaux Café

This Bordeaux Mountain favorite is renowned for its unparalleled views over Coral Bay. Recently reopened, the family-run café specializes in authentic West Indian recipes (caramelized plantains; conch chowder) culled from owner Lorelei Monsanto's 94-year-old mother's collection. After a morning hike along the nearby Reef Bay Trail, opt for a restorative lunch of savory grouper burgers followed by the legend-in-the-making Dirty Monkey. Its contents remain a secret (Lorelei mixes a batch each morning before her staff arrives), but we're betting rum and bananas round out the brew.
Estate Bordeaux; 340/776-6611. **$**

Skinny Legs

St. John's "No shirt, no shoes, no problem" credo is on full display at Skinny Legs, a divey Coral Bay beach shack where locals gather for live music, stiff rum punches, and a rousing game of horseshoes. Standouts on the menu, which is scrawled across old surfboards and faded driftwood, include the blue-cheese burger and grilled mahimahi sandwich.
Coral Bay; 340/779-4982; skinnylegs.com. **$**

Zero Sushi

On the second floor of the Marketplace shopping center, the creative team behind La Plancha del Mar has opened a raw-fish temple that serves rolls and sashimi, plus such island-friendly twists as tempura-fried rainbow runner and the Katsura, a tuna-and-king-crab combo with *shiso* and sprouts wrapped in ribbons of cucumber. To drink, order the Pai Mai, made with almond-green-tea gin.
Cruz Bay; 340/777-9376; zerosushi.com. **$$**

Yachting off Waterlemon Cay. Left: Fatty Crab's steamed spiny lobster with kimchi.

Lunch at Fatty Crab. Left: A hawksbill turtle swimming over a colony of finger coral.

VIRGIN GORDA

Laid-back decadence in the British Virgin Islands

THINK OF VIRGIN GORDA AS THE ULTIMATE Caribbean paradox—an island that manages to be a jet-set draw without losing any of its subdued charm. Much of the action takes place around the funky outdoor cafés that surround the modest marina in Spanish Town. But despite its unpretentious atmosphere, this 8½-mile-long speck is one of the most exclusive destinations in the world. Several properties are now upping the ante for barefoot luxury.

Laurance Rockefeller pioneered development on Virgin Gorda when he opened Little Dix Bay along a crescent beach near Spanish Town in 1964. Four decades later, a $25 million overhaul by the Rosewood group infused the resort with a tropical Asian sensibility, adding a cliffside spa, a two-tiered pool, and five hilltop villas. On a coveted North Sound strand, the Bitter End Yacht Club—another longtime favorite—unveiled its own multimillion-dollar renovation four years ago, complete with an 18-yacht marina.

Much of today's buzz is centered on two newcomers to North Sound. YCCS Marina Virgin Gorda, with its sleek clubhouse and Bond-villain–worthy infinity pool, is a hub for superyacht regattas. A skiff ride away, the soon-to-be-completed gated community of Oil Nut Bay, powered by wind and solar energy, comprises 88 residences and rentals staffed with private chefs.

And of course no accommodation is more exclusive than Aquamare, further south on Mahoe Bay. With just three villas, each measuring 8,000 square feet, the beachfront enclave is understated yet luxe—the essence of Virgin Gorda.

GUIDE

STAY
Aquamare
787/461-2638;
villaaquamare.com.
$$$$$

Bitter End Yacht Club
800/872-2392;
beyc.com. **$$$$**

Little Dix Bay
888/767-3966;
littledixbay.com. **$$$**

Oil Nut Bay
800/761-0377;
oilnutbay.com. **$$$$$**

DO
YCCS Marina
Virgin Gorda
284/346-2000;
yccsmarina.com.

An ocean-facing pool terrace at Aquamare, on Mahoe Bay.

CARIBBEAN HOTELS

Ten secret hideaways worth discovering

A sandy swath outside St. Martin's Love hotel. Opposite: Objets d'art on display at La Banane, in St. Bart's.

S URE, THE CARIBBEAN CAN justly accommodate fans of big, brash luxury resorts, complete with celebrity-chef restaurants and world-class spas. But for the rest of us, there's a lesser-known Caribbean—where pampering is about peace and quiet, local flair, and sophisticated design. For those who prefer the inconspicuous allure of staying small, here are 10 intimate finds on six idyllic islands.

ANGUILLA

For decades, the 16-mile-long island of Anguilla, in the British West Indies, has had what is arguably the densest concentration of luxury properties in the Caribbean. Among the original movers and shakers were Robin and Sue Ricketts, who helped create and manage such legendary hotels as Malliouhana and Cap Juluca. Now they have embarked upon a new project: the 27-room Anacaona Boutique Hotel, a surprisingly affordable option on an island known for sky-high prices. The Anacaona's modern, tropical rooms (with Frette linens, gold and lime pillows, and iPod docking stations) have views over one of the two swimming pools from lower levels; upper floors offer vistas of the sea. Best of all, mile-long Meads Bay beach is just steps away.

ANTIGUA

The formerly British island of Antigua had a slightly stuffy reputation until hotelier Gordon Campbell Gray opened the sexy Carlisle Bay in 2009. Another game changer has burst onto the scene. Overlooking two square miles of reef-protected waters, Nonsuch Bay has been designed with the sailing set in mind. Spacious terraces and wood-shingled roofs reflect the island's Georgian architectural tradition, while the high-ceilinged interiors offer a blend of classic colonial (plantation chairs) and contemporary (crisp white sofas). There's never a dull

moment here thanks to guided snorkeling trips and private sailing and kite-surfing classes. But relaxing is encouraged as well: take a dip in one of three infinity pools, stroll along the private beach, or simply gaze at the landscape from the pergola-shaded restaurant.

High in the hills above Jolly Harbour, on Antigua's western side, the Sugar Ridge resort makes up for its lack of beachfront with spellbinding views over the sea and the neighboring islands of Redonda, Nevis, and Montserrat. A shuttle takes guests to local beaches three times a day. Muslin-draped beds, honey-colored marble bathrooms, and garden terraces—some with plunge pools—are par for the course. The star attraction is the breezy hilltop restaurant, Carmichael's, where residents and expats go for the fresh seafood and knockout desserts, such as bread-and-butter pudding with Antiguan rum sauce or coconut rice with mango purée.

DOMINICA

With its verdant rain forests, rushing rivers, and charcoal-colored sand, Dominica feels like some primordial lost world: all that's missing is the dinosaurs. Until recently, however, there was no decent place to stay. The opening of Rosalie Bay, an eco-friendly property that seems a microcosm of the island itself, changes all that. Scattered across 22 lush acres, the 28 gingerbread-trimmed cottages—each with carved mahogany and red-cedar four-poster beds—look out onto a rocky beach or over the Rosalie River. Relying on solar panels and its own wind turbine for power, Rosalie Bay is one of the world's few carbon-negative resorts. Other standout features include a spring-fed onyx-colored swimming pool, organic vegetable gardens, and a restaurant designed to resemble a plantation house, where most dishes are made using regional ingredients—from the Kalinago porridge with cassava root to the smoked cod on fried green plantains.

Opposite, clockwise from top left: One of the villas at Secret Bay, in Dominica; on the patio at Hotel Chocolat's Rabot Estate, in St. Lucia; a pool at Anguilla's Anacaona Boutique Hotel; breakfast in Hotel Chocolat's Boucan restaurant.

Another eco-luxury retreat, Secret Bay seems to rise from the bush like a mirage. Designed by Venezuelan architect Fruto Vivas, the four stilted villas, made from native hardwood, are outfitted with kitchenettes, floor-to-ceiling windows, and outdoor showers. Hammocks are ideal for watching the sun dip below the azure water. The staff can arrange a guided tour of the Emerald Pool or the nearby Kalinago territory to see centuries-old traditions of pottery and basket-weaving by one of the region's few remaining indigenous peoples. Care to stay put? Two secluded beaches and a hidden sea cave—not to mention a chef at your disposal for en suite meals—offer the perfect excuse never to leave the property.

ST. BART'S

It should come as no surprise that this French West Indies island, with its over-the-top villas and celebrity devotees, is home to one of the Caribbean's most stylishly revamped hotels. Once owned by the late cabaret impresario Jean-Marie Rivière, La Banane was long known for its campy vibe (showgirls and drag queens provided nightly entertainment). Then, in 2009, dynamic new French owner Jean-Marc Israel and manager Benjamin Fabbri set about creating a Midcentury Modern–inspired oasis. A two-tiered pool gives way to nine white bungalows with pastel interiors, custom-designed geometric tiles, and furniture made by Swiss-born architect Pierre Jeanneret for his cousin Le Corbusier. As if the design weren't enough reason to stay, La Banane's ace in the hole is the lively Chandi' Bar, where crowds gather on Thursday evenings to dance to live flamenco music. For sustenance before the big event, head to Le Bonito restaurant for sunset cocktails and ceviche.

Things are quieter across the island at the Hotel Le Village St.-Barth. Forty-three years after the pioneering Charneau family opened the bayside retreat, bordered by fragrant frangipani and palm trees, the hotel has a fresh look. What to expect? Colorful paintings by native artists; wood-beamed

ceilings and teak furniture; and large, Zen-inspired marble bathrooms. There's also a library full of travel classics that the Charneaus have collected over the years, as well as a glass-walled spa offering deep-tissue massages and yoga classes (better yet, have a treatment on your private terrace, overlooking Baie de St.-Jean). Despite the upgrades, Le Village's stone cottages and suites are still among the island's best deals during high season.

ST. LUCIA

One could easily mistake the area of Soufrière for an island in the South Seas: the lush landscape is made even more spectacular by the two conical Piton mountains rising up where the jungle meets the water. Already the site of St. Lucia's top resorts, Soufrière has just welcomed one of the sweetest hotels in the Caribbean. The 14 villas at Hotel Chocolat are set on a 140-acre cacao plantation that aims to make cocoa production a sustainable industry on the isle. Under the expert guidance of chef Jon Bentham, guests learn to make their own chocolate bars. The theme continues at Boucan restaurant, with dishes such as cacao-marinated red snapper accompanied by—what else?—a chocolate daiquiri.

ST. MARTIN

In one of the low-key fishing villages that dot French St. Martin, the hillside Karibuni Lodge resembles an upscale African safari camp. The six rustic-chic studios incorporate rough concrete walls, Guyanese redwood bookcases, and just the right mix of Caribbean and sub-Saharan objets, from mirrors framed in corrugated metal to hand-carved wooden elephants. Large doors open onto wide terraces with in-your-face views of Cul de Sac Bay and its islets. Although there's no restaurant at the hotel, owners Marion and Erick Clement are on hand to take guests by boat to the nearby island of Pinel so they can get first dibs on tables at Le Karibuni, the couple's perennially packed beachside haunt. If you prefer to stay on the "mainland," don't miss the grilled-to-perfection scallops and broad-bean risotto on the Victorian veranda at Le Ti' Bouchon, down the road.

Another husband-and-wife team is the force behind the understated Love hotel. When William and Muriel Demy first visited St. Martin, they fell in love with the tiny town of Grand Case, a cluster of picket-fenced pastel shacks facing a long, secluded stretch of sand. On Tuesdays, Grand Case Boulevard turns into a huge block party with calypso music, dancing, and the island's best street-food vendors. The Demys eventually bought a ramshackle beachfront villa and gave the seven-room property a top-to-bottom overhaul that makes it feel like an updated version of the charming, bare-bones hotel you used to find in the Greek islands 20 years ago. Airy, light-flooded suites are simply decorated with dark wood furniture built by William himself. For lunch, order from the hotel café's chalkboard menu of salads, croque-monsieur, and carpaccios, and toast with a Carib beer or a bottle of Ruinart champagne.

GUIDE

STAY

Anacaona Boutique Hotel
*Meads Bay, Anguilla;
877/647-4736;
anacaonahotel.com.* **$$**

Hotel Chocolat
*Soufrière, St. Lucia;
800/757-7132;
thehotelchocolat.com.*
$$$

Hotel Le Village
St.-Barth
*Baie de St.-Jean, St. Bart's;
800/651-8366;
villagestjeanhotel.com.* **$**

Karibuni Lodge
*Cul de Sac, St. Martin;
590-690/643-858;
lekaribuni.com.* **$$**

La Banane
*Baie de Lorient, St. Bart's;
590-590/520-330;
labanane.com.* **$$$**

Love
*Grand Case, St. Martin;
590-590/298-714;
love-sxm.com.* **$**

Nonsuch Bay
*Hughes Point, Antigua;
268/562-8000;
nonsuchbayresort.com.* **$$**

Rosalie Bay
*Roseau, Dominica;
877/397 0257;
rosaliebay.com.* **$**

Secret Bay
Portsmouth, Dominica;

*767/445-4444;
secretbay.dm.* **$$**

Sugar Ridge
*Jolly Harbour, Antigua;
866/591-4881;
sugarridgeantigua.com.*
$$$

EAT

Le Bonito
*Rue Lubin Brin, St. Bart's;
590-590/279-696.* **$$$$**

Le Karibuni
*Pinel, St. Martin;
590-690/396-700;
karibunipinel.com.* **$$$**

Le Ti' Bouchon
*Cul de Sac, St. Martin;
590-690/648-464.* **$$$**

*Adapted from "10 Caribbean Hideaways,"
by Richard Alleman.*

Petit St. Vincent's open-air beach bar and restaurant, overlooking the Caribbean Sea.

ST. VINCENT AND THE GRENADINES

New takes on "Privacy, please"

A STRING OF 32 ISLANDS just south of St. Lucia, St. Vincent and the Grenadines has long been a low-profile getaway for the rich and famous. But recent developments—including a $240 million airport set to open on St. Vincent in 2013— are making the region accessible to a broader audience.

Built on volcanic black sand, the Buccament Bay Resort has 90 light-filled villas that gaze out on a secluded white-sand beach. Twenty miles south, tiny Mustique remains a playground for the likes of Mick Jagger and Tommy Hilfiger (and was a runner-up honeymoon pick for the Duke and Duchess of Cambridge). A handful of new villas are now available to rent from the Mustique Company, including the four-bedroom Mimosa, a contemporary affair with a pebbled infinity pool, private chef, and dedicated utility vehicle for exploring the isle. A more affordable option is the four-bedroom Liselund, on a hillside overlooking the sea. Nearby, the 44-year-old private-island resort of Petit St. Vincent has reopened after a top-to-bottom makeover: 22 stone-walled, thatched-roof cottages are done up in earthy tones and driftwood *palapas* now line the beach. There's also a waterside restaurant and a tree-house-style spa, where an open-air hot-stone massage is the perfect end to the day.

GUIDE

STAY

Buccament Bay Resort
St. Vincent; 877/502-2022; buccamentbay.com; all-inclusive, three-night minimum. **$$$$**

Mustique Company
mustique-island.com. **$$$$$** *per week.*

Petit St. Vincent Private Island
800/654-9326; petitstvincent.com; meals included. **$$$$$**

A private bungalow at the Luna Lodge, on Costa Rica's Osa Peninsula.

MEXICO+
CENTRAL+
SOUTH
AMERICA

CITYCOSTARICAMACHUPICCHUBAHIARIODEJANEIROSALTA
ACAREYESBELIZEPANAMACITYCOSTARICAMACHUPICCHU

MINERAL DE POZOS, MEXICO

A transformed village where the past lingers

Above, from left: The view from El Secreto de Pozos hotel; Camino de Piedra's handmade musical instruments. Opposite: The interior patio at Posada de las Minas.

W HEN PEOPLE BUZZ ABOUT this or that newly "discovered" colonial Mexican town as "the next San Miguel," they usually mean the pre-malls and pre-traffic city of 10, 20, or 30 years ago. In recent years, the buzz has hovered over the central highlands *pueblo fantasma* (ghost town) of Mineral de Pozos, an hour's drive from San Miguel. Pozos (the locals' shorthand) was nearly lost to history until the 1990's, when artists fled here from the urban overgrowth of its famous neighbor. They opened their own galleries and restaurants and were followed by other solitude and spaciousness seekers, including discerning shop owners and hoteliers. By the 2000's, the inevitable weekend visitors had arrived, and for good reason: the town was charming, small, and had far more Mexican residents than newcomers. The spectral ruins of mines strewn over cactus-thick hillsides nearby deepened the atmosphere.

If Pozos is the next San Miguel, it's not the San Miguel of 30 years ago, the already well established American expat destination, but the San Miguel of 80 years ago: the seminal slumbering village woken up by artists of a different, post-revolutionary stripe. Without knowing exactly what I was looking for, I had found it here—the small-town Mexico of long ago: before *maquiladora*-labor horrors, international-drug-cartel violence, and globalized type-A-ism had forever changed the landscape. This was the old Mexico that a foreigner can blend in to, the Mexico that still sleeps when it is sleepy.

De-stressing in the garden of El Secreto de Pozos. Right: Inside the town's Church of San Pedro.

The pyramid-shaped furnaces of the Santa Brígida mine. Right: Chiles rellenos at Posada de las Minas's restaurant.

110

The town—which all but died in the early 20th century from successive blows to the silver-mining industry—started to stir in 1982, when President José López Portillo designated it a national historic treasure. But it wasn't until 2010, when the town was promised Pueblo Mágico status, that federal and local investment began to materialize. Wealthy Mexicans are now buying land, and new places to stay have increased the town's stock from three to six hotels: a quartet of luxury suites called Su Casa en Pozos was opened by gallerist Eva Axelsson, and the expats originally behind the LavenDar Farms collective are now renting out their own houses on the property.

> ■ THIS IS THE MEXICO OF LONG AGO, THE MEXICO THAT STILL SLEEPS WHEN IT IS SLEEPY.

But a trip to Pozos is still an exercise in slowing down, helped along by the steep cobblestoned streets and narrow sidewalks rising from the shaded Jardín Principal as if from a canyon floor. Wherever I went, I had all the attention of the proprietors of the tiendas selling crafts, cotton clothes, or handmade pre-Hispanic musical instruments (a Pozos specialty)—whistles, drums with carved cases, and percussive round pots to tap with sticks. At the shop Camino de Piedra, I met artisan/musician Marco Antonio Sánchez García, who took me through the ruins of the 16th-century Santa Brígida mine a few days later.

The galleries that bring outsiders to Pozos show work that reflects a wide range of styles, but all of it seems drawn from Mexico's texture, color, and light—a light that you can almost touch. For the newer residents, the connection to the local landscape and culture is crucial. "We moved here to be in Mexico," says Nick Hamblen, owner of Galería No. 6, who arrived in Pozos from Dallas in 2004. The moment I walked into his gallery, I understood the rapport between Pozos old and new.

There is nothing in Galería No. 6 that fails to suggest *take me home*—from the wooden casement windows in foot-thick walls to Janice Freeman's splashy paintings of agave cactus. Hamblen's restored 200-year-old house is both gallery and residence. The first meanders into the second's outdoor living room and a small open-air kitchen decorated floor-to-ceiling in blue tiles. The space is shared with guests of El Secreto de Pozos, a sophisticated three-room B&B hidden in the exuberant but orderly gardens designed by Hamblen's partner, horticulturist ManRey Silva. This corner of Pozos fills in all the details of a fantasy of heading down to Mexico for good.

Which is not to say I was unhappy staying at the eight-room Posada de las Minas, a former mansion and adjacent factory restored by Houstonians David and Julie Winslow. Posada's courtyard restaurant serves typical Mexican dishes and Mexican-American mash-ups like fried asparagus with a lime-butter sauce. In Pozos, hospitality flaunts its personality—a right afforded to quiet towns that remain under the travel radar.

Midweek at Posada de las Minas, things were slow enough for me to play Goldilocks and sleep in two rooms. In the one named for Santa Brígida, the view from my bed was of sky and mountains, and electrical wires dotted with birds. Pueblo Mágico status will ensure that those wires are buried. It likely, eventually, will bring more development, and more hubbub. The birds of Pozos will look for other places to alight.

Adapted from "Hidden Mexico," by Alice Gordon.

GUIDE

STAY
El Secreto de Pozos
*6 Jardín Principal;
52-442/293-0200;
elsecretomexico.com.* **$**

LavenDar Farms
Hacienda
Las Barrancas; 723/429-4475; lavendar farmsofpozos.com. **$**

Posada de las Minas
1 Manuel Doblado;
*52-442/293-0213;
posadadelasminas.com.* **$**

Su Casa en Pozos
*19 Manuel Doblado;
52-442/293-0284;
sucasaenpozos.com.* **$**

EAT
Posada de las Minas
*1 Manuel Doblado;
52-442/293-0213;
posadadelasminas.com.*
$$

DO
Camino de Piedra
*13 Leandro Valle;
52-442/293-0123.*

Galería No. 6
*6 Jardín Principal;
52-442/293-0200.*

Santa Brígida
Take a tour of the mine with local guide Marco Antonio Sánchez García from Camino de Piedra.

MEXICO CITY

An insider's guide to the greatest dining in town

You can read a Kindle's worth of tour books, Yelp your way around the globe, and put your concierge on speed dial, but you'll never get better local eating advice than from a resident chef. We turned to top toque Enrique Olvera of hotel hot spot Distrito Capital for the scoop on Mexico City's best-kept secrets, from outdoor markets to old-fashioned ice cream parlors.

Azul y Oro
Ricardo Muñoz Zurita may be the most important food scholar in Mexico (he has authored nine books on the country's cooking), so it's fitting that the gastro-historian set up shop on the campus of the national university. His menu is splashed with Oaxacan flourishes: hibiscus enchiladas blanketed in a tomato-and-chipotle salsa; duck empanadas with smoky *mole negro* ("They're amazing," Olvera says). The highlight, however, occurs at Zurita's monthly "festivals," where a single ingredient—mango, say, or pumpkin—becomes the star in every course.
3000 Insurgentes; 52-55/5622-7135. **$$**

Distrito Capital
Given the success of his first restaurant, Pujol, where he was renowned for modernizing Mexican cuisine, Olvera's name alone is enough to kick-start a Mexico City food craze. That's what's happening at the chef's new fifth-story dining room inside the minimalist Distrito Capital hotel. The contemporary menu features items like chicken-and-pumpkin-flower soup and marinated sea-bass lettuce tacos. The slate-gray space is equally cutting-edge, adorned with glossy black-and-white marble tables and pearly Alvar Aalto lamps.
37 Avda. Juan Salvador Agraz; 52-55/5257-1300; hoteldistritocapital.com. **$$**

La Merced
You can easily lose an afternoon weaving through the stalls of La Merced, an indoor and outdoor market—Mexico City's largest—whose expansive collection runs from exotic spices and zesty peppers to piñatas and hand-woven blankets made nearby. The street vendors are top-notch, dishing out authentic bites such as spicy *cabrito* (goat) tacos. "I go on Saturdays," Olvera says, "for blue-corn quesadillas with zucchini blossoms, Oaxacan cheese, and epazote," a lemony Mexican herb.
180 Rosario; no phone.

Merotoro
Located among Condesa's Art Nouveau buildings and tree-lined avenues is Merotoro. From the owners of the much-lauded seafood destination Contramar, the restaurant specializes in upscale Baja cuisine: braised abalone, grilled octopus, and *percebes* (gooseneck barnacles) with salicornia greens.
204 Amsterdam; 52-55/5564-7799; merotoro.com.

Nevería Roxy
On steamy summer days, lines wind around the block at this old-school ice cream parlor, a 1960's relic with a few tables out front. Inside, the flavors of *helados* (ice cream) are listed on a blackboard—opt for the prickly guava or the *zapote negro,* Olvera's favorite, made from native black persimmon.

161 Tamaulipas; 52-55/5256-1854.

Nicos
Family-owned Nicos has been drawing patrons for more than 50 years. Chef Gerardo Vázquez Lugo locally sources the ingredients for his regional classics and promotes an all-Mexican wine list. But it's the authentic breakfast recipes that epicures swear by. "They use free-range eggs for the *huevos a la Mexicana* and *huevos montuleño,* plus all the most flavorful chiles," Olvera says. Don't leave without trying their famous *concha,* sticky buns made with French-style dough.
3102 Avda. Cuitlahuac; 52-55/5396-6510.

Racing past the Metropolitan Cathedral, in downtown Mexico City.

Chef Enrique Olvera. Right: House-made breakfast pastries at Nicos.

The bar in Distrito Capital. Left: La Merced food market.

Pacific Ocean vistas from Casita de las Flores, a villa at Costa Careyes Resort.

COSTA CAREYES, MEXICO

An under-the-radar resort comes into focus

AN ABUNDANCE OF BOUGAINVILLEA has made fuchsia the unofficial color of Costa Careyes, a laid-back Pacific-coast hideaway that has somehow evaded the tourist hordes. Over the years, guests have run the gamut from film directors (Francis Ford Coppola) and prime ministers (Silvio Berlusconi) to models (Heidi Klum), all looking for a paparazzi-free bolt-hole among the bold-hued casitas. Despite the luxe trappings—butler service; lavish infinity pools—Costa Careyes is more famous for what it doesn't have: yachts, Jet Skis, nightclubs, and high-end boutiques. Italian artist and entrepreneur Gian Franco Brignone bought up the property in the 1960's—and has shielded it from overdevelopment ever since.

Still, quiet doesn't necessarily mean sleepy. By day, socializing revolves around outings to Playa Rosa; come sundown, you'll likely find Brignone and his cohorts down at Punto Como—one of three on-site restaurants—sipping a guayaba (guava) margarita. During polo season, you can linger after a match at the hotel's Polo Club Grill, the Argentinean-style *parrilla* that keeps the Porteño players pacified with steak and tequila. Night owls might prefer an after-hours dance party on the beach at Cocodrilo Azul, an atmospheric sushi restaurant where the only prying eyes come from a lagoon filled with crocodiles.

GUIDE

STAY
Casita de las Flores
52-315/351-0320;
careyes.com. **$$**

Costa Careyes Resort
52-315/351-0320;
careyes.com. **$$**

EAT
Cocodrilo Azul
52-315/351-0320. **$$**

Polo Club Grill
52-315/351-0320. **$$**

Punto Como
52-315/351-0320. **$$**

PUNTA GORDA, BELIZE

Farm-to-table, meet jungle-to-table

Fish tacos with papaya salsa and black-bean salad at Belcampo Lodge.

Kayaking on
the Rio Grande.
Below: Setting
the table
on Belcampo's
Sunset Deck.

M Y VERY FIRST NIGHT AT Belcampo Lodge is punctuated by what sounds like Ozzy Osbourne being strangled in the pitch dark. The cottage is suspended in a dense canopy of hanging vines and gumbo-limbo trees, providing natural privacy, so I've traded my bed for a hammock on the screened porch to feel closer to this forest primeval. A breeze rattles palm fronds as a rain shower sweeps through, carrying the scent of jasmine. Nuts hit the corrugated zinc roof and roll to the ground far below. Suddenly, just before dawn, that Ozzy-like roar from a troop of howler monkeys bolts me upright—and it's resoundingly clear that I'm bivouacking beyond my comfort zone.

By first light, their screeching has faded, giving way to the soft clicks of keel-billed toucans. Soon I'm seated on the lodge's veranda with a pair of binoculars, keeping an eye on the cotton tree where these colorful birds hop from branch to branch, until breakfast arrives: a plate of "fry jacks" (puffy tortillas), sour-orange marmalade, nutty granola sweetened with coconut, and cinnamon-bark-smoked bacon. I could linger long into the morning, watching the toucans play, but I want to see where baby chocolate bars are born.

At the end of a steep driveway lined with torch ginger and flowering trumpet vine, the landscape opens up to a broad valley that the Belcampo farm team has planted with cassava and banana cover crops. Inside the nursery I meet head forager Kenny Ramos, a man with a passion for vanilla orchids and rare varieties of cacao. In his spare time he hunts for wild plants in untrammeled corners of Belize.

Surrounding us are hundreds of cacao saplings. Ramos picks one up and points to a pale green bud grafted onto its woody stem.

"Criollo," he says quietly.

"*That's* what you hiked three days into the jungle to find?"

Ramos simply shrugs, implying it was a walk in the park, albeit a park populated with coral snakes and deadly fer-de-lance. I touch the tender criollo shoot carefully. Might this be a direct descendant of the mysterious "white cacao" that the Maya first domesticated 2,500 years ago? The fabled lost bean that Columbus tasted on his fourth voyage to the New World? The holy flavor grail among artisanal confectioners? It is enough to make a chocoholic go weak in the knees.

Belcampo belongs in the vanguard of the next culinary travel trend: more field expedition than farm stay, a full-immersion experience for intrepid foragers who want to walk on the wilder side, discovering and tasting exotic edibles on a 1,000-acre plantation and adjacent 12,000-acre wilderness reserve complete with jaguars and lots of snakes. Its 12 guest cottages are scattered along a hill that drops abruptly to the banks of the slow-moving Rio Grande, which flows from the Maya Mountains on the Belize-Guatemala border to a mangrove-lined outlet on the Caribbean Sea, just eight miles away as the crocodile swims. The rain forest unfolds in every direction: a vast green mansion that shelters more than 80 percent of the country.

Guiding Belcampo's ongoing transformation are owner Todd Robinson, a conservation-minded investor from California, and CEO Anya Fernald, a former Slow Food director. They have embarked on an ambitious "farm of origin" project, proving that the concept of *terroir* doesn't apply just to wine. Fernald has forged relationships with discerning cacao and coffee buyers, including Katrina Markoff of Vosges Haut-Chocolat and James Freeman of Blue Bottle Coffee. They come to Belcampo to source rarefied ingredients as well as to share their expertise during culinary excursions and master classes. (When Belcampo's criollo trees mature—they're still five years from first harvest—the estate will be the single-largest grower of cacao in the country.) Belcampo also plans to produce

its own rum, from cane that is raised on the property. Meanwhile, the estate is swiftly becoming self-sufficient: raising chickens and pigs; growing herbs and produce in a three-acre kitchen garden; even harvesting rosewood to craft service pieces for the dining room. Belcampo is the source for nearly everything on the menu, from the poached eggs served at breakfast to the mint muddled for the mojitos during cocktail hour.

Market days start early in Punta Gorda, the regional capital. Fortunately, the howler monkeys are a fail-safe alarm clock. I ride into town just after sunrise on Saturday, in the company of one of the guides. All around me, vendors are selling provisions unavailable in the outlying villages: fresh seafood, Tupperware, yards of lace, secondhand jeans. Children hawk frozen bananas dipped in chocolate and toasted coconut. In the shade of makeshift stalls, Mayan women sit next to piles of cassava, dried beans, turmeric, and bottles of homemade habanero sauce, while on the opposite sidewalk, bearded Mennonite farmers, in their straw hats and suspenders, unload juicy watermelons and broccoli. It is the weirdest juxtaposition of agriculture. And of cultures. Belize isn't so much a melting pot as a hotbed of runaways and renegades, a place where descendants of Confederates, Caribbean slaves, indentured East Indians, British buccaneers, and indigenous Mesoamericans all cling to their own culinary traditions under one shared jungle canopy.

Along Punta Gorda's waterfront, I'm lured by the sweet aroma issuing from Cotton Tree Chocolate. They do it all here, from roasting beans to molding candies. The shopkeeper gives me a sample of intensely dark chocolate that melts on my tongue. It's as good as any from Paris or New York confectioners—better, maybe, for being tasted so close to the source.

■ BELCAMPO BELONGS IN THE VANGUARD OF THE NEXT CULINARY TRAVEL TREND: MORE FIELD EXPEDITION THAN FARM STAY.

Back at the lodge, my next horticulture lesson involves a 27-inch machete. Bumping through a cleared field at the base of Machaca Hill, Kenny Ramos steers into a twilight zone of tangled vegetation. Francisco Ack, another farmhand, climbs off and sizes up several cohune palms. This is a mother plant: the fronds are used by the Maya for thatch; the nuts produce cooking oil; the inner bark provides food for pigs and chickens. Nothing goes to waste. After a few rasps of the blade on a whetstone, Ack hacks away at the cohune until the core is exposed. He chops the palm down and sections out its heart in a matter of minutes.

At a family-style dinner at the lodge that evening, the palm heart is prepared two ways: slivered over salad greens and boiled to a pulp with fresh turmeric root until it resembles an East Indian *palak paneer*. Kimchi made from garden cabbage is served alongside johnnycakes and black-bean dip. Barbecued chicken glazed with rum and brown sugar and a pork loin simmered in coconut cream are luscious and homey. There's even a ceviche of lionfish, a spiny little invasive that has been rapidly overwhelming local reef species; the flesh is surprisingly delicate and flavorful when filleted and cured with lime.

On my final afternoon I go out on the river with Emmanuel Chan, one of Belcampo's resident bird experts. He launches two kayaks from the dock, and we paddle against the current. The banks are thick with blooming swamp iris and jipijapa palms. A heron startles and flies off.

Chan points to a dark, furry silhouette high in a mahogany tree. "You don't see lone howlers often," he says. "That's probably a juvenile male who's been pushed out of the troop." Chan tries to get the monkey's attention, but it ignores us, asleep in the heat of the day. No doubt the onset of dusk will change that. I'm just glad to finally spot one of these raucous jungle creatures, whose night music has colored my dreams.

Adapted from "The Wild Heart of Belize," by Shane Mitchell.

GUIDE

STAY
Belcampo Lodge
Punta Gorda;
belcampoinc.com. **$$$**

SHOP
Cotton Tree Chocolate
Punta Gorda;
cottontreechocolate.com.

Punta Gorda Farmers'
Market
Front St.; open Monday,
Wednesday, Friday, and
Saturday.

PANAMA CITY

An emerging outpost blends the old and the new

Once known as a sunny haven for shady characters—and not much else—Panama is shedding its rather seedy reputation by courting high fliers with chic new hotels and a Frank Gehry–designed nature museum. Even the canal is getting an upgrade—a $5.2 billion expansion will double its capacity. And just like that, the capital is humming with business travelers, curious cultural tourists, and South Americans on weekend jaunts.

Exploring Casco Viejo's colonial architecture.

Panama Canal

In 2014—just in time for the landmark waterway's 100th birthday—the final stages of a groundbreaking expansion will be completed. Built in 1914 as a direct trade route between the Atlantic and Pacific oceans, the passage will now fit supersize cruise liners, such as Cunard's flagship *Queen Mary 2* and nine Princess Grand Class vessels. The Miraflores Visitor Center, located canalside 30 minutes from downtown, sheds light on the project's history, from the Teddy Roosevelt years through the present day.
Avda. Omar Torrijos; 011-507/276-8617; pancanal.com.

Biomuseo

Frank Gehry—whose wife is Panamanian—designed this series of rain-forest-like gardens and biosphere galleries on Panama City's Amador Causeway after decades of fits and starts. He was aided by industrial designer Bruce Mau and landscape architect Edwina von Gal in the $90 million project.
Edificio 136, Calzada de Amador; 011-507/314-0097; biomuseopanama.org.

Casco Viejo

Looking for the next great neighborhood? Panama City's atmospheric Casco Viejo (Old Town) is being scrubbed up for travelers lured by its 17th-century cathedral and crumbling mansions. The six-room Las Clementinas—whose owner is a pioneer in the area's preservation efforts—captures the colonial-chic vibe with romantic terra-cotta-tiled interior green spaces (don't miss the Secret Garden, hidden two stories below street level between sections of an old fort wall). The restaurant dishes up Panamanian comfort food such as coconut-spiked risotto and *ropa vieja*.
Calle 11 and Avda. B; 011-507/228-7613; lasclementinas.com. **$$**

The Luxury Hotel Boom

Five-star hotels are rising to meet travelers' growing demand. Everything is over-the-top at the sail-shaped Trump Ocean Club *(Calle Punta Colón; 855/878-6700; trumphotelcollection.com;* **$$***),* from the slick service (customized mini-bars; personalized stationery) to the soon-to-open private island beach accessible by catamaran. Guests spend most of their time on the 13th-floor deck, where cabanas surround two pools (one with an infinity edge and a glass wall) with views of the water and the tony Punta Pacifica neighborhood. In nearby Bella Vista, the South Beach–style Hotel Manrey *(Calle Uruguay; 011-507/203-0000; manrey*

panama.com; **$$***)* claims a bold, Modernist design scheme and a neon-lit rooftop lounge. And on the rim of the Bay of Panama lies Le Méridien *(Calle Uruguay and Avda. Balboa; 800/543-4300; lemeridien.com;* **$$***),* a sleek option with an inverted mosaic-glass pyramid that lights up the lobby in a rainbow of colors. At the hotel's Latitudes restaurant, fresh concoctions like mango-chili lime juice served in shot glasses and braided coconut bread spiked with green tea make for the ultimate reinvention of the continental breakfast.

The view from a private pool deck at Trump Ocean Club. Left: One of the bedrooms at Las Clementinas.

The 17th-century church of Santo Domingo, in Casco Viejo. Right: French toast for breakfast at Las Clementinas restaurant.

GUIDE

STAY

Lapa Rios
*506/2735-5130;
laparios.com; some
meals and activities
included.* **$$$**

Luna Lodge
*888/762-4069;
lunalodge.com.* **$$**

DO

Buena Esperanza
(Martina's)
Carbonera

Corcovado National Park
*Osa Conservation Area;
506/2735-5036;
pncorcovado@gmail.com;
reservations required.*

OSA, COSTA RICA

Where the wild things are

JUTTING OFF COSTA RICA'S PACIFIC COAST, the Osa Peninsula is primitive and untamed, a paradise of rain forests, empty beaches, and backwater settlements. Scarlet macaws and tiger herons fly overhead and pumas strut languidly across your field of vision. Here, nature calls all the shots.

Animals outnumber people in the unglamorous town of Puerto Jiménez, the area's main hub. From there it's only 12 miles to one of the Osa's first eco-lodges, the decidedly upscale Lapa Rios. Sixteen stone-and-bamboo cabins are set high on a hillside overlooking the canopy and come with netted beds and outdoor showers. Say the word and the staff will arrange a picnic under one of the waterfalls on the thousand-acre property. If you're looking for interaction of the human variety, join the expat crowd down the hill at Buena Esperanza (known colloquially as Martina's, after the German owner), whose open-air bar is adorned with Chinese lamps, surfboards, and Tibetan prayer flags—and steeped in the natural magic of the Osa.

Beyond Lapa Rios, the roads only get rougher. At the end of a narrow dirt track, Luna Lodge is a hydro- and solar-powered oasis with eight bungalows, five permanent tents, and a spa clinging to the mountainside. Nearby, Corcovado National Park is an ecological hot spot that's home to red-crowned woodpeckers, bull sharks, howler monkeys, and the exotic Baird's tapir, a huge mammal that looks like a cross between a horse and an anteater. Wild, indeed.

Horseback riding along the Osa Peninsula's Pacific shore.

MACHU PICCHU, PERU

Demystifying an ancient city

Whether approached by bus, train, or foot, Machu Picchu never fails to elicit awe. Though it's no longer the overgrown lost city that explorer Hiram Bingham located more than a century ago, the ruins still feel improbably wild and alien despite the droves of visitors that circulate across this green-carpeted ridge (especially in summer). T+L helps you navigate the must-see sites without all the hassle.

A guest house at Inkaterra Machu Picchu Pueblo Hotel.

The Sacred Plaza

The city was abandoned in the mid 1500's, after the Incan empire was conquered by the Spanish. Construction was clearly still under way at the Sacred Plaza, where gables remain incomplete and a stray slab lies in wait. Look for the impressive Temple of Three Windows, with its perfectly fitted stones.

Intipunku

Most tourists choose to take the easy 1¼-mile walk to Intipunku (the Sun Gate) around sunrise, hiking a forested path south from the main site. Instead, head there in the late morning, once the area clears out, and you'll have the landscape to yourself.

The Peak

Allow at least two hours for the trek from the ruins to the peak that towers over them, also called Machu Picchu. You'll be practically alone as you ascend to some 10,000 feet above sea level, where views stretch from the ancient city to the river and snowcapped mountains beyond.

Huayna Picchu

Only 400 tickets are handed out daily for entry to Huayna Picchu, the familiar rounded peak in the north where the Incan high priest is said to have once resided. Beat the lines and buy tickets ahead on machupicchu.gob.pe. The climb to the top is quite steep; you'll want to traverse down the side along the spectacular (if sometimes slippery) path that leads to the lesser-known Temple of the Moon, the city's northern gateway.

The Quarry

At first, the quarry looks like an unremarkable pile of granite, but the abundance of stone may have been a reason the Incas chose this location for their emperor's estate. Poke around to catch their work—halted in mid-chisel—and find the boulder with serpents carved on top, a traditional indicator of an ancient ceremonial site.

The Urban Sector

The eastern urban section is the least visited of Machu Picchu's residential core. Look for the two so-called mortars: carved bowls that still baffle archaeologists. The latest theory holds that they were once pools filled with water to reflect the stars.

Top Guide

There are no tourist signs at the site, so a guide is essential. Peter Frost of Aracari Travel Consulting *(312/239-8726; aracari.com; three-day trips from $300 per person)* has explored the Andes for more than 30 years. His scholarly tours include visits to private residences and adventures tailored to guests' experience levels.

Where to Stay

Spend a night in Machu Picchu Pueblo, the town closest to the site, so you can see it in the tranquil early morning hours and after 3:30 p.m., when day-trippers depart. Inkaterra Machu Picchu Pueblo Hotel *(800/442-5042; inkaterra.com; $$$)* is a peaceful 85-room retreat within walking distance of traditional Peruvian restaurants and a bus station where the 25-minute journey to Machu Picchu begins.

Road Less Traveled

To travel on foot, as the Incas did, secure a permit in Cuzco and take a train to Km 104, arriving no later than 10 a.m. for access. The five-hour hike will get you to the ruins after the crowds depart but with enough time to explore before dark.

Huayna Picchu and the ruins of Machu Picchu.

BAHIA, BRAZIL

Beach towns on the verge

A reclaimed-timber
room in one of
Vila Naiá's casas.

THE PATAXÓ PEOPLE GOT IT RIGHT when they named their Bahian village Corumbau—"far from everything." Bumpy dirt roads make the 30-mile drive from Porto Seguro airport a jarring four-hour trek. Yet that hasn't deterred the same venturesome Brazilians who transformed nearby party capital Trancoso from declaring Corumbau and neighboring Caraíva as the country's next hot spots.

In the former, fishing boats bob in the surf and birds sing in coconut groves. You may want nothing more than to lie on the shore sipping açai juice, but there's plenty to keep the adventurous busy: snorkeling the reef off Itacolomi beach; mastering the local spearfishing technique; hiking through dense tropical forest. Take it all in from clothing designer Renata Mellão's hotel Vila Naiá, eight bold-hued bungalows and suites outfitted in recycled driftwood. A more secluded option is Fazenda São Francisco do Corumbau, where 10 light-filled cabins face nine miles of deserted coast; fresh seafood is paired with organic produce from the garden.

Six miles north, Caraíva epitomizes Brazil's no-fuss seaside attitude. Wooden houses splashed in shades of mustard, lime, and peach line a tangled web of streets too sandy for cars; the chief mode of transportation is mule. An authentic *moqueca* (fish stew) is served under an almond tree at low-key Boteco do Pará. Afterward, settle into one of the five brightly painted cottages scattered across a lush garden at the rustic Pousada Lagoa. On the other end of the spectrum, the three-bedroom Fazenda Caraíva sits on a forested promontory, a natural draw for—and a well-kept secret among—publicity-shy execs and celebrities alike.

GUIDE

STAY

Fazenda Caraíva
*Caraíva; 55-21/
2225-9476; brazilian
beachhouse.com;
breakfast and dinner
included.* **$$$$$**

Fazenda São Francisco
do Corumbau
*Corumbau; 55-11/3078-
4411; corumbau.com.br;
meals included.* **$$$$**

Pousada Lagoa
*Caraíva;
55-73/9985-6862;
lagoacaraiva.com.br.* **$**

Vila Naiá
*Corumbau;
55-11/3061-187;
vilanaia.com.br.* **$$$$**

EAT
Boteco do Pará
*Caraíva;
55-73/9991-9804.* **$$**

RIO DE JANEIRO

The capital of hope

AT A TIME WHEN MUCH OF the world is in some form of decline, Rio de Janeiro is the view looking forward. The wave of change owes something to the booming Brazilian economy, something to the discovery of offshore oil, something to the energy brought to the city when it was chosen for the 2014 World Cup finals and the 2016 Olympics, and most of all to the dramatic reduction in crime. The city has not achieved the placidity of Zurich or Reykjavík, but the improvement in Rio has an aura of fiesta, even of miracle, that those serene towns will never know.

A great many cities sit beside the sea, but no other integrates the ocean as Rio does. To imagine Rio without the waterfront is like imagining New York without tall buildings, L.A. without celebrities. "If you don't go to the beach you don't know anything that's happening," said the Rio- and New York–based artist Vik Muniz. "No matter if you have Twitter, or if you have a cell phone, you have to go to the beach, every day at four o'clock until sundown." Beaches are inherently democratic institutions; when you're in a bathing suit, there's no way to show off anything much besides your body, your skill at volleyball. It's pointless being a snob in Rio.

Rio's topography has dictated another social anomaly. People of privilege live in the flat seaside areas in the Zona Sul, the southern district that encompasses the famous beaches of Copacabana, Ipanema, and Leblon. These neighborhoods are punctuated by abrupt hills, which have been settled by the poor over the past century or so. These steep favelas do not appear in detail on most maps of the city, and have historically had no utilities, no garbage collection, no closed sewers, and no police protection. The social distances in Rio outpace the geographic ones. Muniz said, "You're sitting in St.-Tropez surrounded by Mogadishu."

Nowhere is this unusual arrangement more apparent than from the air. My husband and I went hang-gliding one morning from the Tijuca Forest, soaring above the snaking alleys of Vidigal on one side and luxury oceanfront hotels on the other. A few days later, we took a helicopter ride over the city at sunset, observing the Olympic facilities under construction and the Italianate Escola de Artes

The scene on Rio de Janeiro's Ipanema Beach.

Visuais, noting how the favelas are distributed like chocolate chips in a cookie, rich and poor alike under the gaze of the towering Christ of Corcovado.

We stayed in fine hotels; when we arrived at the Fasano with our two-year-old, a pillow embroidered with his name was waiting in the crib. We ate at chic restaurants such as Gero and Satyricon. But for me, Rio at this moment is not about tourist attractions; it is about renaissance. As in Moscow at the end of communism, Johannesburg at the end of apartheid, and Beijing when China opened to capitalism, the sights are secondary to the electrifying current of transformation.

A frenzy of construction precedes any international mega-event, and Rio natives—Cariocas—are fiercely opinionated about the rejuvenation of historic sites: the Maracanã soccer stadium, which is either being ruined or being saved, and the Hotel Gloria, which is getting a face-lift from billionaire Eike Batista. The Theatro Muncipal, modeled on the Garnier, in Paris, has just been refurbished. "In Rio now," said biographer Luciana Medeiros, "it's like what happens when you fall in love. It's a sparkle. One of the most symbolic things about Rio was that the street was so dirty. All of a sudden, everybody takes care."

The city's street life has been reborn now that the streets are relatively safe, and there are whole neighborhoods given over to the fun between dusk and dawn. The center of nightlife is glamorously seedy Lapa. In the small hours, music pours out of every other door; the caliber of décor of any particular spot and the quality of the musicians who play there are unrelated, so you have to pause and listen up and down the street before choosing where you want to go. We decided to check out what appeared to be a small chapel only to find that it was a tiny bar, presided over by a middle-aged transgender woman who had moved to Rio from Minas Gerais, to the north. She offered us a liqueur from her home state, hot and redolent of cinnamon, and told us howlingly funny tales about figuring out her gender identity on a farm in

the jungle. It's not only the sun that's warm so close to the equator; friendship happens fast in Rio, and you continually find yourself in intimate conversation with people you've just met. They, in turn, introduce you to their friends—some of whom they've just met themselves—and after a few nights, you are juggling invitations to parties, dinners, rain forests.

One such new friend invited us to an early-evening samba party. People often gather to play music informally; anyone can bring an instrument and join in. Our party was in a downtown area where it attracted both businessmen on their way home from the office and favela residents on their way to clean those offices. Musically and socially, improvisation was the style. Two women from Bahia were frying *acarajé*, delicious fritters of seafood and black-eyed peas, and a bar was serving caipirinhas in plastic cups. Rio is not Rio without a sound track; music salts all the other senses.

Much of Brazilian culture originated in Rio's favelas. Samba evolved here, and the new funk music, too. Many soccer stars came out of the favelas, and some of Brazil's famous models were born there. Carnival in Rio depends on their "samba schools," which compete to put on the most glittering display. French aristocrats never say that France would be nothing without the slums of Paris; hip-hop culture notwithstanding, most Americans opt for the suburbs. But in Rio, those who have privilege admire those who don't.

Some tourists choose to stay in hostels in the favelas. Travel companies offer safari-like favela tours; the new Museu de Favela is one of the most dynamic spaces in Rio. There seems to be consensus that the favelas must be preserved. There have always been NGO's trying to fix them; now, people from the favelas are starting their own organizations. Luiz Carlos Dumontt and Dudu de Morro Agudo founded Enraizados, whose artists make graffiti murals to beautify grim neighborhoods. The operation has established a "street library": You find a book on the road, log on to the website stamped opposite the title page, and make a note of where you found it, whether you liked it, and where you're leaving it so someone else can find it.

Marcus Vinicius Faustini left the favelas to become an actor and theater director, but he's now back there, helping kids to realize their dreams. One of the kids I met in the pacified favela of Batan, where Faustini is working, said, "If you could bottle the joy in this place, you could sell it in the Zona Sul."

The glamorous television star Regina Casé, the Oprah Winfrey of Brazil, received me in her extravagant mansion. "Have you been in our Atlantic rain forest?" she said. "You have a hundred kinds of trees, everything is growing on top of everything else, it's all competing for the sun and the water, and somehow it all survives, more lush than anywhere else in the world. That's the social structure of Rio, too. And just as our Amazon is providing the oxygen for the world, we make social oxygen here. If you don't learn to integrate your societies the way we've integrated ours, you're going to fail. In America, you have a lot of problems, a lot of injustice, a lot of conflict. You try to solve the problems." She threw up her hands in mock horror. "In Rio, we invite all the problems to a big party and we let them dance together," she said. "And we're inviting the world to come here and dance, too."

Adapted from "City of Hope," by Andrew Solomon.

GUIDE

STAY
Fasano
*80 Avda. Vieira Souto;
55-21/3202-4000;
fasano.com.br.* **$$$**

EAT
Gero
*157 Rua Aníbal de
Mendonça; 55-21/2239-
8158; fasano.com.br.* **$$$$**

Satyricon
*192 Rua Barão da Torre;
55-21/2521-0627;
satyricon.com.br.* **$$$**

DO
Escola de Artes Visuais
*414 Rua Jardim Botânico,
Jardim Botânico;
55-21/3257-1800;
eavparquelage.rj.gov.br.*

Museu de Favela
*Rua Nossa Senhora
de Fátima, 7 Igrejinha,
Morro do Cantagalo,
55-21/2267-6374;
museudefavela.org.*

Theatro Municipal
*Praça Marechal Floriano;
5-21/2332-9191;
theatromunicipal.rj.gov.br.*

SALTA, ARGENTINA

A journey into the rugged northwest

Stable manager
Ernesto González
on the grounds of
Estancia Colomé.
Opposite: A ravine
on the road from
Cafayate to Salta.

THE WEEK HAD PASSED LIKE A fever dream. Perhaps it was the altitude, or the heat from an unfiltered sun. Or maybe this just happens to anyone who tackles an eight-day drive around the province of Salta, in Argentina's mountainous northwest.

In proximity, physicality, culture, and spirit, Salta is closer to the Andes than to the rest of the country. The cosmopolitan airs of Buenos Aires seem a world away. The province's topography is remarkably diverse: a jumble of red rock and green rivers, vineyards and thorny cacti, snowcapped peaks and arid deserts—as if God had crumpled a map and squeezed a continent's worth of landscapes into one remote corner of Argentina.

My wife, Nilou, and I had caught the two-hour flight from B.A. to the city of Salta, the provincial capital. It was the end of South America's summer, and the tobacco fields were lush from rain, the alfalfa blooming vibrant purple. From Salta we set out on a 330-mile loop: over an alpine pass to the pueblo of Cachi; onward to the fabulous wine estate of Colomé; then north through rust-colored canyons. And on the eighth day, as we pulled into the rental lot to return our mud-spattered 4x4, we had trouble fathoming all we'd encountered: a series of vivid, almost surreal moments, strange enough to make the trip seem half-imagined.

Had all that really happened?

THE PASS

"Nothing grows here but scrub and resentment," Nilou observed as we rounded Hairpin Turn No. 472. We were inching along the Cuesta del Obispo, a near-vertical series of switchbacks in the Sierra del Obispo, en route from Salta to Cachi. We had risen above the treeline, though it was hard to say for sure; you couldn't see 10 yards for the mist clinging to the road. It looked like Venus out there.

"Are we sure this road is even open?" Nilou wondered aloud.

The fog was thick, the air dizzyingly thin: we were wending our way up to 11,000 feet. At the height of the pass, a stone chapel materialized out of the mist, poised on the edge of a cliff. Nearby stood several primitive crosses, no doubt marking where someone had fallen into the void.

We pushed on into the murk, the SUV now pointed downward. I rode the brake. Our ears popped; the rain stopped. In an instant the fog fell away, revealing an arrow-straight highway and a vast plain dotted with cardon cacti. Along the roadside grazed a herd of curious, fuzzy-eared donkeys. Two ambled toward us as we idled on the shoulder. The ears were so ridiculously outsize that the donkeys seemed to stoop under their weight; they looked like helicopter rotors.

THE RODEO

I could hear them approaching from the ravine below. It began as far-off thunder, a rumble that became a roar—the deafening drumbeat of a hundred hooves. The herd rounded the corner: 25 unbridled criollo horses at full gallop. Trailing was a boy no older than 14, riding bareback and wielding a *rebenque*, the braided-leather riding crop of the gaucho. The crowd cheered as he drove in the last of the herd. The *doma* could begin.

After the Cuesta del Obispo we had dropped down, down into the Calchaquí Valley, where lush pastures and llama farms sidle up to Georgia O'Keeffe hills striated pink, chalk-white, and green. At last we'd pulled into Cachi, a low-slung frontier town that, despite the dust, manages to keep its adobe façades blindingly white.

By sheer luck, we'd arrived on the day of the *doma*, a gaucho rodeo festival that draws crowds from around the valley: families in pickup trucks, ranchers on horseback, and a whole cavalry of gauchos, with their flat wool brims, their baggy *bombacha* trousers, their faces like rock formations.

We joined the spectators at the rim of a gravel pit that doubled as the rodeo ground. Salteño folk

music began to blare over the tinny loudspeakers, and one by one the horses were set loose into the pit, to be lassoed and mounted by the gauchos. Most riders were tossed within seconds, but a few hung on for a minute or more, whereupon the men in the audience would murmur their approval. Under the shade of a eucalyptus tree, a cluster of bowlegged gauchos sharpened their facon knives and studied their BlackBerrys. Their horses lapped at a nearby water trough, their stiff leather *guardamontes* (saddle guards) flared out like butterfly wings—the mounts of flying cowboys.

THE RIVER

"When you get to the river, go straight," they told us when we called for directions to Colomé.

"You mean the bridge?"

"No—there is no bridge. You'll have to cross the river yourself." The man paused. "You do have four-wheel drive, yes?"

Late-summer rains had raised the river to unusual heights. The water was a hundred yards across and rushing at a good clip. "Turn your wheel into the current," the man on the phone had advised. "And whatever you do, don't slow down."

Nilou unbuckled her seat belt in case she needed to get out quickly and swim. I shifted into first. With a jerk we launched off the muddy bank and into the current. At this point, for reasons that still remain unclear, I began to yodel. Nilou seemed to agree this was the thing to do, and soon both of us were yodeling as we bounced and splashed our way across the river, until at last we reached the shore.

THE ESTANCIA

If any place is worth fording a river for, Estancia Colomé is it.

The 96,000-acre estate was bought in 2001 by Donald Hess, a Swiss entrepreneur and art collector whose primary intention was to make wine.

Above, from left: The fountain in the courtyard of Estancia Colomé; young llamas spotted on the drive from Cachi to Colomé.

Colomé's vineyards are some of the oldest in Argentina (one plot dates to the 1850's), and among the highest in the world, averaging 7,200 feet above sea level. The elevation and the increased UV-ray exposure result in more concentrated, intensely flavored wines. Colomé's Malbecs, Syrahs, and Tannats now rank among the country's finest.

That a state-of-the-art winery could exist here seems a minor miracle. That Colomé would house an 18,000-square-foot James Turrell museum veers into the absurd. Hess built the museum in 2009, working from a design by Turrell himself. It is the world's only museum devoted to the California-born artist, whose cunning light installations toy with infinitesimal variations in color. The exhibition is mesmerizing, and Turrell's works take full advantage of the setting. The final installation, *Unseen Blue 2002*, occupies an entire room, with a rectangular portal in the ceiling: a massive skylight framed by ever-shifting colored lights. During our sunset tour of the museum, the docent instructed us to find a spot on the marble floor, lie on our backs, and watch. Watch what? The sky, for the last minutes of twilight, as it shifted imperceptibly from blue to cobalt, deep indigo to inky black.

■ IT'S AS IF GOD HAD SQUEEZED A CONTINENT'S WORTH OF LANDSCAPES INTO ONE REMOTE CORNER OF ARGENTINA.

LA ZAMBA

Wine, empanadas, and colonial architecture notwithstanding, Salta is most famous for its music. The signature form is the *zamba*, a stirring waltz-time dance that showcases the *bombo legüero*, a traditional fur-skinned drum. The lyrics typically name-check provincial villages and landmarks. Like American country music, *folklorico Salteño* is nothing if not hometown proud.

So on our final night in Salta City, we wanted to hear some live music. La Casona del Molino sits on the outskirts of town in a crumbling old mill complex that dates from 1671. It's a bar, but far more than that: in five cozy salas surrounding an open courtyard, musicians gather to play informal sets, hootenanny-style.

At 11 p.m. on a Wednesday, the place was just beginning to fill up—with students, old men in canvas caps, mothers nursing babies. Tabletops were already crowded with Fernet-and-Cokes (Argentina's national cocktail) and pop-top bottles of wine. Every man in the place was wearing a gingham shirt; some carried satchels of coca leaves.

We found a table in the torchlit courtyard; around midnight a quartet of musicians came out. The guitarist unleashed a flurry of manic strumming, and the crowd, recognizing the tune, went nuts. Soon everyone was singing along to the triumphant chorus. The only words I could make out were *Salta*, *Salta*, and *Salta*. It was a fist-pumping tribute to the place they called home—the "Empire State of Mind" of folk anthems.

Hearing that song, watching that crowd, I once again had the impression of Salta as a land apart from the rest of Argentina—or at least the sense that Salteños see it that way. Their pride is infectious.

Adapted from "Argentina's Northwest Passage," by Peter Jon Lindberg.

GUIDE

STAY

Hotel Hacienda de Molinos
A renovated historic house featuring a beautiful courtyard, sweeping views, and indigenous touches like algarrobo (black carob) ceilings. *Molinos; 54-3868/494-094; haciendademolinos. com.ar.* **$**

House of Jasmines Estancia de Charme
This early 1900's hacienda has 14 rooms and suites on a 370-acre ranch just outside of Salta. *800/735-2478; houseofjasmines.com.* **$**

Legado Mítico Hotel
An 11-suite boutique hotel in a restored colonial town house whose rooms are themed around notable Salteños. *647 General Mitre, Salta; 54-387/422-8786; legadomitico.com.* **$**

La Merced del Alto
Cachi's most luxurious property often doubles as a contemporary art gallery. *Cachi; 54-3868/490-030; lamerceddelalto.com.* **$**

Patios de Cafayate Hotel & Winespa
One mile northeast of Cafayate, this resort has fussy interiors but lovely grounds. *54-3868/422-229; patiosdecafayate.com.* **$$**

DRINK

La Casona del Molino
1 Luís Burela, Salta; 54-387/434-2835.

DO

Bodega y Estancia Colomé
Tours of the estate's winery, museum, and horseback-riding trails must be booked in advance. *54-3868/ 494-200; bodegacolome. com; tours from $70.*

BUENOS AIRES

South America's cultural hub steps up

A dizzying combination of Europe and Latin America, colonial and contemporary, laid-back and fast-paced, Buenos Aires has an energy all its own. In recent years, forward-thinking shop owners and chefs have reinvigorated the city's Palermo barrio; its edgy restaurants and bars, set in ivy-covered town houses, make it more appealing than ever to the young and hip. The neighborhood at your fingertips? Look no further.

A café on one of Palermo's cobblestoned streets.

Bolivia

Fashionable Porteños choose men's clothing shop Bolivia for of-the-moment pieces by owner Gustavo Samuelian, including floral-print shirts, slim-cut jeans, and sharp tailored suits.
1581 Gurruchaga; 54-11/4832-6284; boliviaparatodos.com.ar.

Experiencia del Fin del Mundo

At the limestone-clad tasting room of Patagonian winery Bodega del Fin del Mundo, flights follow a single varietal through several vintages. Pair them with regional items from the adjoining restaurant's menu such as Neuquén venison with smoked apples and bacon.
5673 Honduras; 54-11/4852-6661; bodegadelfindelmundo.com. **$$**

La Cabrera

Pretty young things sip champagne outside on the sidewalk while they wait for tables at La Cabrera, a classic *parrilla* where waiters in berets serve gargantuan sides—mashed squash; Andean potatoes; broiled onions—along with cuts of sizzling grilled beef.
5099 Cabrera; 54-11/4831-7002; parrillalacabrera.com.ar. **$$**

La Pulpería (El Federal)

For lunch, locals go to La Pulpería, an old-fashioned diner that serves delicious oyster-and-mushroom sandwiches and fresh-baked *alfajores,* a traditional sugar-dusted pastry made by joining shortbread cookies with jam or creamy *dulce de leche* filling.
1667 Uriarte; 54-11/4833-6039. **$$**

Leopoldo

Chef Diego Gera whips up intensely flavored specialties such as crisp-skinned suckling pig paired with quince purée and rib eye—dry-aged in-house—with truffled potatoes and sautéed mushrooms, at the purple-hued Leopoldo. After dinner in the velvet-and-wood dining room, head to the restaurant's patio for cocktails and live DJ music.
3732 Avda. Cerviño; 54-11/4805-5576; leopoldorestaurante.com.ar. **$$$**

MALBA

Here you'll find a permanent collection of more than 500 paintings, sculptures, and objects from top Latin American talent. There's also a screening room that showcases independent films.
3415 Avda. Figueroa Alcorta; 54-11/4808-6500; malba.org.ar.

Mundo Bizarro

For a cocktail lounge with a retro rock-and-roll vibe—and an appropriately vampy red-and-black color palette—head to neighborhood stalwart Mundo Bizarro. The bar features an ever-changing selection of original artwork on the walls (most are for sale) and plays little-known B-movies on a screen in the back.
1222 Serrano; 54-11/4773-1967; mundobizarrobar.com.

Social Paraíso

Renowned Argentine chef Darío Gualtieri recently took the reins at the long-loved bistro Social Paraíso. His mission: to shake up the menu with cutting-edge dishes like Patagonian prawns cooked in palm oil and coconut milk and Sichuan-pepper ice cream with passion-fruit mousse.
5182 Honduras; 54-11/4831-4556. **$$**

An *ojo de bife* steak at La Cabrera. Left: Inside the MALBA museum.

Happy hour at Mundo Bizarro. Right: Men's-wear store Bolivia's off-the-rack fashions.

PATAGONIA

Observing Chilean glaciers by land, sea, and air

PATAGONIA HAS ALWAYS BEEN the haunt of the wanderer, the exile, the outlaw—souls drawn to a land where one can disappear into the sheer enormousness of physical space. The name alone conjures images of cloud-veiled peaks, electric-blue lakes, and endless steppes unpopulated for hundreds of miles.

The best way to take in this spectacular scenery is by water, cruising to see the glaciers of Chilean Patagonia's southern Lake District. Modern-day journeyers with a penchant for the finer things should book passage on Nomads of the Seas' 150-foot *Atmosphere,* a 14-cabin yacht that departs from the bay of Puerto Montt en route to the Taitao peninsula. On the way, watch whales from the boat's deck—or from its six-person helicopter—then disembark to go fly-fishing and hike through miles of pristine rain forest with guides. At day's end, the windowed dining room serves regional wines alongside Patagonian specialties made with local ingredients such as ostrich, grouper, and king crab. And that's just the tip of the iceberg.

A colony of sunbathing sea lions, as seen from the Nomads of the Seas ship *Atmosphere.*

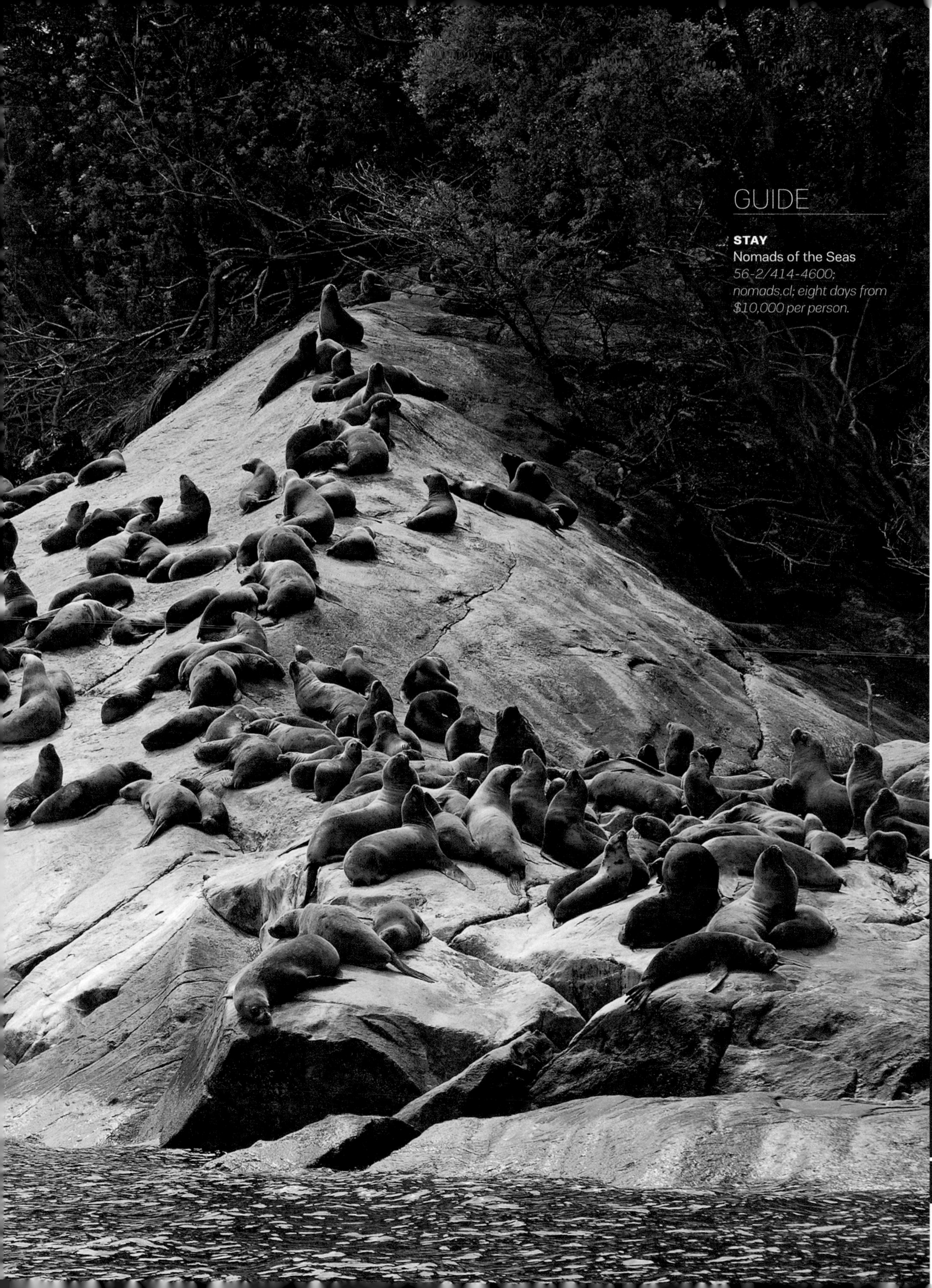

GUIDE

STAY
Nomads of the Seas
56-2/414-4600; nomads.cl; eight days from $10,000 per person.

Looking out over the rooftops of Milan from the Duomo.

ENGLANDLONDONMADRIDPORTUGALPROVENCEPARISMIL
BRUSSELSEUROPEANROADTRIPTHEMEDITERRANEANISTA

EUROPE

AREMMANAPLESTRIESTEBERLINNETHERLANDSCOPENHAGEN
AEGEANCOASTMOSCOWENGLANDLONDONMADRIDPORTUGAL

ENGLAND

A stylish resurgence by the sea

Wild and windswept, England's southwestern coast has long been a magnet for the artistically inclined—the preeminent sculptor Barbara Hepworth, for one, moved to St. Ives in 1949. Today, Cornwall, Devon, and Dorset are in the midst of a transformation that has brought sophisticated new inns and restaurateurs such as Mark Hix (who opened the Hix Oyster & Fish House in Dorset) to these quiet shores. On a drive through the region you can easily spend a week hotel-hopping—one tiny, handsome port town at a time.

DAY 1
London to St. Ives
(300 miles)

Exit off the A30 at St. Ives, an idyllic seaside resort with winding narrow lanes that's something of an art mecca amid Cornwall's old tin mines. Pulling up to the Salt House, on a street lined with traditional rendered cottages, you might think you've taken a turn for Palm Springs.

The two-room inn is a contemporary cube constructed out of concrete, wood, and floor-to-ceiling glass windows high above St. Ives Bay—the work of chic London transplants Alan and Sharon Spencer. One guest suite is decorated with a pair of cherry Ligne Roset mini-Pop chairs and a red, hand-shaped bag hanger giving the A-OK sign.

A coastal path leads from the Salt House to a town full of art galleries. Compared with its London counterparts, the gleaming-white Tate St. Ives is small and easily navigable—and across the street from a pristine stretch of sand. Not far away, stop to take in the abstract bronze and stone sculptures at Barbara Hepworth's namesake museum and garden. Then retire to the Salt House for the night and spend the evening on your room's private terrace, watching the sun disappear below the horizon.

DAY 2
St. Ives to Mousehole
(15 miles)

"The remarkable pagan landscape" is how Hepworth once described the tip of Cornwall. You'll see why as you drive down Route B3306 toward Land's End, England's westernmost point. The road becomes a swirl of black in an expanse of green as you cut through pastures of grazing cattle toward the Gurnard's Head, a "dining pub with rooms" in

Right, from top: Tate St. Ives; the South Bedroom at the Salt House, in St. Ives. Opposite: Durdle Door Beach, on Dorset's Jurassic Coast.

Zennor, that serves fresh fish and potatoes. Its owners have also taken over the Old Coast Guard hotel in the fishing port of Mousehole, 10 miles away.

For a place the size of Mousehole, the Old Coast Guard is huge. Still, it feels intimate. After you have dinner in a distressed-oak dining room, the general manager clears your plates; the housekeeper tells you about the hotel's local art for sale. The 14 guest rooms are snug, with warm yellow walls and thoughtful touches such as old-school Roberts radios and Cornish tea. Settle in for the night or venture 10 miles west to see the classics performed at the open-air Minack Theatre.

DAY 3

Mousehole to Fowey
(60 miles)

The next morning, boat over to St. Michael's Mount—an isle with a legendary medieval castle— then get back on the main roads through farmland toward the historic harbor town of Fowey.

The village hosts an annual festival celebrating *Rebecca* author and former resident Daphne du Maurier; hotelier Angelique Thompson, who greets you at her quirky Upton House wearing a silk frock and fishnets, seems to capture the Gothic mood. Opt for the Snow Bubble room, a study in whites with a dose of kitsch. A peek into the bathroom reveals an egg-shaped tub and an illuminated Bossini

Left, from top:
Nautical gear at Quba & Co.; sipping pints on the patio of the Pigs Nose Inn, in East Prawle.

146

Beauty and the Beast, performed at the Minack Theatre, in Porthcurno.

showerhead that pours out beams of light with the water. Like everything else, you can buy one in the downstairs boutique.

DAY 4
Fowey to Salcombe
(60 miles)

After crossing the river Exe into Devon, you'll reach Salcombe, a sailing resort in the South Hams.

The South Sands Hotel sits on a golden beach and has 27 airy rooms with a nautical-chic blue-and-white décor that calls to mind Nantucket. Waiters clad in checkered crew shirts and khakis serve mussels harvested from the river Exe. From here, ride the resort's own ferry over to Salcombe's high street for some shopping. Taking inspiration from the hotel's upscale-preppy style, you can buy stripes at both Quba & Co. and Jack Wills, two U.K. brands influenced by the region's sailing heritage.

DAY 5
Salcombe to Bridport
(80 miles)

Start with an early lunch nearby in East Prawle at the eclectic Pigs Nose Inn (prawn curry; calamari salad). From there, the scenic route on the A379 toward Dorset passes through Slapton Sands, an unusual swath of beach (and road) that's flanked by water on both sides. Only a few major motorways run into the county, so it feels more remote than Devon and Cornwall.

But thanks to such restaurateurs as native son Mark Hix, there's been an influx of foodies. At Hix Oyster & Fish House, a glass-walled restaurant overlooking Lyme Regis's harbor, staffers forage for ingredients daily.

Along Dorset's shoreline is the Jurassic Coast, England's only natural UNESCO World Heritage site. Another great spot: Bridport, nicknamed Notting Hill on Sea for its antiques shops. At the center of the action is the 19-room Bull Hotel, a 16th-century coaching inn filled with one-of-a-kind gems such as an Indian-cane sofa and a stained-glass window—more evidence that this coast is becoming one of Europe's next great beach escapes.

GUIDE

STAY

Bull Hotel
*Bridport;
44-1308/422-878;
thebullhotel.co.uk.* **$$**

Old Coast Guard
*Mousehole; 44 1736/
731-222; oldcoastguard
hotel.co.uk.* **$**

Salt House
*St. Ives; 44-1736/
791-857; salthousestives.
co.uk.* **$$**

South Sands Boutique
Hotel & Beachside
Restaurant
*Salcombe;
44-1548/845-900;
southsands.com.* **$$**

Upton House
*Fowey; 44-1726/832-
732; upton-house.com.* **$$**

EAT

Gurnard's Head
*Zennor;
44-1736/796-928;
gurnardshead.co.uk.* **$$**

Hix Oyster & Fish House
*Lyme Regis;
44-1297/446-910;
hixoysterandfishhouse.
co.uk.* **$$$**

Pigs Nose Inn
*East Prawle;
44-1548/511-209;
pigsnose.co.uk.* **$**

DO

Minack Theatre
*Porthcurno; 44-1736/
810-181; minack.com.*

St. Michael's Mount
*Marazion;
stmichaelsmount.co.uk.*

Tate St. Ives
*St. Ives; 44-1736/
796-226; tate.org.uk.*

SHOP

Jack Wills
*Salcombe;
44-1548/842-007;
jackwills.com.*

Quba & Co.
*Salcombe; 44-1548/
844-599; quba.com.*

LONDON

A trove of shops hidden in plain sight

Every Sunday morning, East London's favorite flower market takes on a distinctly Dickensian air, as vendors along Columbia Road cajole browsers with hyperbolic sales pitches delivered in semi-ironic Cockney accents. People pack in among the stalls, jostling and bargaining for the week's best varieties of Dutch tulips, Kenya-grown lisianthus, and English garden roses. Just behind this fragrant scene, however, is a row of singular boutiques that just might be the city's best-kept shopping secret.

Bob & Blossom
Affordable wooden toys crowd the floor of this whitewashed children's store, from multi-colored spinning tops to alphabet stamp kits; cozy crocheted bunnies are perfect fillers for the assemble-it-yourself gift boxes. On the racks you'll find a cool-kids' clothing line of skull-and-crossbones tees, pink-and-white-striped cotton dresses, and star-patterned beanies.
No. 140; 44-127/367-9497; bobandblossom.co.uk.

Openhouse
Openhouse is the only place in East London to sell planting pots bearing the crest of the Royal Botanic Garden, in Kew. The rest of the eclectic collection includes gardening sets, watering cans, and alarm clocks ablaze with William Morris–designed prints; worn wooden farm tables; and steel birdcages. Locals also love co-owner Alex Grayburn's handmade flower baskets.
No. 152; 44-797/985-1593.

Powder Room
This retro 1950's salon is run by a pack of baby-pink-clad stylists dubbed the Powderpuff Girls, renowned throughout London for their artistry. They'll preen you with a makeover (try the transforming Make Him Look Twice treatment), manicure, or blowout while you sip tea and eat cake in their Art Deco–style parlor.
No. 136; 44-20/7729-1365; thepowderpuffgirls.com.

Ryantown
From his book-lined studio in Bethnal Green, Cyprus-born artist Rob Ryan creates whimsical paper-cut bird and flower designs for his diminutive turquoise boutique—everything from handprinted plates and silk-screened urns to limited-edition silk scarves and laser-cut calendars. Pick up one of his original illustrations or a more affordable printed tile etched with Ryan's poetic musings on life and love.
No. 126; 44-20/7613-1510; ryantownshop.blogspot.com.

Suck & Chew
Craving sweets? At Vicki Maguire's confectionery, Union Jack flags hang above old-fashioned dressers stocked with jars of proper British candies such as Rhubarb & Custards, Cola Cubes, and Rosy Apples. The company counts Paul Smith as a fan; the British design stalwart raves about the toffee tins festooned with pictures of motocross bikers, Santa Claus, and the Queen.
No. 130; 44-20/8983-3504; suckandchew.co.uk.

Treacle
The owners of Treacle are passionate about cupcakes—theirs are topped in a delicious buttercream frosting and sprinkled with edible flowers—but there's more to this Midcentury Modern bakery than sweets. Contemporary ceramics by Keith Brymer Jones and restored school desks and church pews are part of the vintage collection for sale.
Nos. 110–112; 44-20/7729-0538; treacleworld.com.

Vintage Heaven
The shelves of this unassuming lavender-fronted shop practically teeter with crockery, glassware, and objets d'art adorned in faded 1950's floral patterns. After picking over the gold-rimmed teapots and blue-toile tableware, sample the tangy lemon-drizzle cake and cream tea at the store's charming Cakehole Café, outfitted in funky David Hicks wallpaper and antique mirrors.
No. 82; 44-127/721-5968; vintageheaven.co.uk.

Above: Vendors at the Columbia Road Flower Market.

Ryantown boutique. Left: Children's fashions at Bob & Blossom.

Treacle's vanilla sponge cake. Right: One of the Powder Room salon's Powderpuff Girls.

EUROPE

MADRID

Hungry for the Spanish capital

Flamenco dancer Gerardo Ferrero Sánchez on Calle Gran Vía in downtown Madrid.

T'S 4 A.M. ON A TUESDAY NIGHT—NEW YORK and London are mostly asleep, Berlin and Barcelona are getting tired, Hong Kong and Frankfurt are completely tuckered out—and here I am surrounded by throaty, amorous singers, some in their sixties and seventies, jammed around a piano at a bar called Toni2, hollering lustily about *amor* and *besos* and all that good stuff. Where am I? Where could I possibly be? *Madrid*, of course. And nowhere else.

My companion on this journey is Diego Salazar, a Peruvian writer and foodie who came to Madrid a decade ago and never looked back. He tells me of a right-wing pundit who got into a fine mess at Toni2 after touching someone's ass. Many stories in Madrid seem to end this way. In any case, some 30 years from now, if I decide *not* to go gently into that good night, if I decide to push the limits of mortality and common sense, this is where I want to be, crooning and drinking and being goosed by a right-wing pundit and generally just being alive.

"You go to Barcelona to have children," Salazar tells me in a way that makes me understand that he's not quite ready to reproduce. Great cities need archrivals. St. Petersburgers routinely hate Moscow. Bostonians still can't seem to get over the rise of New York. But nothing in the world beats the rivalry between Madrid and Barcelona, the two competing faces of Spain. The truth is both cities are worthy of respect, sometimes love. But Barcelona is ruthlessly gorgeous, while Madrid's beauty has to be uncovered, her sweltering summers and freezing winters endured. And then there's the pollution cloaking the place, watering your eyes and tickling your throat.

And yet, Madrid is on the rise! The city has been going to the gym, cutting out the trans fats, and taking summer courses. Today's Madrid is both lean and welcoming, with a recently reclaimed river, a burgeoning arts district within the walls of an old slaughterhouse, oodles of creative cuisine, and, yes, nocturnal 70-year-olds gathered around

a piano in the rollicking Chueca neighborhood waiting for the sun to come up.

The first time I came to Spain I was recovering from a mild nervous breakdown. The year was 1996, and I had just barely survived 13 months of my first postcollege job as a paralegal in New York. I recall stepping off a crowded Spanish train, walking into a bar near Valencia, and getting misty-eyed at the sight of used napkins and shrimp shells on the floor. What a terrific, easygoing lifestyle awaited me! I befriended a clutch of young miscreants in a small village and was invited to join their little club, the Penya Colpet (roughly "Club Shot Glass"). Together we welcomed the summer fiestas, taunted a bull, ate enough *pulpo a la gallega* to empty out Galicia, and slept maybe four hours during the entire month of July.

IN MADRID, THE FEAST IS NOT JUST MOVABLE; IT IS ENDLESS.

My other memory of Madrid consisted of being chased down in the city center by a heroin-addicted transvestite clamoring for my patronage.

Downtown Madrid will now have none of that, thank you. The city has gentrified tremendously, but you can still catch a little grit in your peripheral vision. There are fancy new olive-oil stores next to shoe-repair shops whose proprietors live in darkened holes illuminated only by the flicker of the TV behind thick curtains. In TriBall, short for Triángulo de Ballesta, prostitutes are being edged out by fashion boutiques, cooking schools, artisanal hamburger joints, and the Belgian-owned Al Cuadrado Taglio & Bar pizza shop. The remainder of TriBall's streetwalkers like to cluster outside Al Cuadrado, perhaps getting a whiff of the spicy salami, rosemary, caramelized sweet onion, and potato slices, a nice addition to the Roman *pizza al taglio* canon.

A stroll through Lavapiés reveals a palimpsest of the waves of immigration that have washed over this barrio, an indicator of how tolerant Madrid is perceived to be. "First the Arabs, now

the Pakistanis and Chinese," Lawrence Schimel, a New York–born author who now speaks English with a slight *castellano* accent, tells me over excellent Basque *pintxos* and a *caña* of Mahou beer.

We're at Lamiak, a tapas establishment at the center of Lavapiés, the pleasant muted yellows and the exposed brick lending the bar a cheerful demeanor. Schimel is a vegan, but that doesn't stop me from viciously attacking a three-bite tartare of bacalao and tomato, along with a little *solomillo de cerdo al oporto,* pork tenderloin marinated in port and covered in pineapple and onion, which tastes classier than it sounds. Outside, vegan stores jostle with dark Chinese markets. An overwhelmingly Pakistani street gives way to an array of local hippies. We are far from the land of bullfighting and beachfront siestas, yet we do manage to find flamenco.

The Mercado de Antón Martín is a vital neighborhood market. The second floor of this vast building is an odd place to put the exquisitely named Amor de Dios flamenco school. But there it is: crowded with Japanese girls (flamenco is another unlikely Japanese obsession), resounding with castanets. I wish Renoir were here to capture a half-dozen women standing in a row, their postures perfect, practicing their clicks. Directly downstairs, an olive shop dispenses buckets of tasty pickles and marinated baby eggplant (*berenjenas de Almagro*) stuffed with red pepper and fennel.

In Madrid the feast is not just movable; it is endless, with much of it boiled down to 10 square city blocks. Malasaña, directly north of Calle Gran Vía and northwest of gay-friendly Chueca, is still the hippest stretch of town. I'm strolling through with my friend, the wonderful Spanish writer Mercedes Cebrián. We cross Malasaña's main plaza and make our way to Casa Fidel, where I am introduced to *salmorejo,* a gazpacho substitute from Córdoba made from tomato and bread and the holy trinity of oil, garlic, and vinegar, garnished with *jamón serrano* and hard-boiled egg. Next up, porky *lomo embuchado,* which Cebrián

Opposite, clockwise from top left: Tapas and beer at La Castela, near Retiro Park; schoolchildren pose for the camera in front of the CaixaForum Madrid arts center; Casa Fidel, in the Malasaña neighborhood; outside the Matadero Madrid art space.

says "tastes like the bastard child of *jamón* and chorizo." Appropriately enough for a place called Fidel, most of the men are wearing thick, lovingly maintained beards. Finally, *chipirones en su tinta con arroz*, squid in its own ink with rice; the squid is as dark as night, darker than Goya's black paintings. Javier Blasco, the friendly owner, comes around with a bottle of *orujo*, a Galician spirit, somewhat grappa-like. After drinking it, I'm told: "You sleep very bad." Sleep very bad? The problem with Madrid is there is no sleep *at all*.

Madrid may have embraced edgy pizzas by Belgian newcomers, but there's still nothing like an old-fashioned tapas crawl. First stop is La Castela, a noisy, cheek-by-jowl, napkins-on-the-floor kind of place in the middle-class part of Retiro. The Thursday rush is crazy. We eat *garbanzos con langostino*, enjoying prawns and the poor man's bean doused in olive oil and studded with *ajete*, the green stalk of the young garlic plant.

Walking down the Calle del Doctor Castelo, we nightcap at the Antigua Taberna Arzábal. We are looking for some cava to "cleanse the palate." After the madness of the previous place this one is over-polished and slick, with champagne in silver buckets. We eat the olive-oil-soaked *anchoa* and sip the bubbly, while next to us some wannabe urbanites are posing with a bottle of Tanqueray.

This is perhaps the right place to talk about Spain's newfound love of the Gin and Tonic. If I were a juniper berry I'd be scared of the Spaniards. Rivers of gin are consumed in Madrid. The best place to do so is La Chula de Valverde, in TriBall, a sweet, exposed-brick kind of place with the Johnny Cash version of "Personal Jesus" on the stereo. The preparation of the sacred Gin and Tonic lasts five minutes, as the bartender moves the lime around the rim, gently, oh-so-gently pouring in the tonic.

After a few G&T's, the question: straight to dinner, or tapas? We stop at the modernized Mercado de San Miguel, the wrought-iron foodie's paradise off the Plaza Mayor. Here are some fine little things to pick on: the mussel canapés and garlic brandade from La Casa del Bacalao, and the heavenly, eggy *tortilla* from an outpost of good old Lhardy restaurant (*desde* 1839, no less!).

And then there's Sergi Arola Gastro, the Michelin two-starred Art Deco tunnel of fun over in the quiet Chamberí district. I'm thinking of their play on the *bocadillo de calamares*, the squid sandwich that is a Madrid tradition, here reduced to a handful of bread and thoughtfully fried seafood;

■ THIRTY YEARS FROM NOW, IF I DECIDE *NOT* TO GO GENTLY INTO THAT GOOD NIGHT, THIS IS WHERE I WANT TO BE.

GUIDE

STAY

Hotel de las Letras
Handwoven rugs and punchy, modern furniture fill this Belle Époque mansion. *11 Calle Gran Vía; 34/91-523-7980; hoteldelasletras.com.* **$**

Hotel Villa Magna
Centrally located, the 150-room property was extensively renovated in 2009. *22 Paseo de la Castellana; 34/91-587-1234; villamagna.es.* **$$$**

EAT AND DRINK

Al Cuadrado Taglio & Bar
10 Calle de la Ballesta; 34/91-521-3515. **$$**

Antigua Taberna Arzábal
2 Calle del Doctor Castelo; 34/91-557-2691; arzabal.com. **$$**

Casa Fidel
6 Calle del Escorial; 34/91-531-7736. **$$**

La Casa del Bacalao
Plaza de San Miguel; 34/91-542-6473. **$**

La Castela
22 Calle del Doctor Castelo; 34/91-573-5590; lacastela.com. **$$**

La Chula de Valverde
11 Calle de Valverde; 34/91-523-9044.

Lamiak
10 Calle de la Rosa; 34/91-539-7450; lamiak.com. **$**

Lhardy
8 Carr. de San Jerónimo;

34/91-522-2207; lhardy.com. **$$$**

Sergi Arola Gastro
31 Calle de Zurbano; 34/91-310-2169; sergiarola.es. **$$$$**

Toni2
9 Calle del Almirante; 34/91-532-0011; toni2.es.

DO

Centro de Arte Flamenco y Danza Española Amor de Dios
5 Calle de Santa Isabel;

34/91-360-0434; amordedios.com.

Matadero Madrid
8 Plaza de Legazpi; 34/91-517-7309; mataderomadrid.org.

SHOP

Mercado de Antón Martín
5 Calle de Santa Isabel; mercadoantonmartin.com.

Mercado de San Miguel
Plaza de San Miguel; 34/91-548-1214; mercadodesanmiguel.es.

the "bread nougat," a thin tube of caramelized bread filled with tomato and ham; and a counter-intuitive cornet of trout roe and wasabi ice cream. Down the menu, the king prawns with peaches are simple and delicious, as are the roasted sardines. I've never been inducted into the wonders of the powerful Priorat wines, such as the plummy and chocolaty 2004 Francesc Sánchez-Bas Montgarnatx, but there's no looking back after the first sip. And I'm not the only person falling in love. The woman in tight sequins next to me, looking like she just stepped off the set of an Almodóvar movie, is making out hard with her date, one hand deep into the opening of his blue oxford shirt, her mini-dress rustling under the table. In their defense, it is well past midnight, almost time for the main course.

Daylight reveals Madrid's new gems. The 79-foot-tall "vertical garden" makes Herzog & de Meuron's CaixaForum Madrid a true example of Cool España. And Matadero Madrid, the re-purposed municipal slaughterhouse by the

Manzanares river, buzzes with art and is already a crowd-pleaser. The river park, Madrid Río, is itself worthy of a detour. Snaking through large apartment blocks on its way to the royal palace, the river has become a truly democratic space—older women wearing hats made out of newspaper lounge around with their Sunday beers, children play under sprays of water, and the whole thing is threaded with happy-looking poplar trees.

But, as far as I'm concerned, the best architecture in Madrid is still the Richard Rogers–designed Terminal 4 at Madrid-Barajas Airport. Muscular but sinuous, flooded with natural light, the design reminds you that Spain—a country that sent so many of its citizens abroad during its worst days and now welcomes so many immigrants from across the globe—has mastered both the art of greeting and, sadly, the art of farewell.

*Adapted from "Hungry for Madrid,"
by Gary Shteyngart.*

Above: Revelers at the Toni2 piano bar, in the Chueca neighborhood.

DÃO, PORTUGAL

Encounters in an unknown wine region

Napa, Champagne, Rioja—these are the destinations American oenophiles have come to revere. The Dão? Not so much. Yet this little-known area in central Portugal produces some of the finest reds on the Iberian peninsula. Like the nearby Forest of Buçaco, with its enchanting age-old cork oaks and Carmelite monk traditions, the Dão is a secretive place whose charms, from stylish pousadas to medieval settlements, must be sought out to be savored.

The courtyard at Quinta das Lágrimas. Opposite: Convento do Desagravo's on-site vineyard.

DAY 1

Porto to Coimbra
(90 miles)

Cruise down the A1 Auto Estrada from Porto to the ancient town of Coimbra. The core of the city occupies a promontory crowned by two cathedrals—one Romanesque and fortresslike, the other grand and Baroque— and a university that's among the oldest in Europe. Cobblestoned streets and alleys drop precipitously to a district lined with hotels, shops, and sidewalk cafés, many of them in creamy Belle Époque buildings.

On the other side of the river, check in to Quinta das Lágrimas (Villa of Tears), which takes its name from the macabre legend of Prince Pedro and his mistress Inês de Castro, who was ordered assassinated by the king. The cult of the ill-fated lovers is everywhere: downstairs at the Michelin-starred Arcadas, order your choice of Pedro & Inês wines to go with a tangy goat-cheese ravioli. Or settle down to dinner at A Portuguesa, a casual waterside restaurant overlooking the placid Mondego River, where you can feast on *cataplana,* a traditional fish stew cooked in a special copper pan.

DAY 2

Coimbra to Vila Pouca da Beira
(47 miles)

Beyond Coimbra lies the Dão itself, a verdant plateau of two-lane roads, piney woods, and fields dotted with little hamlets

**Left, from top:
Paço dos Cunhas
de Santar's chef,
Diogo Rocha; the
lobby at Quinta
das Lágrimas.**

The Dão River, slicing through the Douro Valley.

residence turned restaurant serves grilled spare ribs and crisp fries from an unpretentious menu; pair them with a glass of Casa de Santar, an herby red from the village of the same name.

Santar, in fact, is just a half-hour away, and is one of the most beautiful villages in the Dão, with stone-and-stucco houses on narrow lanes and Baroque villas hidden behind high gates. The Casa de Santar itself is a long, white manor house with its back to the street. Its gardens are a terraced fantasia of topiary and boxwood parterres and roses in full flower.

From here, drive onward to Viseu, the hub of the Dão wine industry, and drop your bags at the dramatically restored Pousada de Viseu. A fitting end to your trip: spend the evening dining at the secluded Paço dos Cunhas de Santar, a hard-to-find estate transformed by Dão Sul into a showcase of *enoturismo*, with an inspiring passion-fruit-glazed grilled duck breast and a sweet goat-cheese custard flecked with orange and mint.

shielded by mountain ranges. Stop in tiny Lourosa to see the 10th-century church of São Pedro. A mile south at Vila Pouca da Beira—a relative metropolis of 400 residents—the 18th-century Convento do Desagravo pousada provides a soft landing, combining the minimalist and the Baroque: vast expanses of whitewashed plaster interrupted by polychromed saints in ecstasy. Perch yourself on the hotel's terrace overlooking the Serra da Estrela mountains and order

a Quinta da Bica, a supple red from nearby. Tomorrow, it's on to the vineyards.

DAY 3

Vila Pouca da Beira to Viseu
(43 miles)

A 45-minute drive on back roads brings you to Carregal do Sal and the Quinta de Cabriz, the headquarters of Dão Sul, one of the leading wine producers in the region. Under a stand of pines at the edge of town, the winery's 17th-century foliage-draped

GUIDE

STAY
Pousada de Vila Pouca da Beira, Convento do Desagravo
Calçada do Convento; 351/218-442-001; pousadas.pt. **$**

Pousada de Viseu
Rua do Hospital, Viseu; 351/291-721-405; pousadadeviseu.com. **$**

Quinta das Lágrimas
Rua António Augusto Gonçalves, Coimbra; 351/239-802-380; quintadaslagrimas.pt. **$$**

EAT
A Portuguesa
Parque Verde do Mondego, Avda. da Lousã, Coimbra; 351/239-842-140; aportuguesa.pt. **$$**

Arcadas
Rua António Augusto Gonçalves, Coimbra; 351/239-802-380; quintadaslagrimas.pt. **$$$**

Paço dos Cunhas de Santar
Largo do Paço de Santar, Santar; 351/232-960-140. **$$$**

Quinta de Cabriz Restaurant
Estrada Nacional N234, Carregal do Sal; 351/232-961-222. **$$**

DO
Casa de Santar
Avda. Viscondessa de Taveiro, Santar; 351/232-942-937.

Church of São Pedro
Oliveira do Hospital, Lourosa.

University of Coimbra
Largo da Porta Ferrea, Coimbra; 351/239-859-900; uc.pt.

BANDOL, FRANCE

Sipping rosé in Provence

Above, from left: One of the region's *calanques*; a sleepy corner of Bandol. Opposite: A dish of tuna tartare and rosé at Restaurant Nino, in Cassis.

THE SUN STARTED TO TURN back for the day. I chose a bar and settled into a red canvas-backed chair outside. Every table on the promenade now had on it a glass or a bottle of rosé. A little more sun seeped out of the day, like air slowly let out of a balloon. Finally, as if in deference to the hour and the wine of choice, the last of the light fell off the cliffs and the sky above the sea settled into an uncannily familiar shade of perfect pale pink.

I'd come to Provence for exactly this—for rosé and its context. Some wines invite you to reflect on their expression of *goût de terroir*, to ponder what message is delivered to the palate by this alignment of place and soil and vines. Another wine might ask special consideration for the refining artistry of its vintner or the noble lineage of its grand château. Rosé makes no such demands.

Summer in a bottle, it beckons. Rosé says: follow me to the south of France. A table by the sea. A simple lunch. Tapenade. Grilled sardines. Sweet tomato salad. Ripe green figs and goat cheese for dessert. Wine chilling in a plastic bucket of ice...

Rosé is kryptonite to clichés. Rosé is all, like, *whatèvre*. Let the wine nerds wrestle with one another. Rosé rolls its eyes and says: Relax, pass the aioli, take a swim, have another glass.

About half of the rosé made in France comes from Provence. Much of this is vacuous stuff, produced in quantity to be drunk too cold to notice by masses of holidaymakers. Good rosé, though, is something altogether different: natural, elegant, and encouraging of a summery sense of slowed time. Some of the best come out of the Mourvèdre-dense terraced hills above Bandol.

Just a hundred miles separate the still-gritty port of Marseilles from St.-Tropez and the beginnings of the French Riviera, with its glitz and gridlock and manifold ooh-la-la enchantments. Just a hundred miles, but, man, is it a rich and varied terrain, this in-between place: twisty coastal roads, empty islands, and wild, craggy *calanques*. This is not the soft-focus, landlocked Provence of quaint market towns and sweet fields of lavender and thyme. It is ragged, rocky, less-traveled country, more Pagnol than Peter Mayle.

If I had a mission when I started my trip it was to ask why: why does the texture, color, and taste of rosé complement and transport us to this season? What's so special about this wine?

One day after lunch in Cassis at Restaurant Nino (once you've fallen under the spell of its unstoppably convivial proprietor, Bruno Brezzo, it's hard to eat anywhere else in town), I set out on foot from the port. A short walk brought me to the gate of Clos Sainte Magdeleine. The entrance may look like a normal door, but it acts as a portal to a hidden, better planet. Stepping through it, you gain access to a privileged compound: 30 lush acres of high peninsula running down to the sparkly sea.

"It's a good job, eh?" François Sack, the owner, said, leading me on a tour around the grounds. The prismatic light coming through the trees and radiant blueness of the Mediterranean left me in a kind of dizzy state. I wanted to stretch out in the hammock and never go back out that gate.

I was forgetting my plan. What had I come for? Ah—my rosé inquiry! Talk about these vines—Cinsault, Grenache, Mourvèdre—planted so close to the sea. What was the secret of great rosé?

"Because, well, I don't know," Sack said. "The earth. The sun. It's enough. It's a very good reason."

"Let me ask you something," Kermit Lynch said.

Lynch, who splits his time between Provence and Berkeley, California, is a wine merchant and

importer, folk hero of the funky and unfiltered, defender of honestly crafted, family-run vineyards. He is also the author of *Adventures on the Wine Route*, one of the most readable books about wine you will ever find.

Lynch's pressing question now: did I prefer a *fromage de tête* or a cold leg of lamb with mustard for our lunch? "Both" seemed the obvious but impolitic answer. I told him about the Bath chaps I'd made at home—a British variant of deboned, brined, rolled, poached, and seared pig's head.

"He's a pig's head kind of guy," Lynch called to his wife, Gail Skoff, who was preparing lunch.

Skoff set down a salad of ripe tomatoes from the garden. Then eggs, contributed by the family's chickens, topped with a bit of salty anchovy. The terrine was made by Lynch's old friend Marcel Lapierre, the great Beaujolais winemaker from Villié Morgon.

Here we came to an unfortunate but unavoidable subject that might be dubbed The Other French Paradox. Which is: the apparent disappearance of good Provençal food from the very place we most associate it with. Restaurants in pretty coastal towns tend to be seasonal; the owners head north in winter to run cafés in ski towns. Another explanation is cultural: young, worldly French people don't want to eat the *cuisine bourgeoise* their grandmothers made; they would prefer such insipid novelties as the Thai-spiced steak tartare presented to me in a restaurant in Bandol.

But there we were, eating like enlightened Californians in Provence. The food was perfect. We cut into the wobbly pork, its long-cooked meaty bits suspended in dark jelly, and toasted its maker with a bottle of old Morgon.

Driving around the Rosé Coast (a name I just made up), I had time to ponder the dilemma about the so-so food. It was a bummer, but did it matter? Watching the sparkle of the sea, I decided to take a rosé outlook on things.

The truth is that anyone hoping to find an unspoiled culinary nirvana in the south of France was engaging in a bit of fantasy. Bandol is kind of a cheesy place. But that's okay because you could avoid all that. Above the resorts they are making beautiful wines in still-wild hills where the sun-seeking tourists never bother to venture.

There was one more place that I had to see. In my Fiat 500, from Bandol I headed past Toulon, turning toward Hyères and south past salt marshes and increasingly scrubby seaside roads. Finally the D97 terminates at a small port with little more than a convenience store and a ferry dock.

Île de Porquerolles is the nicest place you've never heard of. The island is small—about five square miles, much of it protected nature reserve—redolent of pine forests and olive trees. It is almost too perfect to believe. There is one square with a church and a group of rosé-nursing locals playing *pétanque*. There are bicycle-rental shops and ice cream stands and soft white-sand beaches. There are a few small inns in the village and one clubby resort at the western end of the island. The hotel, Le Mas du Langoustier, is reached by the Porquerolles's lone bus over mostly dirt roads.

I rode my rented bike over knobby, sandy paths to visit Domaine de la Courtade, one of the isle's three small wineries. Laurent Vidal, the life force behind the place, is an engineer by training and a Parisian by birth. When his father passed away he moved here to look after the business. "We are building something new every time—it's the alchemy of the salty air and the soil." Courtade makes an excellent, crisp, citrusy rosé. Pedaling away, I had the feeling I'd stumbled onto a fantasy island, pristine and beautiful and just a little odd.

After dinner I bicycled under moonlight over a path of pine needles, dropped the bike in the sand, took off my clothes on the empty beach, and ran into the warm water. Maybe it was the full moon or the bottle of Courtade I'd drunk with dinner. Or maybe, just maybe, the unfortunate image of your wine-seeking correspondent frolicking naked in the sea will turn enough people off to keep this place a secret. Then, I will have done my job.

Adapted from "La Vie en Rosé," by Adam Sachs.

GUIDE

STAY
Le Mas du Langoustier
*Île de Porquerolles;
33-4/94-58-30-09;
langoustier.com.* **$$$$**

EAT AND DRINK
Clos Sainte Magdeleine
*Ave. de Revestel, Cassis;
33-4/42-01-70-28;
clossaintemagdeleine.fr.*

Domaine de la Courtade
*Île de Porquerolles;
33-4/94-58-31-44;
lacourtade.com.*

Restaurant Nino
*1 Quai Jean-Jacques
Barthélemy, Cassis;
33-4/42-01-74-32;
nino-cassis.com.* **$$$**

PARIS

Bonhomie and *bistronomie* in the City of Light

Parisian bistros—those strongholds of hearty, affordable cuisine where residents practice their *art de vivre* and stoke their *tête de porc* addictions—are as iconically French as berets and Brigitte Bardot. Now five young and seriously credentialed chefs are reinventing the classics, stretching the limits, rewriting the rules—and still making a damn good *steak frites*.

Bistrot Paul Bert

Ask local critics for a favorite and one name pops up. Run by food hero, wine maven, and bon vivant Bertrand Auboyneau, Bistrot Paul Bert—tucked away in the 11th Arrondissement—has traditionally humdrum décor and food that's anything but: don't miss the crumbly galette with parsleyed snails or the excellent headcheese with shaved cauliflower and *moutarde violette* vinaigrette. For dessert, save room for the oversize pink *macaron* stuffed with fresh raspberries or the signature Paris-Brest: *choux* pastry oozing with chocolate-hazelnut cream. *18 Rue Paul Bert, 11th Arr.; 33-1/43-72-24-01.* **$$$**

Chez l'Ami Jean

Celebrated La Regalade alum Stéphane Jego aces both rustic and refined dishes at his boisterous rugby-themed spot in the Seventh where the lights are low and the tables so intimately spaced that strangers are soon playing footsie. Waiters ferry Staub pots of dizzyingly good roast chicken in sausage-dotted bouillon; clutches of dime-size scallops, barely braised and still tasting of Brittany; and gigantic white bowls of creamy *riz au lait* scattered with pralines—more than enough to feed a ravenous rugby team. *27 Rue Malar, Seventh Arr.; 33-1/47-05-86-89; lamijean.fr.* **$$$**

Jadis

Guillaume Delage may have trained with the avant-garde French master Pierre Gagnaire, but the name of his spartan neo-bistro in the Vaugirard neighborhood means Back in the Day, and there he hews to his roots. The abbreviated menu surprises with fresh updates on the classics, including a tender leg of lamb with bitter chard, roast suckling pig spiced with pickled lemons and date leaves, and pan-fried foie gras on a bed of sweet squash purée. Of course, no meal is complete without a platter of cheeses; the varieties here are so ripe they practically walk onto your plate. *208 Rue de la Croix Nivert, 15th Arr.; 33-1/45-57-73-20; bistrot-jadis.com.* **$$$**

Le Severo

At his 30-seat alcove in Montparnasse, ex-butcher-to-the-star-chefs William Bernet gives meat the VIP treatment. There are crisp-edged coins of boudin noir from Basque über-charcutier Christian Parra; Limousin beef from current butcher-to-the-star-chefs Hugo Desnoyer, aged by Bernet himself; an expertly charred faux-filet; and the Platonic ideal of *steak frites,* served with double-fried *belles grosses frites*—irregularly shaped for that authentic hand-cut effect. Apart from that, an extensive listing of earthy Rhônes and noble Burgundies, hand-lettered on a large blackboard, dominates the cozy brown room. *8 Rue des Plantes, 14th Arr.; 33-1/45-40-40-91.* **$$$**

Septime

Opened by sommelier Théo Pourriat and chef Bertrand Grébaut, a greens-worshipping disciple of Alain Passard, this produce-centric gem in the 11th is a modern take on the bistros of old. The room's simplified *fermier*-chic vibe (butcher-block tables; whitewashed walls) belies the inventiveness of the cod brandade, floating atop an emerald parsley emulsion and potato purée and scattered with tiny white flowers; and of the fat white asparagus stalks tricked out in a puckery sauce *gribiche* and drizzled with minced oyster and trout roe. *80 Rue de Charonne, 11th Arr.; 33-1/43-67-38-29; septime-charonne.fr.* **$$$$**

Above: Sampling a pared-down feast at Septime, in the 11th Arrondissement. Opposite: Bistrot Paul Bert's classic dining room, also in the 11th.

MILAN

Timeless treasures in an au courant city

The Imperial Suite at the Park Hyatt Milan. Above: Gazing out over the city from the Duomo's rooftop.

G O LOOKING FOR THE NEW in Milan and you doom yourself to disappointment. I say this with a confidence that results from the fact that my job has carried me to this millennium-old city four times every year for more than a decade.

True, there is the occasional glimmer of progress, far from least the political broom sweep that finally pushed Italy's scandal-plagued prime minister Silvio Berlusconi to the curb. Even before the European debt crisis forced the media mogul—who had weathered accusations of corruption and an unwholesome appetite for teen prostitutes—to step down, there were subtle signs in Berlusconi's hometown of Milan that change was afoot.

Some of this had to do with the construction of Porta Nuova Varesine, a much-ballyhooed urban renewal project on the site of an old rail station, built to bring millions of square feet of retail, office, and cultural space to the city, along with some shiny new starchitecture by the American firm Kohn Pedersen Fox Associates.

But as a New Yorker, I find it hard to generate the requisite excitement for a bunch of glass towers. Far more thrilling was the Duomo's emergence from a seemingly never-ending renovation. When the scaffolding finally came down from the main façade, it was as if a film star you'd always loved had emerged from a face-lift as dewy and gorgeous as she'd ever been. The same was substantially the case with the legendary Teatro alla Scala, which also reappeared newly gilded and gleaming after its own long renovation.

On a more domestic scale, intrepid newcomers periodically show up to import something unexpected to Milan's perennially conservative dining scene. In the case of Genoa natives Marco Bruni and Paul Lips, it was the introduction of regional home cooking served in a setting almost too casual to fit a city so formal and prim. "Am I in Milan," one wonders at U Barba, "or Brooklyn?"

A former sporting club turned restaurant, U Barba (the name is Genovese dialect for *uncle*) has a kitchen filled with the reconditioned pasta cutters and blending apparatuses Bruni collects. "I don't want things too perfect, and with the old machines you get more texture in the food," he said. The restaurant has a bocce court active in all but the coldest of seasons. Watching people play there, one can't help but recall the Jane Jacobs dictum that old buildings make good settings for new ideas. Old cities do, too.

Despite the fact that Milan plays host to the prestigious annual Salone del Mobile and the twice-yearly ready-to-wear fashion shows—events that use the city as a changeable scrim against which, season after season, designers offer up the latest in furniture and clothing—there's no escaping the sense that in Milan cutting-edge is an alien concept. Hip can't happen here.

I struggled with this at first. I made fruitless efforts to cozy up to a city bent on preserving an enigmatic northern distance. Spending as much time there as I did, it seemed necessary to discover the spring that opens the secret drawer. And, as with most revelations of this sort, when I finally happened upon the key to understanding, it turned out to have been hidden in plain sight.

I was looking for novelty in Milan when all along the allure of the place was its inverse. Few cities hold as fast to the time-tested as Milan does, and few places so fetishize that most conservative of virtues, refinement. In Milan it is no hardship to find a specialty cutlery store selling a mind-boggling array of, say, horn-handled hunting knives (G. Lorenzi) or one that offers gloves in wrist, driving, and opera lengths (Sermoneta Gloves).

There is a confectionery shop I often visit in a storefront little altered since it opened in the 19th century. Standing at a minute zinc-topped coffee bar, you order bite-size sandwiches while a clerk wraps your purchase of sweets that must have seemed anachronistic even in your grandmother's time. Candied violets? Pasticceria Marchesi has them, and not only that but candied rose petals

and lilacs. If you happen to be there around All Souls' Day, you can find the delicious small seasonal loaves of sugar-dusted *pan dei morti*, although the ones I prefer come from Giovanni Galli, a rival shop. It says something about a city that it can sustain real competition between bakeries with house recipes for cakes for the dead.

A venerable engraver (Ditta Raimondi di Pettinaroli) tucked amid the emporiums on the bustling high street of Corso Venezia stocks copperplates that date to the company's founding, which corresponds with the signing of the Declaration of Independence. At Pettinaroli one can order correspondence cards and have them personalized using a blind embossing technique so subtle one's initials seem written in braille.

In Milan it is still possible to fall upon what must be among one of the last great troves of secondhand goods in Europe at the Mercatone dell'Antiquariato. On the last Sunday of each month, hundreds of dealers set up at dawn with offerings including the kind of reconditioned kitchen equipment that Mr. Bruni collects, but also Venini glass or bridal linens or Mussolini memorabilia or industrial material such as the jointed-metal 1950's doormat I snapped up that looks like a piece of contemporary art.

I WAS LOOKING FOR NOVELTY IN MILAN WHEN ALL ALONG THE ALLURE WAS ITS INVERSE.

Not only is there a shop (Mercatores) specializing in uniforms for household domestics, it does a volume of sales any fashion retailer might envy. The anachronism of Mercatores might seem bizarre in any other city. Houseman jackets with epaulets? Starched caps for the parlor maid? Yet it's probably worth knowing that before every fashion show she presents, the designer Miuccia Prada—a discreet child of the Milanese haute bourgeoisie if ever there was one—sends waiters wearing crisply starched jackets from Mercatores to circulate among the buyers and press.

As a sage American friend who lived in Milan once pointed out, it is fairly pointless to try to

Opposite, clockwise from top left: A sampling of Peck's famed confections; an engraved map for sale at Ditta Raimondi di Pettinaroli; lunchtime at U Barba; a bike rider in the *centro*.

"squeeze out" newness there. "Time would be better spent," this woman said, "unearthing the buried treasures in the land that time forgot."

It happens that, when my friend made this remark, we were seated in a restaurant that is one of my haunts in the city, eating bowls of vivid green soup made from stinging nettles. This hearty first course had been prepared by Arturo Maggi, a man with a head like a public monument and the habit of referring to himself not as a chef but as an "alchemist." Maggi, his wife, Maria, and their sons, Roberto and Marco, run La Latteria, an eight-table den a short walk from San Marco, a church where, in a side altar, is installed a credible copy of Caravaggio's *Deposition*, a masterpiece that allegedly hung here at one time. Whenever I am in Milan, I make plans to have dinner at La Latteria, stopping en route at San Marco to light one of the pale wax candles that have not yet been replaced by feebly flickering electric lights.

On my most recent trip, I stayed at the hyper-efficient Park Hyatt. It's adjacent to the 19th-century Galleria Vittorio Emanuele II, an immense glass-roofed cathedral to consumerism erected, with a certain impertinence, alongside the Duomo, Milan's foremost house of God. The Galleria functions as a kind of geographic pivot point for central Milan and the streets that radiate outward into the area called the Golden Quadrilateral; from whichever direction you exit the place, you come face to face with a monument.

I often advise friends to stop for a moment to observe the small army of workers seemingly always repairing the Galleria's pavement. Curious as the advice may seem, there's good reason to cast an eye downward at the gorgeous mosaics, so rich and symbolic. (It's considered lucky to execute a circle atop a bull inset there, heel planted where its testicles might be if generations of Milanese hadn't worn them away, leaving a hole in the floor.)

Above, from left: Men's-wear boutique AD56 Milano; the Galleria Vittorio Emanuele II.

It takes time to unearth the city's wonders—a decade in my case. I make a point of having drinks in the tranquil garden at the Bulgari Hotel. Its air of exclusive remove is so earnest even cabdrivers are challenged to find its private cul-de-sac.

I stop each time at that great Milanese deli Peck and AD56 Milano, a haberdashery I walked past for years before a comment by Lapo Elkann, the Fiat heir famed for a style both chic and raffish, finally sent me inside. I kick myself now for the years that I squandered shopping elsewhere when all along I might have been capitalizing on Guido Vergani, the expert whose advice I now seek whenever decisions are to be made about clothes.

Last time I visited, I piled my purchases into a car and hurried off to keep an appointment I'd been trying to get for years. It was on the way to Santa Maria delle Grazie, where Leonardo's *Last Supper* sits, that Milan produced a bit of serendipity in an offhand remark made by my driver.

Did I know, Massimo asked, that San Maurizio al Monastero Maggiore had reopened? I did not. He explained that this ecclesiastical complex, hidden from public view for years, boasts a masterpiece that rivals that of Leonardo: a fresco cycle executed in the early 16th century by the undersung genius Bernardino Luini and his sons that has been undergoing major surgery since the 1980's.

When Massimo told me this, I decided on a whim to forgo my allotted 15 minutes with the *Last Supper* and stop into San Maurizio instead. Both Ruskin and Nabokov, I knew, were unified in praise of a painter some art historians wrote off as a Lombard bumpkin. Could both be wrong?

For an hour that brisk afternoon, I took in the assorted ascensions and annunciations; lunar Madonnas and bloody-fanged demons; martyrs beheaded, impaled, or fricasseed in oil. I wandered among the idealized virgins and puzzled over an ark onto which Noah herded a wacky menagerie that included a pair of unicorns.

That the church should be so eerily empty felt hard to explain, until I remembered a defining feature of a city where talent and wealth has concentrated at least since Roman times. In Milan, there are so many riches it would take a lifetime to scratch the surface of them all.

Adapted from "Mysteries of Milan," by Guy Trebay.

> ■ FEW PLACES SO FETISHIZE THAT MOST CONSERVATIVE OF VIRTUES, REFINEMENT, AS MILAN DOES.

GUIDE

STAY

Bulgari Hotel
7/b Via Privata Fratelli Gabba; 800/628-5427; bulgarihotels.com. **$$$$**

Four Seasons Hotel Milano
A luxury conversion of a 15th-century convent.
6/8 Via Gesù; 800/332-3442; fourseasons.com. **$$$$**

Park Hyatt Milan
1 Via Tommaso Grossi; 877/875-4658; park.hyatt.com. **$$$$**

EAT

La Latteria
24 Via San Marco; 39-02/659-7653. **$$$**

U Barba
33 Via Pier Candido Decembrio; 39-02/4548-7032; ubarba.it. **$$**

DO

San Marco
2 Piazza San Marco; 39-02/2900-2598.

San Maurizio al Monastero Maggiore
15 Corso Magenta; 39-02/8645-0011.

Teatro alla Scala
2 Via Filodrammatici; 39-02/7200-3744; teatroallascala.org.

SHOP

AD56 Milano
2 Via Marco de Marchi; 39-02/654-030; ad56milano.it.

Ditta Raimondi di Pettinaroli
43 Corso Venezia; 39-02/7600-2412; pettinaroli.it.

Giovanni Galli
2 Via Victor Hugo; 39-02/8646-4833; giovannigalli.com.

G. Lorenzi
9 Via Montenapoleone; 39-02/7602-2848; lorenzi.it.

Mercatone dell'Antiquariato
Naviglio Grande; 39-02/8940-9971; navigliogrande.mi.it.

Mercatores
3 Via Filippo Turati; 39-02/7600-1177.

Pasticceria Marchesi
11/a Via S. Maria alla Porta; 39-02/862-770; pasticceriamarchesi.it.

Peck
9 Via Spadari; 39-02/802-3161; peck.it.

Sermoneta Gloves
46 Via della Spiga; 39-02/7631-8303; sermonetagloves.com.

Spazio Rossana Orlandi
14 Via Matteo Bandello; 39-02/467-4471; rossanaorlandi.com.

MAREMMA

Undiscovered gems in a lesser-known corner of Italy

ACCORDING TO LOCALS, THE HEART of the Maremma runs along the Tyrrhenian coast, from Grosseto to Capalbio, and 30 miles inland to Mount Amiata. A hub for stylish new hotels and restaurants, it is also one of the most unspoiled regions in Italy, marked by pristine beaches fringed with umbrella-shaped maritime pines and cork-oak woodlands where aristocratic families still hunt wild boar.

The medieval village of Capalbio is the Maremma's epicenter, and come summer, Italian politicians and actors fill its sidewalk trattorias and artisanal shops. Until a few years ago there weren't many decent places to stay. Enter the eco-conscious Locanda Rossa, a modern Tuscan-red country house with 12 beige-and-taupe rooms and four apartments set on a 50-acre olive farm. To live like royalty, opt for neighboring Manciano's Tenuta Marsiliana, an estate owned by the Corsini family. The highlight: one of the five accommodations is a seven-bedroom hunting lodge with a collection of mounted boar heads and sketches by Corsini princesses.

Days are filled with rustic-chic exploits throughout the area. Oenophiles won't want to miss Fattoria Le Pupille, one of the Maremma's most prestigious vineyards, in Istia D'Ambrosia; book a tasting of Saffredi, an award-winning red. Ready to get in the saddle? Join the traditional *butteri* (Maremmani cowboys) as they herd semi-wild cattle and horses at the 11,366-acre Azienda Regionale Agricola di Alberese, a publicly owned coastal ranch in the protected Ente Parco Regionale della Maremma. For the less adventurous, there are guided tours of the farm that end with samplings of—what else?—native pecorino cheese and salt-free Tuscan bread.

STAY
Locanda Rossa
*11B Strada Capalbio-
Pescia Fiorentina,
Capalbio;
39-0564/890-462;
locandarossa.com.* **$$**

Tenuta Marsiliana
*Localitá Castello,
Manaiano;
39-339/566-1326;
tenutamarsiliana.it;
seven-day minimum.*
$$$$

DO
Azienda Regionale
Agricola di Alberese
*Localitá Spergolaia,
Alberese; 39-0564/
407-108; alberese.com.*

Fattoria Le Pupille
*92A Piagge del Maiano,
Istia D'Ambrosia;
39-0564/409-517;
fattorialepupille.it.*

The volcanic-
rock village of
Pitigliano,
an hour outside
Capalbio.

NAPLES, ITALY

A quest to find the best pizza in town

America may be in the midst of its own artisanal-pizza boom, but having the right pie at the right place on its Italian home turf is like discovering the dish for the very first time. In the *pizzerie* of Naples, both new-wave and old-world recipes—and new-breed *pizzaioli* and old-school bakers—vie for supremacy. Which spots beat out the rest? Read on to find out.

Da Attilio
On a crowded market lane resembling an Arab souk, Da Attilio is a gem of a family trattoria, with Mamma cooking garlicky spaghetti and mussels in the kitchen out back while her son the *pizzaiolo* waits tables. Hungry Napolitanos come for the *pizza-cannolo* (a heady mix of porcini and ricotta and provola cheeses folded into a singed, tender, tubular shell) and the *pizza alle carnevale*—shaped like a star, its stuffed points bursting with ricotta, its middle luscious with tomato sauce, mozzarella, and sausage. *17 Via Pignasecca; 39-081/552-0479.* **$$**

Di Matteo
Pizza lovers head straight for the many counters in the historic Spaccanapoli district, in the *centro storico*. Here, *pizzerie* often double as *friggitorie* (fried-snack joints). Keep an eye out for the three-deep line and you'll have found one of the best: the 1936 Di Matteo, a traditional Neapolitan hole-in-the-wall on narrow Via dei Tribunali with a vast mosaic-tiled *forno*. The *specialità della casa* is a giant golden-fried crescent, oozing ricotta and provola cheese and dotted with *ciccioli* (cracklings), though the *arancini di riso* (rice balls) and *crochette di patate* (potato croquettes) are equally good. Not to be outdone, the classic margherita practically blazes with red sauce and white mozzarella. *94 Via dei Tribunali; 39-081/455-262.* **$**

Gino Sorbillo
Though he churns out nearly 1,000 pies every day, Gino Sorbillo still delivers an exemplary crust at his namesake pizzeria: on the robust, chewy side, but artfully blistered and bubbly. Don't miss the lyrical Mediterranean combo of shaved artichokes, Vesuvian Piennolo cherry tomatoes, aged goat cheese, and basil. Carnivores might opt for the gutsy homage to the black Caserta pig, combining its *strutto* (lard) and salami with a salty, earthy, black-olive flourish. *32 Via dei Tribunali; 39-081/144-6643; accademiadellapizza.it.* **$**

Il Pizzaiolo del Presidente
The late über-*pizzaiolo* Ernesto Cacialli opened Il Pizzaiolo del Presidente in 2000, but it's his son Enzo who now doles out prized rounds of dough to Spaccanapoli pizz-addicts. In the no-fuss, stone-walled dining room, savor the Presidente's pie with smoked Agerola provola cheese, basil, and Vesuvian vine-ripened *pomodorini*, all atop a supple blackened crust. *120-121 Via dei Tribunali; 39-081/210-903; ilpizzaiolodelpresidente.it.* **$**

Pizzaria La Notizia
There's a touch of thermo-dynamics at work inside the beech-and-oak-fueled oven at Pizzaria La Notizia, where third-generation *pizzaiolo* Enzo Coccia creates ethereal, perfectly charred *cornicioni* (that crucial inch of raised crust) in the well-heeled Posillopo quarter. The menu's three dozen *pizze* are essays in smoke, air, and acidity, precisely matched to their toppings: fava, asparagus, and pungent Campanian pecorino from herb-fed Laticauda sheep channel spring on a plate; a pie of yellow tomatoes, green Cilento figs, and buffalo *bresaola* is both dusky and sweet. *94/A Via Michelangelo da Caravaggio; 39-081/1953-1937; enzococcia.it.* **$$**

Speeding by the counter at Di Matteo, on Via dei Tribunali.

The oven at Pizzaria La Notizia. Above: Dining at Gino Sorbillo.

Pizzaiolo Gino Sorbillo in front of his restaurant. Above: Pizzaria La Notizia's Neapolitan pie with anchovies.

TRIESTE, ITALY

A bridge between East and West

Above, from left: Tables at Harry's Grill, in the Grand Hotel Duchi d'Aosta; sailboats docked near the Piazza dell'Unità d'Italia. Opposite: Miramare Castle, on Trieste's Adriatic coast.

T'S LUNCHTIME IN TRIESTE, THE HANDSOME Italian city on the Adriatic, and at Buffet Da Pepi, a genial crowd surges forward toward the serving station, lured by fresh pork simmering in fragrant broth. The guys serving up the food resemble old-time countermen at a New York deli or maybe Tom Cruise as the bartender in *Cocktail*. The art is in the speed, the deft theatrical wielding of carving fork and knife as they haul the meat onto a marble slab, carve off slices, toss some in a bun for a sandwich or onto a plate for a mixed platter.

"This is what you could call a pig pub, and it is pure Trieste," says Picrpaolo Segrè, my guide, a third-generation Triestine who claims Italians, Dalmatians, Austrians, Hungarians, Catholics, and Jews among his ancestors, a mix as characteristically Triestine as the pork and the local Terrano wine, followed by a black espresso at a tiny café.

Segrè, like most natives, is a little obsessed with his city and thrilled that it's currently got a buzz. Its tourist-office people eye the blue bay—dotted with sailboats and rimmed with beaches—lick their lips and, in spite of the fact that Trieste is much more alluring than a mere coastal resort, pronounce the town "Portofino waiting to happen."

Trieste's location on the very edge of the Adriatic Sea has always defined it; it still does. As a modern city it was, in a sense, invented as a port town. From the 1380's to World War I, Trieste belonged to the Hapsburgs—it was Vienna's main route to the sea and the rest of the world.

Sitting in the Piazza dell'Unità d'Italia, I watch a spiffy blue-and-white ferry on its daily run. The sea is the piazza's fourth side, and you can almost taste the salt as speedboats bounce over the water. In early fall, during the Barcolana regatta, the bay is so heavily dappled with white sails you feel you can almost walk out over it.

Everything in Trieste leads to the piazza; this is the city's beating heart, its living room. In the middle is the Fountain of the Four Continents, a place where students loll, yapping into their iPhones in a cacophony of languages. The piazza is flooded with the gilded Triestine sunlight that bounces off the sea and catches the old stones. At night, lit up with operatic grandeur, its splendor is as heart-stopping as any public space in Europe.

Trieste? Where? A lot of people have trouble placing Trieste on the northeastern coast of the Adriatic, up by the fold in the map, its oxygen sucked out by Venice, its more glamorous neighbor 90 miles away. Surrounded by Slovenia and with Croatia, Austria, and Hungary just up the road, this is a border town. In Trieste, geography is everything—language, history, culture, cuisine. After World War II, Trieste became a political football, tossed between East and West. The polyglot city had been Italian on and off for decades, but it wasn't until 1975 that Trieste became absolutely, legally Italian.

I visited Trieste at the end of the Cold War, and it felt a shabby place that had lost its purpose. Wherever I went, a fog of melancholy seemed to cling to me. By the time I got back this year, everything had changed. The city I visited—its gleaming buildings, its street life, its sheer vigor—had been revived. The man responsible, as almost everybody agrees, was Riccardo Illy, who was mayor from 1993 to 2001.

At the Grand Hotel Duchi d'Aosta, I observe a pair of local ladies, Vuitton bags in hand, gossiping over coffee, glancing at the handsome, stubble-jawed young Polish filmmaker looking hungover from the festival the night before. This is Trieste's hotel—everybody calls it the Duchi; in its present shape, the building has been here since the 1870's. Harry's Grill, the hotel restaurant, has a large terrace on the piazza. At teatime in the bar, the waiters

bring drinks on silver trays. At breakfast there is chocolate cake along with the eggs and toast.

"Remember the Austrian Empire," says a mustachioed man on the Duchi steps as he gathers up his cape and disappears into the morning.

Around 1740, it was the Hapsburg empress Maria Theresa who ordered the new town laid out on what had been salt flats, much as Peter the Great built St. Petersburg on a swamp; the cities, built around the same time, are architectural cousins. The Borgo Teresiano, named for the empress, is a lovely quarter, a canal at its heart, the streets full of bookshops, old churches, and small, elegant houses that could be in Prague. My favorite of the city's shops is here: Farmacia Biasoletto all'Orso Nero is a pharmacy founded in 1821 by a botanist, and it retains all the original fittings—fine wood; glass; tile; painted ceramic mortar and pestle.

But of all Trieste's period attractions, the Museo Storico del Castello di Miramare is the most evocative: a little castle and fort that, at night, glows like a mirage in the moonlight. Built in the 1850's by Archduke Maximilian, it is the exact reflection of the naval officer, the Victorian gent.

His study is designed like a ship's cabin; the book-lined library and carefully chosen art collection mirror his intellectual passions.

Coffee is Trieste's drug of choice, its consolation, its memory-making madeleine. The café culture is more reminiscent of Budapest or Vienna than of Rome. I'm tempted to idle away the days at the cafés: in the morning at Caffè degli Specchi, where coffee comes straight, with liqueurs, or with ice cream; before lunch at Caffè Tommaseo for an aperitif among the marble-topped tables and plaster cherubs; in the evening, at the Jugendstil Antico Caffè San Marco.

But my pal Segrè has got food on his mind. Lunch is at Chimera di Bacco. Following the classic *jota* (bean and kraut soup), there's meat stuffed with potatoes and a sampling of strudel. A snack at Trattoria da Giovanni that follows turns out to be tripe and fried *baccalà*. I need to lie down.

That night I get a taxi up to Antica Trattoria Suban, Trieste's famous 19th-century restaurant. The décor is slightly kitschy, a sort of Eastern European farmhouse style, and the food, in keeping, is meat. Families are gathered around platters of succulent beef and lamb just off the grill. It all reminds me of a trip to Bosnia where every meal was meat, sometimes only meat; a sign of prosperity, it also seemed about something less tangible, a kind of peasant culinary macho.

Da Pepi notwithstanding, the best meal I have is at Ristorante Al Bagatto, a deceptively simple fish joint with a little fridge in the middle of the room, the catch of the day on display. I eat octopus stew with soft polenta, snapper tartare with chive ricotta, and the best *fritto misto* I've ever had. At Al Bagatto, eating sublime Italian fish dishes (oh, the dumplings with mullet roe and marinated squid!), I return at last to the modern Italian city, back from my tryst with fin de siècle Mitteleuropa. Slovenia this is not.

Adapted from "The Edge of Italy," by Reggie Nadelson.

GUIDE

STAY
Grand Hotel Duchi d'Aosta
2/1 Piazza dell'Unità d'Italia; 39-040/ 760-0011; duchi.eu. **$**

EAT AND DRINK
Antica Trattoria Suban
2 Via Emilio Comici; 39-040/54368; suban.it. **$$$**

Antico Caffè San Marco
18 Via Cesare Battisti; 39-040/363-538.

Buffet Da Pepi
3 Via della Cassa di Risparmio; 39-040/366-858; buffetdapepi.com. **$$**

Caffè degli Specchi
/ Piazza dell'Unità d'Italia; 39-040/036-5777; caffespecchi.it.

Caffè Tommaseo
4/C Piazza Tommaseo; 39-040/362-666; caffetommaseo.com.

Chimera di Bacco
2 Via del Pane; 39-040/364-023; chimeradibacco.com. **$$$**

Harry's Grill
Grand Hotel Duchi d'Aosta, 2/1 Piazza dell'Unità d'Italia; 39-040/660-606; duchi.eu. **$$**

Ristorante Al Bagatto
7 Via Luigi Cadorna; 39-040/301-771; albagatto.it. **$$$**

Trattoria da Giovanni
14/B Via San Lazzaro; 39-040/639-396; trattoriadagiovanni.com. **$$**

DO
Farmacia Biasoletto all'Orso Nero
16 Via Roma; 39-040/364-330.

Museo Storico del Castello di Miramare
Viale Miramare; 39-040/224-143; castello-miramare.it.

BERLIN

Mitte's polished new edge

Germany's culture capital has always been achingly hip—"poor but sexy" is how mayor Klaus Wowereit described it six years ago. At the time, Mitte, a concrete jungle known for its gritty experimental art galleries and faded Baroque buildings, was in the midst of a resurgence. Now the burg has evolved into a borderline-bourgeois haven full of modern hotels and gastronomic temples that draw throngs of in-the-know locals. Here's a closer look at the locale.

Alpenstueck

The restaurant is awash in cozy charm, from its rustic beech walls to the rotating menu of Alpine/Bavarian fare with a regional and seasonal focus—spaetzle and rabbit, pumpkin-and-beet ravioli, and potato-and-cucumber salad are the next best thing to a mountain getaway. There's even an on-site bakery that whips up flaky apple strudels and sweet rhubarb parfaits.
9 Gartenstrasse; 49-30/2175-1646; alpenstueck.de. **$$$**

Contemporary Fine Arts

Opposite Museum Island, Mitte's airy high-end art space features three stories of oversize sculptures and canvases by the likes of Georg Baselitz, Chris Ofili, and Julian Schnabel. Floor-to-ceiling windows in the light-filled galleries overlook the Fernsehturm and the Berlin Cathedral.
10 Am Kupfergraben; 49-30/288-7870; cfa-berlin.de.

Happy Shop

Berlin's fashion-forward set heads to the black-and-white-checked Happy Shop for of-the-moment pieces (think Christopher Kane stilettos, teeny cocktail blazers from Maison Kitsuné, and gold sunglasses by local stylist Mykita) sold in an ever-changing showroom that resembles theater stages. Clothing racks, shelves, and lighting suspended from above give the space a futuristic feel.
67 Torstrasse; 49-30/2900-9501; happyshop-berlin.com.

Hotel Mani

Cognac leather settees, polished macassar-black glass, and green marble accent the stylish and centrally located Hotel Mani. There are laptops and iPads for rent; put them to use while relaxing in the hotel's fireside lounge. And this being Berlin, bikes are always at the ready.
136 Torstrasse; 49-30/5302-8080; amangroup.de. **$**

Neues Museum

After a painstaking renovation that took nearly 12 years to complete, the Neoclassical Neues Museum has been given new life. It's all thanks to British architect David Chipperfield's impressive revamp. You can still see traces of the edifice's history in brilliantly understated fashion—the serene galleries take advantage of the 19th-century structure's existing frescoes, columns, and brickwork. It serves as a dramatic counterpoint to one of the world's top collections of Egyptian art (the pièce de résistance: the bust of Nefertiti).
1-3 Bodestrasse; 49-30/266-424-242; neues-museum.de.

Soho House Berlin

Creative types who disdain ties but obsess over the cuffs of their selvage denim will find plenty to love at the Soho House Berlin. In a restored Bauhaus building at the border of Mitte and Prenzlauer Berg, the property has seriously spacious rooms with 20th-century furniture and brass lighting fixtures, and a top-notch restaurant serving international comfort dishes such as schnitzel and eggplant parmigiana.
1 Torstrasse; 49-30/405-044; sohohouseberlin.com. **$$**

A George Herold installation on display at Contemporary Fine Arts.

Happy Shop's checkered exterior. Left: The dining room at Alpenstueck.

Outside the Neues Museum. Right: A Large suite at Soho House Berlin.

The colorful Katterugwonigen houses in Almere's residential sector.

ALMERE, NETHERLANDS

A glimpse of things to come

THE CITY OF THE FUTURE doesn't mirror the monolithic skyscrapers of Shanghai or the man-made utopia under construction in Abu Dhabi's desert; rather, it's a small, self-sustaining town 30 minutes outside Amsterdam. Every aspect of Almere's creation was a conscious human invention, and the result—given that the Dutch are world-class planners—is quietly spectacular.

Maybe that's because Almere looks so much like today's idea of how we'd like our cities to someday be: architecturally engaging, humane, and eco-thoughtful. Cars are relegated to underground roadways, weirdly angled pedestrian corridors separate overtly edgy buildings, and bicyclists own the surface roads (there are 285 miles of lanes). There are also odd enclaves of energy-efficient residences, as well as a bold downtown section envisioned by Rem Koolhaas. But the comforts of the present persist. The sleekly practical Apollo Hotel—with its flashy restaurant and bar, Salada Samba—sits strategically in the heart of the city.

Almere's most intriguing element may be the Museum De Paviljoens, an experimental-art institution on the fringe of the city center housed in a pair of industrial-looking structures, leftovers from the 2007 Documenta art fair in Kassel, Germany. To underscore the collection's focus on urban development, the museum erected a 600-foot-long fence so graffiti artists could have a place to work—perhaps the only thing in this cleverly conceived city that has been left to chance.

GUIDE

STAY
Apollo Hotel
2 Koetsierbaan; 31-36/
527-4500; apollohotels
resorts.com. $

COPENHAGEN

Cool new stops on a once-gritty thoroughfare

The now-trendy Nørrebro district has had its share of problems in the past: the multicultural melting pot had been the site of some of Denmark's worst ethnic clashes. But a buzzy corridor called the Jægersborggade is putting a new stamp on the neighborhood. On sunny days, the street is packed with meandering locals seeking out house-made candies, flea-market scores, and everything in between.

CMYK Kld

Even before you step in to it, Maya Langeland's funky multimedia gallery sets the tone with a collection of framed original paintings hanging from the shop's brick exterior. Inside, the space resembles a working studio with disheveled comic-book sketches scattered across drawing desks and walls lined floor-to-ceiling in pieces by emerging Danish artists. The place also serves as a bookshop and print factory, and there's even a small stage for local performers. *No. 51; 45/2162-9563; cmykkld.blogspot.com.*

Coffee Collective

Jonesing for a cup with a conscience? Coffee Collective's tiny kitchen uses direct-trade beans from farmers in the developing world and roasts them on site; taste the difference in an exclusive apricot-and-jasmine-tinged brew made from Panama's Hacienda La Esmerelda variety, which has garnered a cult following and is often cited as the greatest coffee on earth. Or avert the lines—they usually spill out the door—by brushing up on your roasting skills at one of the store's monthly DIY courses. *No. 10; 45/6015-1525; coffeecollective.dk.*

Karamelleríet

In their light-filled shop, former pop icon Charlotte Vigel (a.k.a. Tiggy) and her friend Tina Ipsen produce offbeat flavored caramels (licorice, mint, cinnamon) using a 100-year-old copper cauldron. You can watch as the sticky confections go through the process or browse shelves stocked with handmade greeting cards by Ipsen's aunt Pia Bitsch and handblown glass bowls by Vigel's aunt Aja. *No. 36; 45/7023-7777.*

Mademoistella

Owner Stella Malfilatre scours flea markets outside of town for her inventory of vintage women's clothes, including 1960's-style knitted vests and hippie blouses. An über-cool shoe collection (Pointer sailor loafers; Minnetonka moccasins) rivals the impressive haul of retro American candy (Charleston Chew; Dubble Bubble; Sugar Daddy), but it's her rare bijous that have Malfilatre on treasure hunters' speed dials. *No. 52; 45/5357-5996; mademoistella.tumblr.com.*

Meyers Bageri

Arrive early at the compact café, owned by Claus Meyer, a cofounder of Noma (the world's No. 1 restaurant in 2012, according to *Restaurant Magazine*'s prestigious list). The pumpkin-seed rye bread and the cinnamon buns—made with organic Nordic flour and filled with pockets of Valrhona chocolate—often sell out before 9 a.m. Latecomers will find a worthy consolation prize in one of the wunderkind baker's raspberry *hindbærsnitter,* the greatest Pop-Tart you'll ever eat. *No. 9; 45/3918-6900; meyersbageri.dk.*

Relæ

Another Noma alum—chef Christian F. Puglisi—is responsible for the surprisingly airy gastro-bistro Relæ, in a basement below the Jægersborggade. Drawers in the dining room's wooden tables reveal silverware that you're meant to set yourself. The two menus (one for vegetarians, the other for omnivores) focus on such seasonal Scandinavian dishes as poached pork with smoked cod roe, baked Bintje potatoes with olives and buttermilk, and risotto ice cream with grated sunchoke. *No. 41; 45/3696-6609; restaurant-relae.dk.* **$$$$**

Scoping out the scene in Nørrebro.

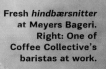
Fresh *hindbærsnitter* at Meyers Bageri. Right: One of Coffee Collective's baristas at work.

Chef Christian Puglisi in his restaurant Relæ. Left: Browsing the art at CMYK Kld gallery.

A laid-back perch for people-watching at the Zebra Bar, on the Place St.-Géry.

BRUSSELS

Shopping, Belgian style

BRUSSELS HAS BEEN SHAKING off a bad rap for the past decade as the Continental redoubt of the well-heeled and slightly stuffy; a resolutely bourgeois town, suffering from a dearth of...well, vitality. There have always been hushed, pricey restaurants aplenty, swathed in stiff white table linens (with squadrons of stiff waiters to match); ditto comically expensive shops for well-groomed but terminally conservative diplos and Eurocrats.

No longer: Brussels has embraced a culture of streetwise cool that's giving its neighbor Antwerp a run for its money. Just head north of Old Town, down the hill toward the Bourse, and then cross Boulevard Anspach. You're in the once-rough, now thoroughly chic Dansaert neighborhood. Named for its main artery, Rue Antoine Dansaert, it roughly comprises Place St.-Géry to the southwest (a super-cool bar at every turn) and Place Ste.-Catherine to the east (stylish boîtes and seafood bistros; a sweet outdoor food and flower market).

The place to rest your head, if you're keen to be at the center of the action, is the 13-room Hôtel Café Pacific. The prevailing aesthetic is blanched austerity: light oak floors, white-dressed beds, and biscuit-colored linens hanging in the windows. So far, so Flemish; but a couple of the rooms harbor raspberry-red interiors or quotations whimsically stenciled onto the walls. Downstairs, Café Pacific is known for its top-notch café crèmes.

Step outside the hotel and you're surrounded by Rue Antoine Dansaert's pioneering clothing and accessories boutiques that collectively lend Brussels its new appeal. The progenitor of the street's cachet is Stijl, where owner Sonia Noël has been stocking her sprawling, high-ceilinged space with designs from Ann Demeulemeester, Kris Van Assche, and the like for years. The prettiest shop interior belongs to Annemie Verbeke, a Flanders native whose Dansaert store is housed in a massive early-20th-century house with aged mosaic floors

Accessories on display at Les Précieuses. Above: Bikes for rent on Rue Antoine Dansaert.

EUROPE

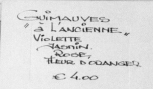

and a curving staircase. Verbeke's deconstructed designs in drapey, sexy fabrics—a bit Dries Van Noten, a bit DvF—are the quiet stars of the show. For a sleek white emporium that showcases Belgium's emerging talent, make your way to Glorybox. A rotating cast of smaller labels mixes with edgy clothing and accessories from Filles à Papa.

Understated chic is the neighborhood's defining aesthetic, and Belgian jeweler Christa Reniers, whose flagship has been on Antoine Dansaert since 1999, embodies it with her elegant designs. Her signature Rainbow 8 rings (thin, hammered-gold stacking rings with tiny tourmalines and moonstones) form gorgeous constellations on the hand. For statement pieces in the manner of Marni and Lanvin—bold, outsize necklaces and cuffs in brass, enamel, and grosgrain—the default is Les Précieuses, a treasure box where owner-designer Pili Collado also stocks Diptyque votives and one-off accessories; you could shop with a blindfold on and still walk away with a perfect choice. Around the corner, on Rue des Chartreux, an outpost of sporty brand Bellerose sells its own Abercrombie & Fitch–like line

for men and women as well as a vast selection of vintage clothes, books, and housewares (yes, that black-lacquered Bobbin bike against the wall is for sale).

With great shops come restaurants appealing to those who want to eat and drink well—in refreshingly dressed-down surroundings. Stalwarts on the street include Bonsoir Clara, a boho space serving an haute menu of Continental standards turned on their heads (goose-liver pâté is paired with vanilla, pears, and dates). Just a few doors up is L'Archiduc, a circa-1937, speakeasy-style bar that's an Art Deco fantasy of slender columns and curvaceous fauteuils, with a dimly lit mezzanine for intimate tête-à-têtes. One of Belgium's loveliest afternoon teas is on offer at AM Sweet, a diminutive, two-story *salon de thé* and confiserie around the corner. It's a favorite for lesser-known artisanal chocolates (including those of local cult producer Laurent Gerbaud), delicate pastries, and obscure teas from all corners of the globe.

But Dansaert's secret weapon is its unexpected wealth of Asian restaurants. Rue Dansaert itself is abutted on one side by Brussels's version of Chinatown and, on the other, by Rue Jules Van Praet, which is lined with Thai and Vietnamese joints serving authentic food at rock-bottom prices. Green curry at Lune de Miel and shredded pork at Thiên-Long are musts. Whatever cuisine you choose, it's de rigueur to end your evening at one of three irrevocably hip bars flanking the Place St.-Géry: Zebra Bar, with its metal-clad interiors and wide terrace for people-watching; Le Roi des Belges, which has Chimay on tap and views onto the square; or Mappa Mundo, all dark-wood rafters and low lighting, but with a stealth Latin spirit in the form of the city's best caipirinha and a thumping samba-remix sound track. Mappa Mundo is thoroughly Flemish, but with a taste of the great wide world—the essence of Dansaert, in other words. Even the Eurocrats are loosening their Hermès ties and lining up at the bar.

GUIDE

STAY
Hôtel Café Pacific
*57 Rue Antoine Dansaert;
32-2/213-0080;
hotelcafepacific.com.* **$**

EAT AND DRINK
AM Sweet
*4 Rue des Chartreux;
32-2/513-5131.*

Bonsoir Clara
*22 Rue Antoine Dansaert;
32-2/502-0990;
bonsoirclara.be.* **$$**

L'Archiduc
*6 Rue Antoine Dansaert;
32-2/512-0652;
archiduc.net.*

Le Roi des Belges
*35 Rue Jules van Praet;
32-2/503-4300.*

Lune de Miel
*15 Rue Jules Van Praet;
32-2/513-9181.* **$$**

Mappa Mundo
*2-6 Rue du Pont de la
Carpe; 32-2/513-5116;
mappamundo.com.*

Thiên-Long
*12 Rue Van Artevelde;
32-2/511-3480.* **$$**

Zebra Bar
*35 Place St.-Géry;
32-2/511-0901;
zebrabar.be.*

SHOP
Annemie Verbeke
*64 Rue Antoine Dansaert;
32-2/511-2171;
annemieverbeke.be.*

Bellerose
*11A Rue des Chartreux;
32-2/502-8953;
bellerose.be.*

Christa Reniers
*196 Rue Antoine
Dansaert;
32-2/510-0660;
christareniers.com.*

Glorybox
*10 Rue Léon Lepage;
32-2/511-0488.*

Les Précieuses
*83 Rue Antoine Dansaert;
32-2/503-2898.*

Stijl
*74 Rue Antoine Dansaert;
32-2/512-0313;
stijl.be.*

---

*Adapted from "Brussels, Revisited,"
by Maria Shollenbarger.*

EUROPEAN ROAD TRIP

Five countries, three days, one epic ride

On the road near Lake Garda, Italy.

One of the most appealing things about Europe—besides its rich culture, rolling panoramas, and unforgettable food—is the sheer physical proximity of its nations. Perhaps no place else on the planet is it easier to country-hop, given the well-marked roads and hassle-free car rentals. Can't decide where to start? This art-centric itinerary snakes through five of our favorite countries, beginning in Belgium and ending in Italy. So trade in your dollars for euros and hit the highway.

DAY 1

Brussels to Frankfurt
(340 miles)

Before getting on the road, head to Place du Grand Sablon for a classic breakfast of Belgian waffles. Angle for a table at Au Vieux Saint-Martin, which serves some of the tastiest in town. Then take the E411 highway going southeast. After about 45 minutes, you'll enter the Belgian Ardennes—which look almost as pristinely wooded and unpopulated as they did decades ago. At the city of Luxembourg, pull off to stretch your legs at the I. M. Pei–designed Musée d'Art Moderne Grand-Duc Jean and have a snack at the café.

Sated, drive northeast into Germany across the hilly state of Rhineland-Palatinate on E44. In Koblenz, take E31 south, then E42 east, following the Rhine toward the city of Mainz, in German wine country. Push on to Frankfurt, and check in to the Gerbermühle. Butter-yellow gemütlichkeit on

the outside, the small hotel (13 rooms; five suites) is all style on the inside. Sip an aperitif in the hotel's Tower Bar before venturing to the Westend-Süd for dinner at Gargantua, where chef Andrea Torresan mixes French and German influences in dishes such as pike perch on lentils with champagne-mustard sauce.

Frankfurt to Munich
(250 miles)

Feel free to linger a bit: today's drive is about 100 miles shorter than yesterday's. Start on E41 going south toward Würzburg, keeping an eye out for the castles and churches that cluster in the surrounding towns. Next, follow E45 south to Nuremberg (about halfway to Munich), and turn off to see one of those majestic buildings up close: the Imperial Castle was home to the Holy Roman emperors from 1050 to 1571.

Hop back on E45; from here on out, the highway widens to eight lanes. Fly past Ingolstadt and soon all signs point to Munich, where you've booked a room at the centrally located Cortiina Hotel, one of the best deals in town, with first-class service to boot. Drop off your bags and grab a taxi to the Alte Pinakothek, which holds a vast collection of European masterpieces by Dürer, da Vinci, and Rubens. Then to dinner: stroll over to Maximilianstrasse— one of the city's four royal avenues—and snag a table at

Left, from top: Ordering lunch at Brenner Grill, in Munich; the city's Alte Pinakothek museum.

192

you'll arrive in Trento, where, in the surrounding hills, some of northern Italy's top wines are produced. You're almost halfway there, so reward yourself with a lunch of porcini risotto from Locanda Margon, helmed by chef Alfio Grezzi. Settle in again on E45; the mountains gradually mellow back into hilly terrain, sloping down to Lake Garda, with Verona near its wide base.

From there, the driving is smooth and fast through rich agricultural flatlands; you pass Mantua, Modena, and finally, Bologna, where you switch to E35 south. It's a winding four-lane joyride through steep hills, until a final crest brings you in sight of the Arno River valley—and Florence, with the Duomo just visible on the horizon. Give up those wheels but don't get too comfortable at the refined Hotel Lungarno, owned by the Ferragamo clan. You'll want to walk across the Ponte Vecchio into the city center to start exploring.

Brenner Grill, a popular northern Italian restaurant.

DAY 3

Munich to Florence
(450 miles)

You've got an eight-hour trip ahead of you, so wake early and order a traditional German breakfast spread in your room. Head south on E45; within half an hour, Bavarian pastorals give way to staggering Alpine peaks. You'll go through Wattens, Austria, home to Swarovski Crystal

Worlds, a grandiose homage to the brand that holds one of the world's largest Swarovski stores.

At Innsbruck, the road swings to Brenner Pass—which is 30 minutes of curves and tunnels cutting through beautiful Tyrolean ranges. On the other side? Italy's Trentino-Alto Adige region. For miles, the towns—bearing dual Italian and German names—cling to precipitous terraced slopes and hide in the shadows of cliff faces. About 90 minutes beyond the pass,

GUIDE

STAY
Cortiina Hotel
8 Ledererstrasse, Munich;
49-89/242-2490;
cortiina.com. **$$**

Gerbermühle
105 Gerbermühlstrasse,
Frankfurt;
49-69/6897-7790;
gerbermuehle.de. **$$**

Hotel Lungarno
14 Borgo San Jacopo,
Florence; 39-055/
2726-4000; lungarno
collection.com. **$$**

EAT
Au Vieux Saint-Martin
38 Place du Grand
Sablon, Brussels;
32-2/512-6476;
auvieuxsaintmartin.be. **$$**

Brenner Grill
15 Maximilianstrasse,
Munich;

49-89/452-2880;
brennergrill.de. **$$$**

Gargantua
Park Gallery, 3 An
der Welle, Frankfurt;
49-69/720-718;
gargantua.de. **$$$**

Locanda Margon
Via Margone di Ravina,
Trento, Italy;
39-0461/349-401;
locandamargon.it. **$$**

DO
Alte Pinakothek
27 Barer Str., Munich;
49-89/2380-5216;
pinakothek.de.

Imperial Castle
13 Auf der Burg,
Nuremberg, Germany;
49-911/244-6590;
nuernberg.de.

Musée d'Art Moderne
Grand-Duc Jean
3 Park Dräi Eechelen,
Luxembourg;
352/453-7851;
mudam.lu.

Swarovski Crystal Worlds
1 Kristallweltenstrasse,
Wattens, Austria;
43-5224/500-3849;
kristallwelten.swarovski.
com.

THE
MEDITERRANEAN

Tracing the footsteps of a 3,000-year-old hero

A seaside village on the island of Gozo, in Malta. Opposite: A view of the Mediterranean from the deck of the *Corinthian II.*

N THE END, WE NEVER GOT TO ITHACA— never followed "in the wake of Odysseus," as the brochure for the cruise had promised; at least, not all the way to this most famous of literary destinations, the small and rocky island of which Homer sings, and where Odysseus had his famously gratifying homecoming.

We saw much that he had seen: Troy, where his war ended and his wanderings began; Malta, where he was imprisoned by the nymph Calypso for seven years; Sicily, where his sailors were devoured by Scylla; the Neapolitan coast, which the ancients believed was close to the entrance to the underworld. But Ithaca turned out to be unattainable. For the hero of legend, that island was the culminating adventure; for us, there were just the inconveniences of modern politics—in this case, a strike that forced us to make a mad dash for Athens to catch our flights home.

But we weren't at all disappointed, those of us who'd signed up for "Journey of Odysseus: Retracing the Odyssey through the Ancient Mediterranean," one of several voyages run by Travel Dynamics International, a small-ship cruise operator. The opening lines of *The Odyssey*, after all, describe Odysseus as someone curiously like us—he's the first tourist, the first person in either legend or recorded history who traveled because he thought the world was interesting, because he wanted to "know the minds and see the cities of many men," as the poem puts it. So did we; and for a brief period, we felt like our hero— for the 10 days we sailed, one day for each year he had to travel before he got to the home we never managed to see.

I was on this cruise less for myself than for my father. As a classicist, I have read and taught *The Odyssey* many times, and have been to many of these sites before, but my dad hadn't. Now in his eighties, a retired research scientist, he decided a couple of years ago that he wanted to read the Greek classics, to know what I've spent much of my career reading and writing about. And so, he's been studying his Homer. When I saw an advertisement for "Journey of Odysseus," it seemed a perfect way to introduce him to the landscapes, the flavors of the eastern Mediterranean, none of which has changed much since Homer first sang his songs.

But I wanted him to have more than just a pleasant vacation. I'd been a guest lecturer on a Travel Dynamics cruise of the eastern Aegean, and had been impressed by the intellectual seriousness of the undertaking. Tours are often conducted by the archaeologists excavating the historical sites, a privilege not available to the average tourist. Our cruise on the 57-suite *Corinthian II* would include daily excursions to archaeological sites in Troy, Pylos, Malta, and Sicily, as well as a full program of onboard lectures given by scholars of classical antiquity and archaeologists.

And then there was the homework. The hefty pre-embarkation packet came complete with a reading list that suggested six "essential" texts and 15 "recommended" texts. Very soon after we set sail from Athens to our first stop, Çanakkale, in northwestern Turkey—the modern-day site of Troy—a nice rhythm established itself, of morning excursions, a leisurely lunch back on the ship's aft sundeck, and a lecture or two. Then there would be cocktails and dinner. It was like a very opulent graduate seminar—rich, but also rigorous.

We began in Troy—the city where *The Iliad* ends, and where Odysseus's homeward-bound adventures begin. Homer calls the city "windy," and it is windy still. On the day we visited, there was a faint, steady breeze, just enough to persuade the spiky acanthus plants to wave their hostile leaves in your direction or the thronging wildflowers to nod their heavy heads. It's a large,

■ ODYSSEUS IS SOMEONE CURIOUSLY LIKE US— HE IS THE FIRST TOURIST, THE FIRST PERSON WHO TRAVELED BECAUSE HE THOUGHT THE WORLD WAS INTERESTING.

Opposite, clockwise from top left: Preparing for departure on the *Corinthian II*; the fortress of Methoni, in Pylos; soaking in the cruise ship's hot tub; fresh seafood served on board.

meandering site, and most of what there is to look at once you get past the pier is walls: the remains of nine successive settlements on the site. Brian Rose, the boyish University of Pennsylvania archaeologist who was one of the cruise leaders and who's been working at the site since 1988, explained to the rapt gaggle of shipmates how the dogleg layout of the walls may have been meant to foil invaders. It seemed pretty good at holding tourists back, too: Troy never feels as crowded as, say, Pompeii, which we later visited.

Rose reminded us that the area was a major attraction in ancient times; wandering around gawking at the famous walls is something people have been doing since the time of the Persian king Xerxes (480 B.C.). That thought—the idea that you, as a tourist, aren't somehow desecrating an ancient site by visiting it, but joining its long history—together with the whispering of that never-dying breeze, makes the place feel alive with

ghosts. Unquiet ghosts, to be sure: across the strait from Çanakkale is Gallipoli. As we first sailed up the strait, Gallipoli on our left—with its heart-wrenching monument to the Australian and Kiwi World War I dead—and Troy on our right, my dad shook his head and said, "Twenty-five hundred years, and it's still the same story."

A few days later, after some bad weather had forced us into an un-Odyssean but delicious detour on the postcard-worthy island of Syros, we landed at Pylos, the legendary stronghold of King Nestor. Already an old man in *The Iliad* and very ancient indeed in *The Odyssey*, Nestor is the hero who enjoys regaling the younger warriors with tales of how much stronger heroes were in his day.

Pylos isn't far from Kalamata: when you arrive at the site known as Nestor's Palace, the landscape shimmers with silver-green olive leaves. The palace is a Mycenaean structure consisting of little more than some thigh-high foundations and an

Above, from left: Diving into the waters near Gozo; the amphitheater at Segesta, on Sicily's coast.

occasional column-base. But every now and then, something extraordinary will pop out at you, an object that draws you into Homer's world. It was here we saw the richly carved, nearly intact bathtub that sits at one end of the palace enclosure and is decorated with an undulating pattern of whorls.

Clustered around this stolid household fixture that had so improbably survived, our little group nodded in eager recognition, remembering the scene in which Odysseus's son is given a bath during a visit to Nestor's Palace, where he goes seeking news of his long-lost father. Clearly, people were doing their homework and enjoying it.

Pylos is typical of the places you encounter on a cruise like this one, where every site has innumerable strata of history; we were always encouraged to explore these post-Homeric layers. Far grander than Nestor's Palace, for instance, is the nearby fortress of Methoni, a relic of the Venetians' ownership of much of Greece during the Middle Ages: its gargantuan stone walls are studded with carvings of the Lion of St. Mark.

I kept worrying secretly that the very richness of these sites and the immensity of their histories threatened, rather pleasantly, to distract us from our Homeric focus at times—although it occurred to me that such distraction was itself very Odyssean. The greatest threat to his homecoming is the pleasure and interest and beauty of so much of what he encounters on his journey: fascinating new cultures; opulent riches; amorous nymphs. The claustrophobia-inducing little grotto on Gozo that has been identified as Calypso's cave is certainly picturesque, but can't possibly compete, for sheer jaw-dropping impact, with the enormous, Stonehenge-like, Neolithic temples nearby. "I know this isn't what we came for," a businesswoman from California turned to me and said as we examined some 19th-century graffiti, as insubstantial as chicken scratches on the man-size

GUIDE

Travel Dynamics International
800/257-5767; travel dynamicsinternational. com; 12-day Journey of Odysseus cruise from $7,995 per person.

■ EVERY NOW AND THEN, SOMETHING EXTRAORDINARY WILL POP OUT AT YOU, AN OBJECT THAT DRAWS YOU INTO HOMER'S WORLD.

stones. "But as far as I'm concerned, it's worth the whole trip."

But maybe it doesn't matter how closely you follow in Odysseus's footsteps, in the end. More than anything, *The Odyssey* is a story about stories—stories about Odysseus; stories that Odysseus hears; stories that, often to save his skin, he tells; stories that we tell about ourselves, often without knowing it.

And then there was the story that I couldn't have made up if I were writing a novel instead of a travel article. One day, while I was sunbathing, I noticed that the elderly gentleman next to me had quite a scar on his leg; when he noticed me noticing it, he smiled. "There's a story to that scar," he said; I settled in to listen. The scar, he began, was why he was on the cruise. He was Dutch, and during the final, most dreadful winter of World War II, when he was a teenager and people in Holland were eating tulip bulbs to stay alive, he went out, weak and underfed as he was, to chop some wood; unable to wield the heavy axe properly, he ended up swinging it into his own leg. For weeks he hovered near death. What saved him was *The Odyssey.* A family friend who was a professor of Greek would come every day and, to distract the teenager from his pain, would recite passages from Homer's epic. "I can still recite parts of it in Greek!" he exclaimed; and did just that, right there on the deck of the *Corinthian II,* nearly seven decades later. He grew quiet and said, "I made a vow that, before I died, I would see what Odysseus saw."

The stories we tell! This was why, when the captain announced that the Corinth Canal had been closed by disgruntled strikers, and that we'd have to skip Ithaca—skip Ithaca!—in order to get back to Athens in time for our flights, I don't think anyone really minded. For Ithaca—as the Greek poet C. P. Cavafy writes—represents the gift of a "beautiful journey." If the island itself disappoints, you're still "rich with all you've gotten on the way."

Adapted from "A Modern Odyssey," by Daniel Mendelsohn.

Karaköy
Lokantasi's
light-filled
dining room.

ISTANBUL

Rooting out Turkey's authentic cuisine

WHEN A NEW GENERATION of travelers began arriving in Istanbul in the 1990's, the city found a glamorous nickname: "Istancool." But beneath all that cosmopolitan gloss, a codified food culture continues to thrive, heedless of global trends. Credit a legacy of Ottoman guild chefs specializing in single genres: kebabs at *kebapçi; balik* (fish) at *balikçi; börek* (flaky, stuffed pastries) at *börekçisi.*

Then there are the *meyhane,* the rollicking drinking dens that unleash rivers of raki with mezes. The *meyhane* of the moment is Karaköy Lokantasi, in the gentrifying docks area by the Galata Bridge, where the dark leather seating is packed with classic Beyoğlu types, from graying filmmakers to young designers in harem pants. They order the lemony braised spinach roots, the smoked octopus, and the cheese *börek,* loaded with shreds of aromatic *pastirma,* a cured beef.

Opposite on the spectrum are the *esnaf lokantas,* humble lunch canteens whose stewy, motherly fare has nourished generations. Near the Nuruosmaniye mosque, Aslan Restaurant serves old-school Ottoman dishes such as "lady's thighs" (minced chicken cylinders fried in lacy batter) and creamy eggplant topped with ground lamb. You could say that Kantin Lokanta is the *esnaf lokanta* of the skinny-jeans-and-status-sneakers brigade—a stop for residents of the boutique-y Nisantasi district. Chef Şemsa Denizsel is the Alice Waters of Turkey, evangelical about everything local and seasonal. Don't miss her braised leeks with marinated green almonds, or the Thrakia lamb stew, made hearty with favas, flat beans, and artichokes. At meal's end, the Turkish coffee comes with a spoonful of mastic gum—a palate-cleanser as old as the Ottoman empire itself.

GUIDE

STAY
Edition Istanbul
This 78-room hotel has design flourishes such as silver-foil ceilings and glassed-in bathrooms. *136 Buyukdere Çad.; 800/466-9695; editionhotels.com.*

EAT
Aslan Restaurant
70 Vezirhan Cad., Fatih; 90-212/513-7610. **$**

Kantin Lokanta
2 Akkavak Sk., Tesvikiye; 90-212/219-3114; kantin.biz. **$$**

Karaköy Lokantasi
37A Kemankeş Cad., Karaköy; 90-212/292-4455; karakoylokantasi.com. **$$**

AEGEAN
COAST,
TURKEY

Ancient pleasures by the sea

In the hazy throes of summer, Istanbullus hop in the car and ditch their urban trappings like so many New Yorkers en route to the Hamptons. Their destination: the country's idyllic north Aegean coast, where the seductive cobalt waters and quiet beaches are matched by an abundance of Turkish delights. Trail their path on a laid-back drive of your own to uncover historic ruins, sublime mezes, and rustic hamlets where you can lose yourself for days.

DAY 1

Istanbul to Assos
(245 miles)

Pick up your car at Istanbul's Atatürk Airport, but don't hit cruise control just yet: a scenic, one-hour car ferry will take you across the Sea of Marmara to Yalova. From there, it's a 40-mile drive to Bursa, the first capital of the Ottoman Empire.

Start your whirlwind tour of the historic district at Ulu Cami, the imposing early Ottoman mosque in the heart of the Old City. Nearby, the 15th-century Koza Han market houses dozens of fabric shops—a reminder that Bursa was once at the center of the global silk trade. A short walk from the market is the elaborate tomb of Osman Gazi, the empire's founder, and his son Orhan.

Stomach starting to growl? Fuel up for the four-hour drive ahead at Kebapçi Iskender. The mouthwatering Iskender kebab—lamb smothered in tomato sauce, brown butter, and yogurt—is a local specialty.

Your next stop is the town of Assos, where you'll find the vast sixth-century-B.C. Temple of Athena. Book a room at the Assos Kervansaray Otel, in a restored historical building that dates from the 1880's and features a sleek ocean-facing pool and alfresco restaurant. Five miles away a languid lunch of grilled sea bass at the harborside Uzun Ev is also on the itinerary.

DAY 2

Assos to Ayvalik
(70 miles)

The region's ruins beckon, but stay right where you are for the lavish breakfast of sheep- and cow-milk cheeses, roasted red peppers, and eggplant-stuffed *börek* pastries. In sleepy Çamlibel, an hour away, be sure to stop at Zeytinbaği, a modest farmhouse with eight stone-walled guest rooms in the resort district of Edremit. The grounds include an ancient olive grove

Above right: The ceremonial fountain at Ulu Cami, a mosque in the historic district of Bursa. Opposite: Outside the mosque.

and an herb-and-vegetable garden and are also home to a friendly black-and-white pup named Çiko. Owner Erhan Şeker leads afternoon cooking classes on *zeytinyağli* (meatless dishes cooked in olive oil) as well as traditional mezes such as red-lentil *köfte*.

Just 15 minutes east of Zeytinbaği is Zeus's Altar, atop what is known in Greek mythology as Mount Ida, from where, according to *The Iliad*, the god kept tabs on the Trojan War. A brisk, tree-shaded hike up to the site leads to dramatic views of the Bay of Edremit and the Greek island of Lesbos. At the foot of the hill, honey-colored Adatepe Village is known for producing the best of the area's fruity, golden olive oil. Stock up on a few bottles at the Adatepe Olive Oil Museum, located in an ancient brick edifice that once housed a soap factory.

A two-hour drive west brings you to Ayvalik Holiday House, a two-story cottage with a private garden that is a convenient base for exploring one of the Aegean's best-preserved Ottoman Greek settlements. Here, deliveries are still made in traditional horse-drawn carts. On Thursdays, a lively market in the Old Town showcases cheese makers, olive-oil purveyors, and farmers in the main square. Fill your basket with dried apricots and olives and sample such cheeses as the ricotta-like *lor* and the sharp goat-milk *tulum peyniri.*

Left, from top: **Colorful Turkish linens for sale at Alaçati's Haremlique; one of Taş Otel's whitewashed guest rooms.**

Alfresco dining at Ferdi Baba, on the Çesme Peninsula.

From there it's a short trip along the causeway to idyllic Cunda Island for dinner. Restaurants line the waterfront, but the best of the bunch is Bay Nihat Restoran, known for its addictive octopus salad and calamari *köfte*.

DAY 3
Ayvalik to the Çesme Peninsula
(150 miles)

After a breakfast of local cheeses, breads, and vine-ripened tomatoes, merge onto the main highway toward Edremit and look for the turnoff for Kozak.

You'll pass pine forests (said to have been planted by Roman soldiers) and sweet little hamlets en route to Bergama, site of Pergamum, a Greek capital dating back to the fifth century B.C. Look out for the sprawling hillside acropolis just outside of town, with a vertigo-inducing amphitheater built into the side of an ocean-facing cliff.

Your final destination is Alaçati, the summer playground of well-heeled Istanbullus: head south on E87 past Izmir and turn onto the 0-32 toll road. After checking in to the seven-room Taş Otel, ask the friendly staff to book you a lunchtime table at Agrilia, an Argentinean- and Italian-inspired restaurant around the corner where the pappardelle with locally grown baby artichokes is enough to make you swoon.

Kemalpaşa Caddesi, the town's main drag, fills with stylish holidaymakers in the warmer months; an outdoor table at the laid-back Köşe Kahve is ideal for people-watching. Indulge in a little retail therapy with finely embroidered Turkish linens and the softest cashmere throws from Haremlique. For your final feast, don't miss the port-side, seafood-centric Ferdi Baba, popular for its just-caught sea bream, octopus, and front-row views of the dazzling Aegean.

GUIDE

STAY
Assos Kervansaray Otel
*Behramkale Village, Assos;
90-266/721-7093;
assoskervansaray.com.* **$**

Ayvalik Holiday House
*100 Mareşal Fevzl
Çakmak Cad., Ayvalik;
90-266/312-2469;
ayvalikholidayhouse.
com.* **$**

Taş Otel
*132 Kemalpaşa Cad.,
Alaçati;
90-232/716-7772;
tasotel.com.* **$$**

EAT
Agrilia
*126 Kemalpaşa Sk.,
Alaçati;
90-232/716-8594;
agriliarestaurant.com.* **$$**

Bay Nihat Restoran
*21 Sahil Boyu, Cunda
Island; 90-266/327-
1063; baynihat.com.tr.* **$$**

Ferdi Baba
*Port Alaçati; 90-232/
716-9001; alacatiferdi
baba.com.* **$$**

Kebapçi Iskender
*7 Ünlü Cad., Bursa;
90-224/221-4615;
kebapciiskender.com.tr.* **$$**

Köşe Kahve
*41A Kemalpaşa Cad.,
Alaçati;
90-232/716-0413.* **$**

Uzun Ev
*Assos; 90-286/721-
7007.* **$$**

DO
Adatepe Olive Oil Museum
*Sahil Mahallesi,
Küçükkuyu; 90-286/
752-1303; adatepe.com.*

Zeytinbaği
*Çamlibel;
90-266/387-3761;
zeytinbagi.com.*

SHOP
Haremlique
*43A Kemalpaşa Cad.,
Alaçati;
90-232//16-0074.*

MOSCOW

The city's youthful infusion

The staff of *Snob* magazine. Opposite: Christ the Savior Cathedral, overlooking the Moscow River.

OVER THE YEARS I HAVE MADE a healthy living poking fun at Russia's over-the-top elites, describing heavyset men in Adidas tracksuits, overripe women tottering beneath wedding cakes of hair, and a nation's general misuse of leather goods. Born in Leningrad, U.S.S.R., in 1972, I have been coming back almost every year since my late twenties to make fun of my birthplace. But I come back for a different reason as well.

I believe we travel not just out of curiosity, but also for selfish reasons. We travel to find out where we come from and who we are, those little shards of identity that fall out of a stall in a Hong Kong market or float up with Proustian clarity from the bottom of a Hungarian goulash. But for those of us from somewhere else, it's not just clarity we seek; a part of us wants to rewrite history. *If Russia can become a normal country, then maybe my past can be normalized, too.* It's a hopeless and romantic task, but then again you don't get to choose where you're born, which language your parents speak to you when they soothe your first cut with iodine and Mishka the Clumsy Bear chocolate candy, and which wooden ladle they use to stir your summer borscht.

My quest for normalcy leads me to a magazine with the unlikely name of *Snob*, a Russian-language glossy that's funded by the mineral wealth of Mikhail Prokhorov. For those who haven't seen him breakfasting alongside Jay-Z and New York's Mayor Michael Bloomberg, Prokhorov is one of Russia's tallest (six foot eight) and more progressive oligarchs, the 32nd-richest man in the world and owner of the Brooklyn Nets. Prokhorov has been critical of the country's sham democracy, but his criticism has been strategic and intermittent—he is unlikely to spend his next 10 years in a frozen labor camp like fellow oligarch Mikhail Khodorkovsky, who didn't quite know when to shut up. His billions have given *Snob* a nice frisson of controversy, but the magazine and the social networks it has sparked through its well-trafficked website are more than just a billionaire's whim. It is an attempt to bring together a strange new animal: the liberal global Russian who is fond of her voluminous culture, her beautiful language, her doting parents, and the pleasant cast of her cheekbones, but doesn't look like she just held up a Neiman Marcus at gunpoint. Can Russian excess and Western reason exist in the same magazine? Can they exist in the same city?

As I fly into Moscow from Rome, the new world order is clear: middle-class Italians gesticulating up a storm in economy, slick Muscovites up front, chatting in hip, sullen tones over their iPads, their luggage bearing tags from Rome's Hotel Hassler. Once landed, I take an express train to this megacity's center and try to get a cab to my hotel. The driver wants a thousand rubles, or roughly $40, for the 10-minute ride. When I protest he says, "A thousand rubles? Young man, that's not even money anymore!" Moscow has more billionaires than any other city in the world. The pain and humiliation of not being one is a part of every interaction here. If I had never

left as a child and then bought a part of some ferrous-metal enterprise at a rigged auction during the Yeltsin era, I wouldn't be bargaining over a $40 cab ride.

The center of the *Snob* universe is Moscow's former Red October (Krasniy Oktyabr) chocolate factory on the Bersenevskaya Embankment of the Moscow River. A red-brick fixture for over a century, the enormous complex once perfumed this gritty city with its sweet, chocolaty smells. Today it is at the heart of Moscow's media elite, home not just to *Snob* but to the influential *Kommersant* daily, oligarch-funded Internet ventures such as Digital October, and an endless array of clubs and restaurants with names like Progressive Daddy and Belka: the First Non-smoking Bar. Day and night, swarms of artsy young people hum along with boundless Wi-Fi energy. As *Snob*'s deputy editor, Masha Gessen, told me, gesturing around us: "If they wanted to bomb all of enlightened Moscow, it would be very easy."

> ■ THIS COULD BE LONDON OR BERLIN, OR ANY OTHER PLACE WHERE THE GOVERNMENT DOESN'T CONTROL THE TELEVISION CHANNELS.

At the chocolate factory, I book a room in the new Red Zarya (Dawn) hotel. Checking in to my spacious new suite, decorated with old Russian hygienic posters, I realize: I'm staying within the factory walls where my beloved Mishka the Clumsy Bear candy was made! The Red Zarya is perfectly indicative of contemporary Moscow—a loftlike boutique hotel with Soviet service. (Sample conversation: "Do you have a map of the city?" "No.") At one point my clothes come back from the laundry soaking wet along with a very honest explanation: "We couldn't locate a dryer."

And yet, this is the place to be. The Red October factory is just a five-minute walk from the Kremlin, and occupies a strategic stretch of the westernmost part of Bolotny (Marshy) Island, an unexpected sliver of cool within the Moscow River. The first place I go is Bar Strelka. Proceeds from this bar-restaurant help fund the brilliant new

Strelka Institute for Media, Architecture & Design, and the amphitheater adjoining the bar is packed in the summer for lectures by the likes of Chilean architect Alejandro Aravena, a champion of quality housing for the poor. Aravena's presence within sight of Moscow's Ostozhenka Street, one of the most obscene pockets of wealth in the world, provides a hopeful contrast.

Strelka is a big win for Moscow's architectural and lifestyle prospects. Glass and metal and wood—wood in all its glorious, Russian abundance—are at work here. Strelka alone goes far in negating the acres of faux–Art Nouveau Moscow built by its recently fired mayor Yuri Luzhkov, who had an 18-year tenure that turned the already-wounded cityscape into a drunk peasant's idea of modernity. From Strelka's roof bar you can see the excesses of the past in Luzhkov's pet architect Zurab Tsereteli's statue of Peter the Great in a toga astride a life-size frigate, a 308-foot-high exercise in reducing the great bloody czar to a minor Disney character. "We shouldn't knock Peter down," the husband of one *Snob* staffer tells me when I gleefully propose doing just that. "We can't keep knocking things down and rebuilding." He's right: towering over the Strelka rooftop is the Cathedral of Christ the Savior, knocked down by Stalin and recently rebuilt by Turkish contractors, a marble-and-granite giant referred to in its first 19th-century incarnation as "The Samovar."

Sipping Strelka's sublime Moscow Beauty cocktail, I look east to the Stalin-era House on the Embankment. If one building in Moscow could talk (the All-Russian Exhibition Center notwithstanding), it would be this one. Stalin's scientists and artists lived and died here during his fickle reign. Peeking through a window I am shocked to see a portrait of Stalin in full battle regalia gracing one living room. It couldn't be! But then again, something needs to counter the massive Mercedes-Benz hood ornament currently affixed to the building's roof.

"How Do We Get Rid of the U.S.S.R.?" an article in a recent issue of *Snob* asks its readers, with one

Opposite,
from top:
Sightseeing in
Red Square;
lounging at the
bar inside
Art Akademiya.

responding, "Why would we get rid of who we are?" Strelka's lemon-poached chicken with fennel purée sure tastes like one way out. Its simplicity stands in contrast to the oversauced, insecure Moscow dishes of the last decade, recalling my grandmother's chicken bouillon, if Grandma knew from fennel. Amid the laptop crowd in Strelka's downstairs bar, which houses a baby grand, I feel as normal as I've felt in Russia in two decades. This could be London or Chicago or Berlin, or any other place where the government doesn't control the television channels. And who cares if Strelka's chef happens to be British?

■ CAN RUSSIAN EXCESS AND WESTERN REASON EXIST IN THE SAME CITY?

Next door to the Brits, Bontempi features chef Valentino Bontempi hollering Italian into his open kitchen or smoking soulfully outside as the sun lights up Christ the Savior. I have the bruschetta with olive-and-anchovy tapenade: it's tarted up with butter in a nod to local tastes, but the Russian bread is an improvement over the Tuscan variety (Bontempi sources many of his ingredients from Moscow markets). There's an oregano-and-rabbit ravioli that would not be derided in his native Brescia.

For another dose of progress, I head down the embankment to the Art Akademiya, nearly 3,000 square feet of art, booze, and decent food "in the style of New York's SoHo." Risotto? Check. Sea bass? Check. Sushi? Check. Plush, cracked-leather couches, scuffed ceilings, outsize nudes, indifferent service? Check, check, check, check! In the risotto-mad capital of the Russians, the dish comes heavy with porcini and is oddly reminiscent of the "white" mushrooms in sour cream our parents made for us. Its self-proclaimed "largest bar-stand in Europe" may be a tad excessive, but a painting composed solely of the words RELATIVISM IS DIALECTICS FOR IDIOTS instructs me not to judge (or is it the other way around?).

You'll find an excellent example of the New Moscow in the Garage Center for Contemporary Culture. Set in a leafy Soviet neighborhood, the 1920's Konstantin Melnikov–designed bus depot has been turned into a major art center by Daria Zhukova, girlfriend of Roman Abramovich, the multinational oligarch and owner of London's Chelsea Football Club. Garage features shows by the likes of Ilya and Emilia Kabakov and, recently, an amazing color light show by James Turrell. There's a packed restaurant and art therapy for kids on weekends.

When the summer sun sets, the creative elite is wont to head to a downtown place like Kvartira 44. After three days without a drop of vodka—my first relatively sober 72 hours in Russia—we start following up many shots with *grenka* (dark rye toast) covered in cheese and garlic, and the best old standard for vodka drinking: herring with potatoes. The conversation gets more ribald and I realize I'm in bizarre world: a kind of mirror image of my friends in New York, only with more Armenians. As the night goes on the table thickens with people, my ancestral name of Igor is invoked, and the Russian summer feels golden.

---

*Adapted from "The New Russia,"
by Gary Shteyngart.*

GUIDE

STAY
Red Zarya
*3/10 Bersenevskiy
Pereulok, Bldg. 8;
7-495/980-4774;
red-zarya.ru.* **$$**

EAT
Art Akademiya
*6 Bersenevskaya Nab.,
Bldg. 3; 7-495/771-
7446; academiya.ru.* **$$**

Bar Strelka
*14 Bersenevskaya Nab.,
Bldg. 5; 7-495/
771-7416; strelka.
com.* **$$$**

Bontempi
*12 Bersenevskaya Nab.,
Bldg. 1;
7-495/223-1387;
bontempirest.ru.* **$$$**

Kvartira 44
*24/8 Ul. Malaya
Yakimanka;
7-499/238-8234;
kv44.ru.* **$$**

DO
Cathedral of Christ
the Savior
*15 Volkhonka Ul.;
no phone; xxc.ru.*

Garage Center for
Contemporary Culture
*19A Obraztsova Ul.;
7-495/645-0520;
garageccc.com.*

House on the
Embankment
*20/2 Bersenevskaya
Nab.; no phone.*

Strelka Institute for
Media, Architecture &
Design
*14 Bersenevskaya Nab.,
Bldg. 5A;
7-495/771-7437;
strelka.com.*

The lobby of the Jumeirah at Etihad Towers hotel, in Abu Dhabi.

JOHANNESBURGSAFARISZANZIBARMOZAMBIQUETELAV
TELAVIVABUDHABIJOHANNESBURGSAFARISZANZIBARMO

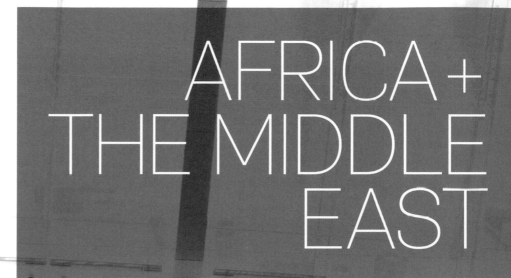

Lamunu Hotel's
colorful façade and
outdoor piazza.

JOHANNESBURG, SOUTH AFRICA

An artistic haven takes root

GUIDE

STAY
Lamunu Hotel
90 De Korte St.;
27-11/242-8600;
lamunu.co.za. **$**

DO
Arts on Main
20 Kruger St.;
27-11/832-451-040;
mabonengprecinct.com.

David West
38 Fourth Ave.;
27-11/71-452-2503;
davidwest.co.za.

Neighbourgoods Market
73 Juta St.; no phone;
neighbourgoodsmarket.
co.za.

What If the World
68 Juta St.; 27-11/23-
0336; whatiftheworld.com.

THE PLAYERS AND FANS may be long gone, but Johannesburg is still basking in the glow of the 2010 World Cup. While futuristic stadiums and billion-dollar rail lines may be the games' most conspicuous legacy, the tournament's transformative influence has reached deep into the historic city center, where anti-apartheid protesters once rallied and youthful entrepreneurs are now raising the creative stakes.

In the western district of Braamfontein, lofts, office buildings, and Victorian row houses have been converted into the galleries, boutiques, ramen joints, and Italian cafés that lend this quarter a distinctive, culture-rich character. Among the highlights are a branch of the Cape Town–based What If the World art gallery, displaying the works of emerging South African artists; the sunlit showroom of fashion designer David West; and the Neighbourgoods Market, an open-air weekend food and crafts bazaar. The crash pad of choice: Lamunu ("orange" in Sesotho), a playful 60-room hotel with giant photo murals splashed across the walls and a convivial piazza as its social hub.

Over in the Maboneng Precinct, on the revitalized eastern edge of the city center, the airy studios and shops at Arts on Main are set in a quintet of century-old red-brick warehouses. Tenants include William Kentridge, South Africa's foremost living artist, as well as the Goodman Gallery, which represents established regional names. Here, too, there's an alfresco weekend market, where artisan-made furniture sits cheek by jowl with vintage fashions and food vendors hawk everything from Indian to Moroccan fare. It's a testament to the city's newfound worldliness— and its ongoing rejuvenation.

SAFARIS

Active pursuits into the wild

An African safari is practically a prerequisite on travel bucket lists. And for good reason: this is the stuff that once-in-a-lifetime adventures are made of, whether it's a romantic sojourn to a tented camp or a rugged, off-the-radar trek in the depths of the savanna. Here, five countries with experiences guaranteed to appeal to both the first-time visitor and the old hand.

Botswana

In Botswana, focus is shifting from ultra-luxe lodges toward active itineraries and comfortably rustic properties. Bring rain boots for a canoe trip along the ancient Selinda Spillway with Great Plains Conservation (*27-11/807-1800; greatplainsconservation.com; four days from $1,760*), where you'll spot elephants and buffalo before setting up camp on the riverbank. In the Kalahari Desert, the Bushmen Initiation Hunt from Uncharted Africa Safari Co. (*27-11/447-1605; unchartedafrica.com; eight days from $11,440*) begins with an introduction to the Juhoansi tribe, followed by eight days spent hunting eland on foot and sleeping in simple fly camps.

Kenya

There's a fresh energy in the Kenyan countryside, evident in a new breed of lodges that emphasize community and preservation. Proceeds from the high-profile, eight-cottage Olarro (*olarrokenya.com;* **$$$$$**) go to build local schools, clinics, and wells. The seven-tent Mara Plains Camp (*254-20/600-0457; greatplainsconservation.com;*

$$$$$**) operates game-viewing trips in a reserve run in partnership with the Masai. And a reclaimed Laikipia cattle ranch is the setting for eight solar-powered villas at Segera Retreat (*wilderness-safaris.com;* **$$$$$).

Namibia

Namibia wins for sheer diversity of landscapes—otherworldly desert; volcanic mountains; dramatic coastal plains. How to navigate the vast distances between attractions and camps? Many visitors are opting for privately guided trips involving helicopters and light planes to access the farthest-flung corners, such as Wilderness Safaris' Serra Cafema (*wilderness-safaris. com;* **$$$$$**), near the Angolan border. More affordable group tours are also available, including eight-person safaris from Geographic Expeditions (*geoex. com; 11 days from $6,215*) that travel to Damaraland, in the northwest, to view desert elephants and fossilized trees. Best value of all: the group tour from Wild About Africa (*wild aboutafrica.com; 11 days from $2,823*), which follows the 100-mile-long Fish River Canyon.

South Africa

Post-apartheid, South Africa established itself as the continent's blue-chip destination with a spate of lodges that brought luxury to the major game regions. Now intimate retreats are enticing safari-goers to make cultural side trips to lesser-known areas. Three hours north of Cape Town, Bushmans Kloof Wilderness Reserve & Wellness Retreat (*27-27/482-8200; bushmans kloof.co.za;* **$$$$**) takes its name from nearby Bushman rock art sites that date back 10,000 years. For a compelling dose of heritage tourism, head east to KwaZulu-Natal, where Fugitives' Drift Lodge (*27-34/642-1843; fugitives-drift-lodge.com;* **$$$$**)—the house of late historian David Rattray—takes visitors on tours of 19th-century Anglo-Zulu War battlefields.

Uganda

Gorillas are the draw in this country's dense jungles, but thanks to sounder conservation policies, wildlife is once again on the rise in Uganda's plains. And with the establishment of the Ziwa Rhino Sanctuary, just south of Murchison Falls National Park, the Big Five are back; base yourself at the rebuilt Chobe Safari Lodge (*chobelodgeuganda. com;* **$$$$**), known for its panoramic Nile River views. For lion and elephant tracking, consider Volcanoes Safaris' Kyambura Gorge Lodge (*866/599-2737; volcanoes safaris.com; four days from $2,036*), on a former coffee estate at the edge of Queen Elizabeth National Park.

Camp Kalahari, in the Botswana desert.

A game drive at Mara Plains Camp, in Kenya. Right: Uganda's Kyambura Gorge Lodge.

The pool at Fugitives' Drift Lodge, in South Africa. Left: Namibia's Serra Cafema camp.

The East Room
at 236 Hurumzi.

GUIDE

STAY
Jafferji House & Spa
178 Gizenga St.;
255-77/374-0888;
jafferjihouse.net. **$$**

236 Hurumzi
236 Hurumzi St.;
255-24/223-2784;
236hurumzi.com. **$$**

DO
Journeys by Design
315/955-6842;
journeysbydesign.com.
$$$$$

ZANZIBAR, TANZANIA

Awakening the senses one bite at a time

IF THERE IS POETRY IN PEPPER, you'll find it in Zanzibar. Off the coast of Tanzania, this low-lying archipelago fringed by coral reefs and white-sand beaches was once a center of the ancient spice trade in East Africa. Even today the scent of cloves, nutmeg, and cinnamon perfumes the air in Stone Town, a sprawling port punctuated by mosques and covered bazaars.

The best way to experience the UNESCO World Heritage capital is on a tasting tour of the tumultuous Darajani Market, where shopkeepers haggle with veiled housewives over piles of peppercorns and sacks of basmati rice. Guide Khamis Sharriff of Journeys by Design will direct you toward the best stands, as well as arrange visits to the Forodhani Gardens to observe street vendors preparing Arab- and Indian-influenced local snacks, including the falafel-like chickpea *bhajia* and *mshikaki* (beef kebabs), on charcoal *jiko* stoves.

For a bird's-eye view of the scene, sample the curried fish cakes and potato *kachori* at the restaurant on the roof of 236 Hurumzi, which has 24 suites outfitted in rich African hardwoods and colorful cotton *kanga* fabrics from nearby stalls. The award for spiciest place in town, however, goes to the residence of photographer Javed Jafferji, who offers Swahili cooking lessons at his coral stone town house. There, 10 guest rooms are filled with items collected during his travels, including carved chests, Moroccan brass tubs, and native folk art. Consider your cultural immersion complete.

MOZAMBIQUE

Alighting on a once forbidden coast

Welcome to the latest enclave of Indian Ocean chic. It wasn't long ago that Mozambique was mired in a decades-long civil war, but now the northern shore has emerged as a destination of choice for post-safari sybarites and private-island connoisseurs. Teak dhows transport visitors through the sandy wisps of the Quirimbas archipelago en route to beach retreats that rival those on Mauritius and the Seychelles.

Azura at Quilalea Private Island

Only 18 guests at a time are allowed on Quilalea, an 86-acre haven for dozens of nesting sea turtles and a dizzying array of marine and bird life. The nine coral-stone-and-thatch bungalows look onto a protected deepwater bay where Portuguese and Arab traders once plied their dhows. Follow the walking trail through the island's dense, age-old baobab groves, then suit up at the dive center for a close encounter with (gentle) whale sharks. *27-76/705-0599; azura-retreats.com.* **$$$$**

Coral Lodge 15.41

A short boat ride from Mozambique Island, the 16th-century Portuguese colonial capital and a UNESCO World Heritage site, Coral Lodge is perfectly sited for explorations of the island's crumbling churches and mosques, as well as the São Sebastião fortress. The 10 villas take a sleek approach to beachy African interiors, with an infinity pool where the lagoon meets the ocean. One highlight: the culinary excursions led by Zimbabwean chef Tessa Bristow, which start at local food markets and end with lessons in traditional Mozambican cooking. *258-266/60003; corallodge 1541.com.* **$$$$$**

Ibo Island Lodge

Snorkel above a century-old shipwreck, kayak through mangrove forests, and meet a *curandeiro* (traditional-medicine healer) on Ibo, the cultural heart of the Quirimbas island chain. At Ibo Island Lodge, the hand-carved teak furnishings and colonial-era architecture reflect the Arab, Indian, and Portuguese heritage of the region. Don't miss the guided night walks, on which you're likely to hear the distinctive thump of humpback whales hunting in the bay. *27-21/702-0285; iboisland.com.* **$$$$**

Nuarro

A rugged panorama of bush-and-baobab forest forms the backdrop for Nuarro's 12 thatched-roof bungalows, tucked into the dunes of the Baixo do Pinda peninsula, 100 miles north of Mozambique Island. The solar- and wind-powered resort has private verandas, complete with hammocks, for spying humpback whales breaching the waves or—if you're truly fortunate—elephants playing in the surf. Even better, proceeds from each stay help fund community projects in the neighboring village of Nanatha. *258-82/301-4294; nuarro.com.* **$$$$**

Vamizi Island Lodge

There's no television or Wi-Fi in the 15 *makuti*-thatch villas at Vamizi, but the samango monkeys and weaver birds that surround the property make lively enough entertainment. On a mile-long beach in the far northern Quirimbas, near the Tanzanian border, the eco-lodge is surrounded by protected coral reefs and some of the best diving sites in the world. Non-divers can book an overnight sea safari on the resort's dhow, *Tusitiri,* staffed by a resident fisherman and a Cordon Bleu–trained chef. *44-1285/762-218; vamizi.com.* **$$$$**

Walking along the beach at Nuarro.

Ibo Island Lodge's understated exterior. Right: The courtyard at Vamizi Island Lodge.

Paddling on the lagoon near Coral Lodge 15.41. Left: A lounge area in Azura at Quilalea Private Island.

TEL AVIV

After hours in a new party capital

"IF YOU THINK COPACABANA IS HOT, you haven't been to Tel Aviv," says Israeli restaurant designer Adam Tihany. A booming dot-com industry (dubbed "Silicon Wadi") and a worldly attitude have made Israel's second city one of the sexiest and most progressive places on the planet, and this ebullient style is on full display in restaurants and cocktail bars across the grid. Take Cantina, an Italian spot on lively Rothschild Boulevard that has become the city's best perch for people-watching. An eclectic mix of models, actors, politicos, and Russian oligarchs tuck in to pastas and salads on the patio, which peers out toward Bauhaus buildings on the tree-lined stretch.

After sundown, Tel Aviv turns up the volume at places like Radio E.P.G.B—a subterranean den that plays host to both the city's fashion set and young bohemian artists. (Think of it as an Israeli take on New York's late, lamented rock club CBGB.) A flirtatious crowd mingles over pitchers of ouzo in the outdoor garden at Taxidermy, a dark boîte where stuffed pheasants and a gazelle head hang prominently above the bar. All epic nights end at the buzzing French-style bistro Brasserie M&R for, as Tihany puts it, "a steak at three a.m. and the latest gossip."

GUIDE

STAY
Brown Hotel
The color scheme stays true to its name—chocolate-hued walls in guest rooms; tobacco leather couches in the library—the better to set off views of the Mediterranean. *25 Kalisher St.; 972-3/717-0200; browntlv.com.* **$**

EAT AND DRINK
Brasserie M&R
70 Ibn Gvirol St.; 972-3/696-7111. **$$$**

Cantina
1 Rothschild Blvd.; 972-3/620-5051. **$$**

Radio E.P.G.B
7 Shadal at Yehuda Halevi St.; 972-3/560-3636.

Taxidermy
33 HaHashmal; no phone.

The Tel Aviv skyline rising above the coast.

ABU DHABI

A 21st-century desert oasis

For years, Abu Dhabi has stood in the shadow of its high-profile neighbor Dubai. But flush with 95 percent of the U.A.E.'s oil, the lesser-known emirate is building its own iconic skyline—and reshaping its image from business destination into cultural hub. Meet a few of the most notable landmarks of the modern Middle East.

Corniche
Running some 1½ miles along the Persian Gulf, the Corniche has been the city's open-air playground for more than half a century. The palm-lined promenade is dotted with cafés, and the beaches are laced with dedicated paths for walkers and cyclists. Currently under way: a long-awaited redevelopment by British architect Markus Jatsch that will add new restaurants, sports facilities, and beach clubs to the mix.

Jumeirah at Etihad Towers
Jaw-dropping hotels are emerging from the sands seemingly overnight. In downtown Abu Dhabi, one of the most impressive is the Jumeirah, a stomping ground for petrodollar dealmakers. Housed in a sky-high glass-and-steel sculptural tower that overlooks the Corniche, the hotel is the pet project of Sheikh Suroor bin Mohammed Al Nahyan, whose personal art collection is displayed throughout. *877/854-8051; jumeirah.com.* **$$$$$**

Monte-Carlo Beach Club
The first beach club on Saadiyat Island (off the coast of Abu Dhabi) takes its cues from its sister property on the French Riviera. The atmosphere around the 7,000-square-foot pool is appropriately extravagant, with canary-striped daybeds and crisp teak-and-sailcloth cabanas that appear to float on the water like a mirage. Reinforcing the members-only club's ultraexclusive reputation: three beachfront bungalows with flat-screen TV's and the requisite butler service. *971-2/656-3500; montecarlo beachclub.ae.* **$$$$$**

Sheikh Zayed Grand Mosque
After a $550 million investment and more than a decade of construction, the Sheikh Zayed Mosque is arguably the city's most dazzling spectacle, clad in white stone and marble and accented with gold inlay. Blending Moorish, Mughal, and Arab designs, 82 domes and four minarets rise 350 feet above a courtyard that features the world's largest marble mosaic. *Sheikh Zayed Grand Mosque Center; 971-2/441-6444; szgmc.ae.*

The courtyard of the Sheikh Zayed Grand Mosque.

World Trade Centre Central Market
While the region awaits the opening of two star-designed museums (Frank Gehry's Guggenheim; Jean Nouvel's outpost of the Louvre), another architectural icon is already up and running. Located in the heart of the commercial core, the World Trade Centre Central Market by London-based architect Norman Foster redefines the typical shopping-mall experience. Stained-glass windows let in multicolored sunlight, soaring wooden-lattice walls and ceilings slide back to create airy corridors, and rooftop gardens make this modern-day souk one of Abu Dhabi's greenest structures. High-end shops specialize in everything from dates to diamonds. *centralmarket.ae.*

Yas Viceroy Hotel
The contemporary hotel boom began with this futuristic structure, created by Asymptote Architecture and recently rebranded as a Viceroy. An audacious departure from the city's palace-style hotels, the two glass buildings are linked by an enclosed bridge and an LED-lit, meshlike canopy made of 5,096 diamond-shaped steel-and-glass panels. Floor-to-ceiling windows overlook the marina and an oceanfront Formula One racecourse that serves as the location for the Abu Dhabi Grand Prix. *Yas Island; 888/622-4567; viceroyhotelsandmarinas.com.* **$$$$$**

A Marine Executive suite at the Yas Viceroy Hotel. Left: A corridor in the World Trade Centre Central Market.

Neatly trimmed hedges in the gardens of the Corniche. Left: The pool area inside the Yas Viceroy.

YAKUSHIMATOKYOSEOULBEIJINGGUANGZHOUXISHUA
HOCHIMINHCITYVIETNAMSINGAPOREPHILIPPINESYA

ASIA

Omoide-Yokocho (Memory Lane), a foodie haven in the Shinjuku district of Tokyo.

YAKUSHIMA, JAPAN

Into the land that time forgot

ANCIENT CEDAR FORESTS AND STORYBOOK hot springs lend the misty island of Yakushima an otherworldly allure. Off the southern coast of Japan, the UNESCO World Heritage site has a one-of-a-kind ecosystem with more than 1,900 species of vegetation—a primeval wilderness nourished by almost 15 feet of rain per year. Needless to say, it's a nature lover's paradise.

A two-hour hydrofoil ride from the port city of Kagoshima brings you within sight of the island, whose granite cliffs jut from the sea like a fortress. Rent a car in the sleepy town of Miyanoura and make your way to Onoaida Onsen, a simple Japanese bathhouse above the coastal road. A good soak prepares you for more downtime to come at the nearby Sankara Hotel & Spa Yakushima. The 28 airy suites and villas have teak furnishings fashioned by Balinese craftsmen, but interiors are decidedly Japanese, with sliding screens and delicate porcelain cups from Kyoto. Joël Robuchon–trained chef Chiharu Takei creates exquisite meals from locally sourced ingredients: a risotto of Asahi crab and bamboo shoots, for example, followed by grilled Nakayama sirloin in a *yuzu*-and-pepper sauce.

Still, it's the Shiratani Unsuikyo forest you've come to see—a surreal universe of moss, infinite rivulets and waterfalls, coiled roots webbing over glistening rocks, and giant cedars that resemble nothing so much as rivers of wood shooting up from the ground. (This was the setting that inspired director Hayao Miyazaki's 1997 animated masterpiece, *Princess Mononoke*.) Here, you can stand beside 48-foot-wide trees called *yaku-sugi,* which have been around for more than a millennium; one stump, named Wilson Kabu after an American botanist, is the size of a small house, with a mini Shinto shrine inside. Follow a slippery trail to the legendary Jomon Sugi cedar, the oldest and most towering tree in the forest. Visitors are restricted to an observation platform, but that doesn't diminish its effect. Standing before it, you feel a keen sense of the passing centuries—and your place as a mere drop in the stream of humanity.

GUIDE

STAY
Sankara Hotel & Spa Yakushima
*553 Haginoue, Mugio;
81-997/473-488;
sankarahotel-spa.com;
meals included.* **$$$$**

DO
Onoaida Onsen
*Kumage-gun Yakushima-cho, Kagoshima;
81-997/472-872.*

Shiratani Unsuikyo Forest
*Miyanoura;
81-977/423-508.*

Kayaking on the Anbo River in the Shiratani Unsuikyo forest.

TOKYO

An atmospheric pub crawl for the ages

In search of the next great eating odyssey? Look no further than Tokyo's *izakaya*—the countless small bars with eclectic menus that provide both a compelling glimpse of local nightlife and some of the most delicious food in town. The casual, unpolished setting is part of the allure; meals are served tapas-style, making it possible to go from one establishment to the next for a progressive meal that's a true epicurean adventure.

En

Hipsters and salarymen alike crowd into this spot in frenetic Shibuya for small plates such as lotus-root *kimpira* and black-pepper chicken. (Unlike many *izakaya*, En has an extensive English menu.) The dining room resembles an indoor park, with bonsai trees scattered through-out, but the best seat is at the counter overlooking the kitchen. *Toei Plaza, 11th floor, 1-24-12 Shibuya, Shibuya-ku; izakaya-en.com.* **$$$**

Kabuto

Think of it as the Japanese version of nose-to-tail gastronomy. This traditional nook has served eel—and only eel—for the past 64 years, every part of it char-grilled on skewers before arriving at your table. Make like the regulars and order the *hito-tori,* a course of seven sticks. *1-2-11 Nishi Shinjuku, Shinjuku-ku; 81-3/3342-7671.* **$$**

Kanae

A nostalgic favorite with an extensive sake list, Kanae serves dishes such as tender pork-stuffed cabbage rolls, grilled duck with mizuna salad, and expertly prepared fried fugu (blowfish) in a dim, wood-clad dining room. *3-12-12 Shinjuku, Shinjuku-ku; 81-3/3352-7646.* **$$$**

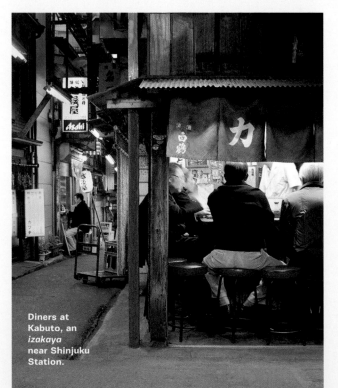

Diners at Kabuto, an *izakaya* near Shinjuku Station.

Kibi

For an only-in-Tokyo experience, visit Shibuya's Nonbei Yokocho (Drunkard's Alley), a warren of narrow lanes marked with glowing red lanterns. Amid the dozens of food-and-drink counters, one standout is the Korean- and Moroccan-inspired Kibi, run by energetic proprietor Ms. Tama. Don't miss her miso-marinated eggplant or classic *karaage,* succulent bits of deep-fried meat. *1-25-9 Nonbei Yokocho, Shibuya, Shibuya-ku.* **$$$**

Konakara

The house specialty here is a refined version of *oden*: sit at the counter, select your favorites (tofu; fish cakes) from a simmering brass cauldron, and sip an *atsu-kan* (hot sake).

Shin-Marunouchi Bldg., fifth floor, 1-5-1 Marunouchi, Chiyoda-ku; 81-3/5220-2281. **$$**

Maru

The *izakaya* goes upscale at Maru, a 15-minute walk away from Kibi but a world away in spirit. Chef-owner Keiji Mori was trained in haute kaiseki cuisine, and he presents his artfully composed dishes—including sweet-corn tempura and a silky, house-made tofu—in a hushed oasis of a dining room awash in muted grays and light woods. *Aoyama KT Bldg., B1, 5-50-8 Jingumae, Shibuya-ku; maru-mayfont.jp.* **$$$**

Rokukakutei

This minimalist gem in Ginza got a Michelin star for its divine *kushiage*. While the wine list is excellent, you'll find native Tokyoites quaffing *happo sake,* a cold, sparkling variety that pairs well with the deep-fried skewered meats and vegetables. *Kojun Bldg., fourth floor, 6-8-7 Ginza, Chuo-ku; 81-3/5537-6008.* **$$$$**

Uoshin

The first thing you'll notice at Uoshin, in Nogizaka, is the day's catch, displayed market-style along the length of the restaurant. This is the rare *izakaya* with a sushi counter—and the eight-piece *kappa maki* roll, topped with heaping portions of tuna belly, sea urchin, crab, and caviar, is stellar. Nevertheless, the *shioyaki* (salt-grilled) fish may be the best seafood you've ever eaten. *9-6-32 Akasaka, Minato-ku; 81-3/3405-0411.* **$$$**

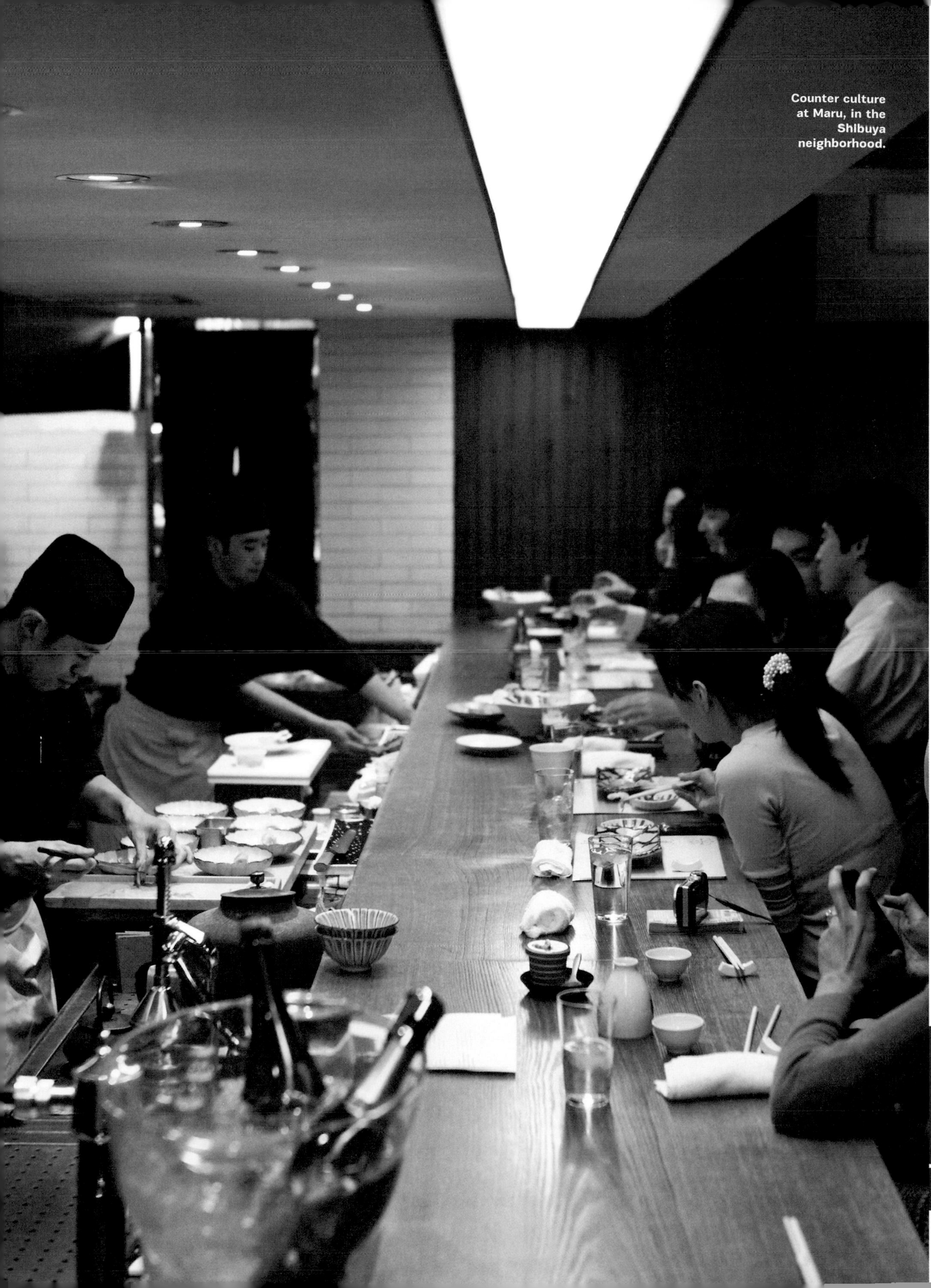

Counter culture at Maru, in the Shibuya neighborhood.

Space Mue's design-centric showroom.

SEOUL

Claiming the spotlight as Asia's Style Central

An embellished handbag by fashion designer Dylan Ryu. Above: A fashionable young local.

E VIDENCE THAT THIS IS SEOUL'S moment? Everyone from Phillip Lim to Tory Burch can't seem to open ambitiously designed outposts fast enough. Prada collaborated with Rem Koolhaas's OMA to create Prada Transformer, a 66-foot-high steel structure that draws an international coterie of gawkers. And Rain, the floppy-haired Korean pop phenomenon, recently topped a *Time* readers' poll of the 100 most influential people in the world.

Some observers have compared Seoul's obsession with high-end products, fueled by new money and a burgeoning upper middle class, to the Japanese hunger for cool consumer goods, dubbing Seoul the new Tokyo. But the city also strikes me as having much in common with Beijing or Shanghai, where the voracious desire for style has an almost liberating character. I have long been fascinated by the far-ranging effects that a powerful love of getting and spending can have on a formerly hidebound culture, so I am deeply curious about this new, much-talked-about Seoul.

I can barely contain my excitement as I head down streets lined in shops crammed with ersatz Birkins rendered in a riot of colors. I go to the store-choked neighborhood of Cheongdam-dong for Boon the Shop, a boutique so glorious that it literally makes me catch my breath. Margiela and Libertine; Gareth Pugh and Vionnet—all are displayed around an atrium dripping with a vast sculpture by French artist Jean-Michel Othoniel called *Ivory Double Necklace*.

Cabs are plentiful and cheap, a good thing in a town that is so spread out. I hop in a taxi to Dosan Park, the Madison Avenue of Seoul—if that street were lined with architectural experiments. The Ann Demeulemeester store's exterior is covered in grass. Tom Greyhound Downstairs has a steep stone staircase between two mossy walls that leads to an underground recess awash in beaded Ashish minidresses from London. And a Ping-Pong table greets you at the entrance (which is on the second floor) to Daily Projects; inside, there are purses shaped like giant silver lips.

At this point, even the least astute shopper will have noticed that Seoul consumers have an obsession with the finest and most rarefied of European and American labels. But did you really travel all this way to purchase Céline and Chloé at even higher prices than in the United States? On Samcheong-dong gil, a boulevard near the Gyeongbokgung palace, I visit the Korean Traditional Folk Dress Museum—not a museum at all, but a shop that will custom-create and ship to you a *hanbok*, Korea's high-waisted, spun-silk version of the kimono. I stop at a rough-hewn spot called Korea Paper, in the Insadong neighborhood, where sheaves straight off the bark are for sale, as far from cool South Korea as you can get but somehow still cooler for it.

I want to go to the famous Dongdaemun night market, which, as I understand it, is really rocking at 2 a.m. Though it's only 9 p.m., the market (a series of warehouse-like malls crammed with everything from shoes to suitcases) is hopping. Here among the supercheap clothes I select my own version of Seoul's tulle tutu with, fortunately, a drawstring waist (clothing here runs small).

"You've picked a hot spot!" says Mun-Soo Kwon when we meet at the awe-inspiring Comme des Garçons store in Hannam-dong, Seoul's newest rediscovered neighborhood, which has been described as the equivalent of Manhattan's Meatpacking District five years ago. Kwon lived in the United States and worked for a number of designers; now he's come home to start his own line.

We taxi back for lunch at the Galleria, Seoul's answer to Bergdorf Goodman. Though we have a bit of trouble finding it, Kwon insists that I must see Space Mue, and he is right. A vast screen on the wall imprints floating pixels on a beige Lanvin coat; a cardigan from the British cult brand Markus Lupfer sports gold sequined lobsters on its pockets.

On my last day, I am being treated to a Korean luncheon courtesy of designer Kuho Jung. Mr.

Kuho, as everyone calls him, is carrying an electric-green schoolbag and has thick nerd-chic spectacles. He wants to take me to 10 Corso Como, and it has required all my strength to avoid entering this temple of mercantile delights earlier in the trip. I have been to the Milan flagship, but this... well...this is something else. The all-white interior is the perfect backdrop for merchandise both obvious (Alaïa, Marni, et al.) and less familiar. I am besotted by a series of vintage crocodile and alligator purses by designer turned artist Dylan Ryu, who finds Chanel and Dior bags at markets in Paris and London, then artfully embellishes them with ribbons and badges.

■ THE VORACIOUS DESIRE FOR STYLE HAS AN ALMOST LIBERATING CHARACTER, AS IF OLD RULES ARE BEING THROWN OFF FOR A NEW WAY OF LIVING.

Kuho and I drive over to Mapo-gu, a low-rise quarter far from the glassy towers that typically define Seoul. The boho residents could pass for Brooklynites, but for the surfeit of Vuittons —real? fake?—dangling from their black-clad arms. We visit Market M, a store famous for its simple wooden furniture. At Mee, the rough-hewn cement entrance gives way to a plethora of plaid trousers and oversize argyle pullovers. When it's time for a break, I shyly suggest Ann House—the uniquely South Korean restaurant chain whose whimsical cottage décor is said to evoke Victorian era dollhouses crossed with *Anne of Green Gables*. I'd love to see one before I leave, I say, and am astonished that Kuho has never heard of it. But persistence—and help from a smart phone—locates a branch right in the heart of this unlikely neighborhood.

Ann House turns out to be a study in saccharine perched on the second floor of an office building. "We call this Princess Style," Kuho tells me. All the other patrons are teenage girls; we sit on pink-and-white floral sofas and eat sugary cakes in our own little room, where a pink Mickey Mouse fan buzzes on the table. As we gaze out the window, Kuho muses that places like this are fast disappearing in a changing landscape of upwardly mobile, sleek Seoul. "Every time I walk down a familiar street, there are new stores, new restaurants I've never seen before," he says. "You go away for a few weeks, and Seoul completely changes."

Adapted from "A Little Bit of Seoul," by Lynn Yaeger.

GUIDE

BEIJING

A culinary tour of the world

No district captures Beijing's globally minded zeitgeist better than sprawling Chaoyang, to the east of Tiananmen Square. Home to the city's embassies and many of its international businesses, the area also comes alive at night with a staggering variety of places to eat and drink—from cutting-edge restaurants to casual spots in shopping malls. These seven places represent some of the most memorable dining in the Chinese capital right now.

Cooking global delicacies in Modo's open kitchen.

Agua

Barcelona chef Jordi Valles has created a temple to Spanish cuisine at this intimate space in Chaoyang's Sanlitun neighborhood. Valles, who trained under Ferran Adrià and Basque master Juan Mari Arzak, showcases his experimental flair in dishes such as steak tartare with salty black-truffle ice cream and a crisp suckling pig served with apricots and shallots. Both are delicious, but don't take our word for it: martial-arts superstar Jackie Chan is reportedly a fan. *Sanlitun Bei Rd.; 86-10/5208-6188; aqua.com.hk.* **$$$**

Bei

At Sanlitun's Opposite House, one of Beijing's flashiest boutique hotels, New Orleans native Max Levy serves up north-Asian-inspired food (smoked Wagyu; silver cod with kimchi; steelhead trout with *shiso* paste) in a series of stylish dining rooms. Levy previously worked at New York City's Sushi Yasuda; his raw-bar selections are appropriately first-rate.

11 Sanlitun Rd.; 86-10/6410-5230; beirestaurant.com. **$$$$**

Fez

For the best view in town—plus equally impressive Mediterranean tapas and expertly mixed cocktails—head to Fez, a Moroccan-themed lounge atop the Nali Patio building in Sanlitun. Be sure to book a table on a Thursday night, when a live DJ spins Caribbean, Latin, and Afro-Cuban beats. *81 Sanlitun North St.; 86-10/5208-6138; aqua.com.hk.* **$$**

Modo

International small plates by Venezuelan chef Daniel Urdaneta are the draw at Modo, a high-energy restaurant in the Sanlitun Village Mall. On the menu: Danish smoked-salmon *smørrebrød,* Spanish-inspired melon gazpacho garnished with *jamón ibérico,* and Italian-Argentinean *malfati* (spinach-and-ricotta dumplings). The wine list runs the gamut from Japanese sake and Chinese *baijiu* to Pinot Noir from the Americas.

19 Sanlitun Rd.; 86-10/6415-7207; mostobj.com. **$$**

Mosto

Urdaneta also heads up the contemporary Latin restaurant Mosto, where the simple yet sophisticated dishes are matched with half-glass wine pours. Start out with the *causa,* made with avocado, blue crab, and yellow potatoes, and a Craggy Range Sauvignon Blanc from New Zealand; follow it up with the Australian rib-eye steak and a Catena Malbec from Argentina's Mendoza region. *81 Sanlitun Bei Rd.; 86-10/5208-6030; mostobj.com.* **$$**

Najia Xiaoguan

Hidden amid the high-rises in the Central Business District, this two-story restaurant offers a respite from Beijing's din. Co-owned by a thirtysomething Manchurian known simply as Zhou, Najia Xiaoguan is known for its exotic fare; the signature dish is the *huangtanzi* soup, made with deer tendon and fish lips. Less adventurous eaters opt for the *hongzhao zhurou* (date-simmered pork) or *zha xia* (fried prawns in crispy shells). *10 Yangan Xili, Jianguomen Wai Dajie; 86-10/6567-3663; najia.com.cn.* **$$$**

Terra

A Beijing *cevicheria* may sound counterintuitive, but Peruvian chef Gaby Alves more than pulls it off. Along with seven varieties of the seafood classic, she serves up creative spins on her country's traditional dishes, including spinach empanadas and cassava croquettes. The five-course brunch features free-flowing caipirinhas and selections from the 20-bottle rum bar. *1 Sanlitun South Rd.; 86-10/6591-9148; terrabeijing.com.* **$$**

Bei's bold dining room. Left: One of the restaurant's sushi chefs.

A drink with a view at Fez bar. Right: Brunch at Agua.

The futuristic lobby of the Guangzhou Opera House.

GUANGZHOU, CHINA

A rising center for the arts

GUIDE

STAY
White Swan Hotel
An 843-room property on Shamian Island with an impressive lobby garden. *86-20/8188-6968; whiteswanhotel.com.* **$$$**

DO
Guangdong Museum
86-20/3804-6886; gdmuseum.com.

Guangzhou New Library
48 Zhongshan Fourth Rd.; 86-20/8334-4408; gzlib.gov.cn.

Guangzhou Opera House
Zhujiang Xi Rd.; 86-20/ 3839-2888; gzdjy.org.

EVEN BY CHINESE STANDARDS, Guangzhou's transformation from gritty industrial port into gleaming metropolis has been lightning-fast. Now the country's third-largest city, 130 miles north of Hong Kong, has become a legitimate player on the international arts stage.

The reason for all the attention? A new cultural complex overlooking the Pearl River that unites cutting-edge architecture and classical treasures. An antique Chinese lacquer box served as inspiration for the Guangdong Museum, designed by Rocco Yim and featuring a light-filled atrium with exquisite ink paintings. (Among the exhibits: dinosaur fossils, centuries-old Buddha figures, and three cannons used to fend off the British during the 19th-century Opium Wars.) Nearby, the zigzag-shaped Guangzhou New Library calls to mind both a towering stack of books and the Chinese character *zhi*. The 10-story structure holds more than 4 million volumes in rooms linked by futuristic skyways.

Most striking of all, however, is the Zaha Hadid–designed Guangzhou Opera House. The contoured building, with its 1,804-seat auditorium and a smaller theater in conjoined granite-and-glass-clad wings, evokes a pair of boulders worn smooth by water. A constellation of twinkling lights glows in the sinuous concert hall, where Spain's National Ballet, the Vienna Boys' Choir, and the London Philharmonic Orchestra have already performed. And the big names keep on coming.

Monks at the Dai Minority Park, in Menghan, a village near Xishuangbanna.

XISHUANGBANNA, CHINA

The next frontier for enlightenment

ROLLING HILLS PLANTED with tea surround ancient Dai villages in remote Xishuangbanna—a corner of southern Yunnan province at the foot of the Himalayas that is still largely overlooked. With dense rain forests, tribal settlements, and China's last remaining wild elephants, it represents a part of the country's heritage that remains timeless and authentic, preserved despite the far-reaching onslaught of urban sprawl.

The prefecture has its share of basic hotels, but the recently opened Anantara Xishuangbanna Resort & Spa has set a new standard for luxury in the region. The gabled retreat—whose 103 rooms are accented with intricate carvings, indigenous woods, and lotus motifs in the marble-and-teak baths—faces the banks of the winding Luosuo River and looks out over the bucolic town of Menglun. At Mekong, one of the resort's five restaurants, the cuisine draws from neighboring Thai influences: lemongrass-roasted snow fish, pineapple sticky rice, and tender steamed chicken with spring onions. It's all served on a riverfront patio.

Hear the chants of Buddhist monks at dawn on a stroll through Manfeilong, a traditional Dai community that feels less Chinese and more like a blend of Thai, Lao, and Burmese cultures. (The area's Dai, Hani, Yi, and other ethnic groups share Southeast Asian ancestry.) Watch the sun rise over an 11th-century pagoda, then visit plantations growing the leaves used to make Yunnan's coveted, smoky Pu-erh tea. Nearby, the 2,200-acre Tropical Botanical Garden has more than 1,000 species, including bamboo, Buddha belly plant, orchids, and jackfruit; lose yourself in its lush canopy, marveling at this undisturbed piece of China.

GUIDE

STAY
Anantara Xishuangbanna Resort & Spa
Menglun; 86-691/871-7777; anantara.com. $$$

DO
Xishuangbanna Tropical Botanical Garden
en.xtbg.ac.cn.

ASIA

241

SRI LANKA

A renaissance in the Indian Ocean

The cool-climate hill towns and pristine beaches of Sri Lanka have long appealed to a certain breed of worldly traveler, but the flare-ups of the country's on-again, off-again, 26-year civil war kept all but the most devoted away. The conflict ended four years ago, and as peace finally takes hold, this teardrop-shaped island is on the cusp of an unexpected tourism boom, with a stylish new batch of hotels for adventure seekers and sybarites alike.

Kandy, Sri Lanka's second-most populous city.

Avani Bentota Resort & Spa

The beach-lined southern coast, centered around the popular town of Bentota, is the country's strongest draw—and big developers have been moving in. The Minor Hotel Group chose the area to debut its sister brand to Anantara with the launch of the 75-room Avani Bentota. Sri Lankan architect Geoffrey Bawa modeled the restored building after an 18th-century Dutch village (a nod to the island's colonial heritage); the coolly contemporary rooms overlook a palm-fringed pool or a sea frequented by suntanned windsurfers. *94-34/227-5353; avanihotels. com.* **$$**

Bar Reef Resort

If Ceylon (as Sri Lanka was once known) did indeed serve as the setting for Robinson Crusoe, then Bar Reef Resort is the best place to summon up that castaway vibe. In the secluded Kalpitiya peninsula, the fuss-free cabanas (there's no running hot water) are set on a one-mile stretch of sand and staffed by local villagers. Nature is the focus: spinner dolphins and sperm whales populate the waters off Alankuda Beach, while the Puttalam lagoon across the isthmus serves as shelter for the rare, manatee-like dugong. *94-77/106-0020; barreef resort.com.* **$**

Maya

Hong Kong interior designer Niki Fairchild turned a century-old manor house into the glamorous Maya, on a two-acre estate outside Tangalle. A tranquil L-shaped pool separates the old and new wings (built 100 years apart); peacocks roam the landscaped grounds, which lead to terraced paddy fields that ripple for miles. The five airy suites (named after trees on the property, such as Amba and Kohomba) have 25-foot ceilings, private courtyards, and four-poster beds from which you can hear the songs of tropical birds. *94-47/567-9025; mayatangallesrilanka.com.* **$**

Ulagalla Resort

Perhaps the biggest peace dividend has been the reopening of the leopard- and elephant-filled Wilpattu National Park, in a secluded part of the northwest. To see it, stay at Ulagalla Resort, composed of 20 thatched-roof bungalows on 58 acres located an hour's drive from the park in an area known as the Cultural Triangle. The eco-hotel strives to maintain its small carbon footprint, with recycled-paddy walls, rainwater showers, an organic garden, and the largest solar farm in the country. Rooms come with private plunge pools; floor-to-ceiling windows overlook a lotus-filled lake. *94-25/567-1000; ulagallaresorts.com.* **$$$**

Villa Bentota

Forty years ago, Geoffrey Bawa turned a decrepit 1880's beach villa into the country's first boutique hotel. Recently, the 15-room property was reimagined by Sri Lankan design guru Shanth Fernando, who renamed it Villa Bentota and added his signature black-and-white stripes to the interiors. Public spaces are especially inviting (frangipani-filled courtyards; a sleek infinity pool; an open-air dining pavilion). Chef Nishantha Liyanage serves up Sri Lankan black pork curry and wasabi-crusted salmon (plus pizzas and salads) at the hotel's streamlined Villa Café, housed in an elegant open-air pavilion. The only thing between you and the beach is an antique railroad track, on which every so often a rickety old locomotive rumbles by with waving passengers on their way to the port town of Galle. *94-34/227-5311; paradiseroadhotels.com.* **$$**

The pool and restaurant at Avani Bentota Resort & Spa. Left: The entryway to one of Bar Reef Resort's villas.

A secluded chalet at Ulagalla Resort. Right: Villa Bentota's Superior suite.

GOA, INDIA

Relaxing pursuits in a party mecca

THERE'S A TRANCELIKE FEELING TO GOA—and that's not even a reference to its hedonistic party scene. This coastal state on the Arabian Sea where international merrymakers descend for all-night raves during the peak months of December and January has a surprisingly serene side. At Nilaya Hermitage, a boutique hotel in the Arpora Hills, hand-cut stone walls curve around a lagoon-like pool, infusing the property with an earthy-chic languor. The 10 guest rooms are furnished with colonial-era antiques from Bombay's Chor Bazaar; the handful of luxe tents have four-poster beds and dressing rooms leading to en suite bathrooms.

Insiders know Goa is rife with shopping finds. In the village of Panjim, Fusion Access— a Portuguese heritage house near the Mandovi River—stocks handcrafted furniture, artifacts, and artwork by the late Goan cartoonist Mario Miranda. Another place not to miss is the Anjuna Flea Market, featuring stalls of tie-dyed sarongs, prayer beads, and local food specialties.

For the most authentic fare in town, however, you'll have to do a little hunting. Tucked into a narrow Latin Quarter alley, the dimly lit Viva Panjim is run by schoolteacher Linda d'Sousa and her husband, who dish up a stellar curried fish fry and a green-chili-garnished chicken *cafreal* (spicy fried chicken). Afterward, follow the revelers to Primrose Café, in Vagator village, where a potent punch—rum, gin, curaçao, fruit juices, and ginger—may be all the impetus you need to dance in the outdoor garden until dawn. This is Goa, after all.

GUIDE

STAY
Nilaya Hermitage
Arpora Bhati;
91-832/227-6793;
nilayahermitage.com. **$$**

EAT
Primrose Café
Vagator Village;
91-832/227-3210. **$**

Viva Panjim
31st January Rd., Panjim;
91-832/242-2405. **$**

SHOP
Fusion Access
Panjim; 91-832/665-
0342; fusionaccess.com.

A view of
Palolem Beach, in
southern Goa.

KOH SAMUI, THAILAND

Can this be paradise?

Daybeds set along the Gulf of Thailand at Banyan Tree Samui.

Above, from left: Shrimp panang curry at the Four Seasons Resort Koh Samui; a pathway on the hotel's grounds.

SOME LOOK IN THE CARIBBEAN. Some search the South Pacific. Others are convinced they'll find it in the Maldives. Or could it be hiding in the Seychelles? Me, I've focused my search on that cerulean-and-green expanse between Indonesia and Indochina, where mangosteens thrive and bamboo is the building material of choice. I've combed the coastlines of the Andaman, Java, and South China seas, hunting for that elusive tropical paradise. Nineteen years ago, for one brief moment, I actually thought I'd found it.

It was the dawn of the Glow Stick Era: late 1993. I was blazing my way across Thailand—Chiang Mai to Chiang Rai, Bangkok to the beach. The question was: which beach? Kayakers went to Ao Phang Nga, snorkelers to Koh Phi Phi. Hat Phra Nang was for cliff divers; Koh Chang drew the nature freaks. Phuket was firmly in the hands of keg-standing lunkheads. Then there was Koh Pha Ngan. If you wanted to skip a rope that was on fire or just freestyle at a Full Moon Party, Pha Ngan was your place.

Alas, the moon was already on the wane as I rode from Bangkok to the coast—and I was too old to skip rope. So I wound up on a boat to Koh Samui.

Koh Samui had no real personality to speak of. But it was by all accounts extremely pretty, with a jungle-draped interior fringed by long, sandy beaches. From the ferry it appeared as a dollop of brilliant green, frosted with creamy white, afloat in a bowl of sapphire blue. I found a family-run guesthouse on Chaweng Beach and stayed for a

week, hardly straying from the path between my bungalow and the sand.

It was no hotbed of culture—but then, most travelers would have already had their dose of that up north. Samui was their reward: a blank slate, defined as much by what it lacked (glow sticks; lunkheads) as by what it had (killer snorkeling; boat trips to a nearby marine park). Who needed flaming jump ropes? Who needed "personality"? Samui was as easy as a summer's day.

The earliest modern-day visitors had arrived in the late sixties—"the First Backpackers," everyone calls them, as if they were talking about the Pilgrims or Lewis and Clark. Given the landscape they encountered, the comparison wasn't so far off: Samui was still remarkably primitive. Roads were rough, where they ran at all. There were no proper hotels; those early vagabond explorers simply flopped down in hammocks on the beach.

As word spread and more travelers arrived, hammocks were replaced by two-buck guesthouses, which in turn gave way to $10 mini-hotels. A tiny airport opened in 1989, and soon mini-hotels made room for maxi-resorts. Despite occasional tensions between locals and tourists, Samui proved an accommodating host.

In 1993, Samui had about 560,000 annual visitors. Today that figure has nearly doubled: almost a million people a year, packed onto an island only 13 miles wide. Scores of hotels now cover the landscape, with increasing numbers on the luxury end. Samui's top-tier resorts rank among the finest in Southeast Asia.

The Banyan Tree occupies a secluded peninsula on the southeastern coast, between Chaweng and Lamai Beach. Its 88 villas are scattered along terraced hillsides that tumble down to a private cove; the highest sit 23 stories above the water. Buggies zip guests up and down vertiginous paths to

Above, from left: Gilded touches in a guest room at Banyan Tree; W Retreat Koh Samui's outdoor WooBar.

the beach, the spa, and the resort's three restaurants. Each villa has its own generously sized infinity pool—lapping at your bedroom door—with views over the lush terrain. There's much to love here: like the easy confidence of your butler, who arranges everything from a half-caf latte to a diving excursion. Or the way the gardeners momentarily stop grooming banana plants or scything back undergrowth and instead smile broadly as you pass. Or the superb spa—where an indefatigable therapist went at my back like it was a sheet of packing bubbles. Best Thai massage I've had in years.

But the real surprise was the W Retreat–Koh Samui, on the island's northern coast. The setting is terrific—on an arrow-shaped headland with a beach along both sides, one facing sunrise and the other sunset; across the bay rises the hazy purple outline of Koh Pha Ngan. One wonders how this plot wasn't snapped up years ago. The suites are airy and spacious and cleverly laid out, with intuitive tech that works, a living area that's actually livable, and an expansive plunge pool. Freestanding stone tubs and outdoor showers are a plus, as are fire-engine-red Illy espresso makers. The mod, youthful vibe carries through to the public areas, where funky amoeba chairs and an outsize Connect 4 game play into the W target demo. And although I'm skeptical of any hotel that thinks it's a nightclub, the W's lobby- and beach-bar stayed on the right side of lively, and the music was not bad.

Both properties show a marked shift in style. Until very recently, Thai resorts made nods to indigenous architecture and design: witness the Four Seasons, with its pitched roofs, sala pavilions, and frangipani-shrouded prayer houses, the embodiment of hotel-as-temple. Samui's newer breed embraces the more secular, urbane-contemporary aesthetic of Singapore and Hong Kong. Their design draws not from the past but from some idealized, pan-Asian future, where there's nary a Buddhist reliquary nor a bolt of Thai silk in sight.

As the east coast fills up with sprawling hotels and villa developments, some locals and expats are fleeing for Samui's rugged southwestern shore. Here it's a whole different island: slower-paced, more traditional—in a word, more Thai. The fishing village of Baan Taling Ngam has even acquired a burgeoning little bohemian community, which gathers at the Five Islands Gallery & Café, tucked inside an 80-year-old wooden house.

I spent a peaceful afternoon there, sipping coffee and sampling house-made ice creams, then drove up the coast to watch the sunset from a near-deserted beach. I lingered late into the evening, savoring the calm. Squid boats began to appear on the darkening horizon, their bow lights glittering like stars. On the hillside behind me, a dog barked, then all went quiet again—until, from somewhere up the shore, came a noisier sound: the pulsing electro-beat of the Black-Eyed Peas. Even here, it seemed, the world was rushing in.

So I walked back to my car, thinking it unlikely that a so-called paradise could exist in this age, what with the thousand rival factions descending on each contender, all clamoring for a piece.

But who knows? Maybe I was wrong.

Maybe it was still out there somewhere—perhaps not so far from where I stood.

Maybe in Koh Lanta.

■ SAMUI'S NEWER BREED OF RESORTS DRAWS NOT FROM THE PAST BUT FROM SOME IDEALIZED, PAN-ASIAN FUTURE.

Adapted from "Can This Be Paradise?" by Peter Jon Lindberg.

GUIDE

STAY
Banyan Tree Samui
99/9 Moo 4, Maret; 800/591-0439; banyantree.com. **$$$$**

Four Seasons Koh Samui
219 Moo 5, Angthong; 800/819-5053; fourseasons.com. **$$$$**

W Retreat–Koh Samui
4/1 Moo 1, Tambol, Maenam; 877/946-8357; whotels.com. **$$$$**

EAT
Five Islands Gallery & Café
34 Moo 3, Tambon Taling Ngam; 66-77/415-360; thefiveislands.com. **$**

DO
Mu Ko Ang Thong National Park
A 42-island archipelago off Samui's northwestern coast with striking rock formations and diverse wildlife. Ask your concierge to advise on boat tours.

BANGKOK

A bargain shopper's nirvana

Packed with authentic surprises at every turn, Chatuchak Weekend Market—one of the largest in the world—sprawls across a staggering 35 acres. More than 15,000 stalls are tucked into narrow *sois* (alleyways) on the city's north side; each Friday they come to riotous life with vendors who hawk seemingly everything under the sun. Rare orchids? Burmese antiques? Exotic animals? Even the hodgepodge trinkets, such as the Zippos left behind by American GI's in Vietnam, are oddly compelling. Here are seven stalls not to miss.

Ajai Silk Art & Décor

You'll find a well-curated collection of handwoven textiles from northeastern Thailand mixed with surprisingly luxe items, like Burmese lacquerware and silk ikat cushions.
No. 137, Soi 1/6, Section 26.

Anyadharu

For a cool reprieve, duck into this air-conditioned oasis filled with soothing natural soaps, perfumes, and essential oils. You can pick up a frangipani-scented candle or a ginger-and-lemongrass sachet, then head to the tiny tearoom in the back for an iced brew.
Nos. 123-124, Soi 3, Section 3.

His & Her Vintage

Weathered white cabinets set the stage for circa-1950's flowered hats and funky eyeglasses, Depression-era dresses, European costume jewelry, and imported frocks from France. There are also old cameras on display. The husband-and-wife team launched their business in Hawaii before moving back to their native Thailand; they recently opened a brick-and-mortar store in Siam Square.
No. 132, Soi 55/1, Section 5.

Lowndoad Me

Tailor-made for the tropics, this jam-packed stall's lightweight linen shirts for men and women come in designs that range from restrained (classic floral pinstripes) to curiously offbeat (polka-dot collars; embroidered cats).
No. 274, Soi 46/1, and No. 284, Soi 46/2, Section 3.

Luksom

Venture to the western edge of the market and quench your thirst at this diminutive stand, where Uncle Ed (as he's known to everyone) makes tart juice to order from Thailand's native green-skinned oranges.
No. 89, Soi 38/2, Section 2.

Pariwat A-nantachina

The gregarious 30-year-old graphic designer showcases his colorful works—including eye-popping 3-D illustrations—at his namesake gallery in the market. A graduate of Bangkok University's School of Fine and Applied Arts, A-nantachina is also known for his panoramic photo collages of the city's street life, which have been exhibited at such high-profile locations as the Alliance Française de Bangkok, a French-Thai language and culture society.
No. 118, Soi 3, Section 7.

R.S.T. Spices

Second-generation spice-monger Surasak Thepa-armonkit scours the country for his delicious merchandise. Take home the zesty lemongrass tea, fragrant white cardamom, or the vacuum-packed green curry paste (the simplest way to cook Thailand's national dish on your own turf).
No. 192, Soi 4, Section 25.

Left: Enjoying a bowl of *mapraw hawn*, a traditional dish of coconut ice cream served in half of the fruit's shell.

Anyadharu's scented candles. Left: One of the many food vendors at Chatuchak market.

Pariwat A-nantachina inside his gallery. Right: Linen shirts for sale at Lowndoad Me.

The Banteay
Srei temple
at Angkor.

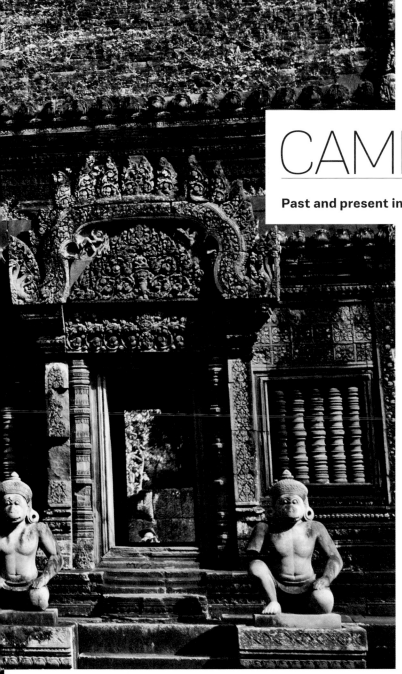

CAMBODIA

Past and present in a forever-changed land

SOME THIRTY YEARS AGO, a traveler arriving in Phnom Penh by air would see a landscape of rice paddies dotted with palm trees, a pastoral image in a parallel universe. But the Khmer Rouge was still in control of much of the country, and the vision was synonymous with memories of Agent Orange and land mines. Today, Phnom Penh is a city teeming with energy and enterprise. There are skyscrapers, high-end hotels and restaurants, hip coffee shops and galleries. What once felt like the drop edge of the world is now a place of opportunity.

The Raffles Hotel Le Royal is but one symbol of this transformation. The storied French-colonial structure, where Charlie Chaplin and Jackie Kennedy were once guests, was left in disarray after the Khmer Rouge takeover, but a revamp by the Raffles Group reinstated its sepia-tinged glamour. Across town in the former Quartier Français, overlooking the river, another colonial-era building was reborn as the Chinese House, a festive bar and restaurant popular with the city's youth. Just getting there is joyous mayhem—at night, the quay throbs with colored lights, food vendors, and groups of people partaking in what seems like an outdoor dance party.

These changes stand in stark contrast to the unaltered environment in Siem Reap province, four hours to the north. The scale of Angkor Wat is both monumental and oddly soothing; viewed from above, the temples seem like a tiny ark in an ocean of jungle. Ta Prohm, a 15-minute *tuk-tuk* ride from Angkor Wat, is akin to a modern-day Atlantis— a setting from myth. Enormous trees have grown over the carvings like a forest that descended from the sky. Giant roots drip down over the structures like candle wax. It feels like a metaphor for the unbelievable complications of telling stories about Cambodia, a place where a dark history has unfolded against a landscape as gentle as a dream.

GUIDE

STAY
Raffles Le Royal
Phnom Penh
92 Rukhak Vithei Daun Penh, Sangkat Wat, Phnom Penh; 800/768-9009; raffles.com. **$$$**

Sojourn Boutique Villas
A gorgeous oasis just outside Angkor and Ta Prohm, staffed by locals from a rural village nearby. *Treak Village Rd., Siem Reap; 855-12/923-137; sojournsiemreap.com.* **$**

EAT
Chinese House
45 Sisowath Quay, *Phnom Penh; 855-23/991-514; chinesehouse.asia.* **$$**

DO
Angkor Archaeological Park
Siem Reap Province; whc.unesco.org.

HO CHI MINH CITY, VIETNAM

A repository of undeniable finds

Imagining a trip to Vietnam invariably summons visions of the purchases that await: custom clothing, one-of-a-kind colonial curios. But expectations often fizzle upon arrival in Ho Chi Minh City (a.k.a. Saigon), thanks to the tchotchke-filled stores that fail to impress on prime Dong Khoi Street. Your best bet? Forgo the well-trammeled corridors for lesser-known addresses where affordable discoveries do justice to the city's reputation as a retail paradise.

Catherine Denoual Maison
Former Parisian fashion editor Catherine Denoual has found her second calling as the doyenne of the perfectly kitted boudoir. Her boutique features delicately embroidered sateen bed linens in chocolates, golds, and caramels.
Saigon Centre, 65 Le Loi Blvd., District 1; 84-8/3914-0269.

Gaya
The white-on-white Modernist building makes a dramatic first impression (yes, those are giant fountain-pen nibs on the façade). Inside, you'll find the best haute souvenirs in all of Saigon. Highlights include Michele de Albert's high-gloss lacquer bowls and trays in psychedelic colors.
1 Nguyen Van Trang St., District 1; 84-8/3925-1495.

Kin Boutique
Many 24-hour tailors hawk cheap silk *ao dai* tunics and promise to copy your Prada sheaths overnight. Instead, follow in-the-know expats to Kin Boutique, where Nguyen Cong Tri designs runway-worthy frocks at ready-to-wear prices. Just don't expect a quick turnaround: it will take up to 10 days and a couple of fittings (shipping is available).
198 Le Thanh Ton St.; 84-8/3502-3090.

L'Usine
Set in a 19th-century garment factory, L'Usine is a light-filled space that houses a café, a gallery, and a bevy of casual-cool clothing labels found only in Vietnam—even a selection of vintage bikes.
151/1 Dong Khoi St., District 1; 84-8/6674-3565.

Massimo Ferrari
For dapper bespoke men's wear—think of New York's Seize Sur Vingt—look for this narrow boutique. Custom-made cotton shirts come with a dozen collar options; chic patchwork pants, deconstructed seersucker jackets, and Hermès-style purple suede loafers offer the urban dandy plenty of choice. An ideal gift for any new baby: crisp white Mao-collared pajamas with frog closures.
42A-1 Tran Quoc St., District 3; 84-8/3930-6213.

Than Thuy
This unassuming shop is heaven for parents of little girls— packed to the rafters in adorable gingham dresses with Peter Pan collars, plaid jumpers, and eyelet nightgowns, all of which are stitched and smocked by hand.
93 Le Thanh Ton St., District 1; 84-8/3822-4893.

Verlim Interior Design
Verlim Interiors abounds with Deco-themed antiques. Visitors fall for the mahogany club chairs and oversize glazed-ceramic lamps; the lacquer tea caddies are luggage-friendly alternatives in oxblood or robin's-egg blue.
152 Le Lai St., District 1; 84-8/3925-3648.

Villa Anupa
Finding it is a challenge. Even harder is deciding which of Anupa Horvil's butter-soft leather bags should come home with you: the white hobo or the metallic-gray clutch? Resort caftans in orange, sapphire, and ikat patterns are ideal for the beach-bound.
17/27 Le Thanh Ton St., District 1; 84-8/3825-7307.

Afternoon tea in L'Usine's airy downstairs café.

Lacquer bowls for
sale at Gaya.
Above: Catherine
Denoual Maison's
whitewashed space.

An employee
modeling
Kin Boutique's
fashions. Above:
A painting on
display at Verlim
Interior Design.

NINH BINH, VIETNAM

A breathtaking detour from the urban bustle

WITH ITS OTHERWORLDLY LANDSCAPE, the northern province of Ninh Binh has been dubbed "Halong Bay on land." But unlike the famed UNESCO World Heritage site, it isn't yet on the main tourist beat, despite being only a 90-minute drive from Hanoi; the region's towering stone karsts and ancient caves remain an insider's secret.

Lacking a high-end place to stay, the area had attracted mostly backpackers or adventurous day-trippers from the capital. That changed with the opening of the Emeralda Resort & Spa, a collection of 172 rustic-luxe villas on 40 acres. Rooms have expansive platform beds, terra-cotta floors, and claw-foot tubs; the organic restaurant serves such local specialties as *bo la lot* (beef wrapped in pepper leaf) made with produce from the garden. Next door, the Van Long Nature Reserve is a postcard-perfect slice of the Vietnamese countryside, with lush rice paddies and wetlands traversed by bamboo boats.

A few miles from the resort lies Ninh Binh's main draw—the Trang An Grottoes. A rowboat takes you from the jetty on a two-hour loop along its waterways, gliding by karsts and pagodas and past a series of rock faces into low-hanging caves. A short ride farther down the road brings you to Hoa Lu, Vietnam's 10th-century capital. Although little of the original citadel remains, you can explore two temples and climb a hill to view the tomb of Emperor Dinh Tien Hoang, the leader of the Dinh dynasty. It's a 15-minute ascent up a steep set of stairs, but the vista is worth it—as stunning as it was more than 1,000 years ago, when this tranquil spot in the countryside was the seat of Vietnam's power.

GUIDE

STAY
Emeralda Resort & Spa
Tap Ninh Hamlet,
Gia Van Commune,
Gia Vien District;
84-303/658-333;
emeraldaresort.com. **$**

Ancient rock formations in Ninh Binh's Van Long Nature Reserve.

The low-key
outdoor patio at
Wild Oats,
in Punggol Park.

SINGAPORE

Tasting your way through an endlessly colorful culture

T WAS NEARLY MIDNIGHT, BUT MANY OF the tables around me at the East Coast Lagoon Food Village were still full. Families lingered over sticky charred skewers of Malay *satay* and platters of Hokkien *mee*, fried noodles slicked with prawn broth, brightened by a stir of chili sauce and a last-minute squeeze of sweet calamansi limes. Kids draped their legs over wooden benches and beat the heat with bowls of *cendol,* a slushy shaved-ice treat.

I considered the relative tranquillity of the scene. Where the hawker stalls and tables ended, the beach began, invisible in the moonless dark. This is not a city that generally encourages quiet reflection. But here at this open-air food court, the city felt more relaxed, intimate, at ease with itself. Uncles and aunties, as everyone calls the older hawkers, stirred woks, fanned charcoal grills, and pressed juice from sugarcane. Late-arriving night snackers passed from stand to stand, hunting alone like owls or ordering in packs.

In Singapore, it's never too late (or too early or too hot or busy or inconvenient or too anything at all) to search for something good to eat. And to earnestly savor it, whether it costs $3 for humble chicken rice at a hawker center like this one, or a hundred times that at Tippling Club, one of the high priced chef-y places of the moment.

Singapore is known as a city of composure, safety; it's a model of the high-functioning modern economic center. But beneath all that is a kinetic energy. The morning after my visit to the food court, I drank iced ginger tea and waited for a chef named Willin Low to pick me up for the day's private tutorial in How to Eat Like a Local. Low is an ideal guide. Like many Singaporeans, he's equally at home at hawker stalls and the globalized brand-name restaurants that have come with the arrival of luxury hotels and casinos. More important, he's a pioneer of the middle ground: his restaurant, Wild Rocket, introduced the city to the concept of dressed-up Singaporean

Hokkien *mee* (fried noodles) at the Maxwell Road Hawker Center. Above: Chef André Chiang at work in Restaurant André's kitchen.

home-style food, as conceived by a former lawyer who taught himself to cook to fend off homesickness and hunger while at school in London.

Our first stop: Maxwell Road Hawker Center for chicken rice at Tian Tian. Chicken rice is the quintessential comfort food of Singapore, humble but exalted—what the unadorned omelette is to the French or the margherita pizza to the Neapolitans. Because it's so simple (poached and blanched chicken; rice moistened with stock and dark soy sauce; a bowl of broth on the side) there is no room for error and infinite room for debate. "If you ask ten Singaporeans about the best chicken rice, you will get ten different answers," Low said, pleased. "This is one of the few places in the world where while we're eating lunch, we are discussing where to go for lunch tomorrow—because we've already planned dinner for sure."

Obviously cities everywhere love their food. What distinguishes Singapore, Low says, is the diversity of cultural (and, by extension, culinary) influence. The population is Chinese, Malay, Indian, and Eurasian, new immigrants and old. What makes the place compelling for travelers who like to eat is that notions of authenticity blur and bend in the transforming heat of the melting pot. Take those Hokkien *mee*: Chinese noodles with a Malay sambal chili sauce and the addition of fried cubes of lard and limes. "The whole thing is just very Singaporean," Low says. "We travel so much, so we're receptive to change." The Singaporization of flavors leads to compelling local variants. "You'll find Chinese crullers dipped in Indonesian peanut sauce and Chinese people doing their own twist on Malay *satay*," a friend had told me. "They'll add five-spice or saffron to the marinade or use pork because they can."

Having established the base knowledge, Low continued our lessons all over town. We paid a visit to an old-school Fuzhou-Chinese place, called

Above, from left: Bartenders at the Tippling Club; a shaved-ice *cendol* from Wild Oats.

Singapura Seafood Restaurant, on the second floor of a government-housing building. It looked a bit like the "Oriental" banquet restaurants in midsize American cities in the 1970's. And for Low it conjured the same sort of nostalgia. "This is the kind of restaurant my grandparents would take us to for a treat," he said. The recipes—including a breaded pork liver on baby kale—belonged to owner Valerie Tang's father, and they were worth preserving.

■ IN SINGAPORE IT'S NEVER TOO LATE (OR TOO EARLY OR TOO HOT OR INCONVENIENT) TO SEARCH FOR SOMETHING GOOD TO EAT.

At the Singapore Food Trail, a hawker center beneath the Singapore Flyer (a gigantic Ferris wheel similar to London's Eye), the stalls have been constructed to look like 1960's pushcarts. Singaporeans come by their fusion food honestly: we ate *satay bee hoon*, a dish of Chinese rice vermicelli covered in a Malay peanut sauce. "I want you to try an oyster omelette," Low said. A loose scramble of eggs and oysters with a fish sauce and vinegary chili sauce, it was fortifying and salty and good.

We ate more and sweated more, and then the world seemed to sweat, too: the bright sky filled with hot afternoon rain. We got back in the car, and Chet Baker sang "Time After Time," and we drove somewhere else and somehow ate more.

One afternoon I found myself transported to the upstairs dining room of Restaurant André, a tiny, serene, white-and-gray cloud of a place, a million miles away from the frenetic world outside. Rather than a traditional menu, chef André Chiang presents diners with his "octa-philosophy," a series of moods or rubrics (Pure, Memory, *Terroir*, etc.). Born in Taiwan and raised and trained in France, Chiang makes French food with hints of Asian influence: tomato sorbet with cured fluke and black seaweed alongside purple sea-urchin risotto and a tartare of razor clams; a foie gras custard topped with a liquid-y truffle jelly that tasted like an earthy Perigordian *chawan mushi*.

From restaurants like André and Fifty Three (a well-choreographed, minimally designed dining room, this one from another homegrown chef and lapsed lawyer, Michael Han), I learned that visitors to Singapore needn't seek out the international Michelin crew from the casino restaurants to have a transportingly good, high-toned meal.

Han has *staged* at Noma and Mugaritz. He tends to his herb plants and edible flowers in the weedy lot next to his restaurant. He takes the whole fine-dining thing seriously. But true to the Singaporean code, he doesn't discriminate on either end of the culinary spectrum. On his night off he drove me out to the old red-light district of Geylang, and we parked ourselves on red plastic chairs on the sidewalk outside the Sin Huat Eating House. "To be really authentic it has to be just a little bit dirty," Han said. We went to the kitchen to pick out the crabs we wanted variously barbecued and wok-fried with noodles. A cook reached into a bucket and retrieved a very large bullfrog, British racing green with a slick underbelly and intelligent black eyes. I felt bad for the big guy, but in the spirit of the city, we'd be eating everything that night.

Adapted from "The New Food Capital," by Adam Sachs.

GUIDE

STAY
Fullerton Bay
On a historic 1930's pier, 100 rooms kitted up in rosewood, leather, and chrome. *80 Collier Quay; 65/6333-8388; fullerton bayhotel.com.* **$$$**

Raffles Hotel
A magnet for A-listers, with 103 colonial-themed suites. *1 Beach Rd.; 800/768-9009; raffles.com.* **$$$**

EAT
East Coast Lagoon
Food Village
1220 East Coast Park Hwy.

Fifty Three
53 Armenian St.; 65/6334-5535; fiftythree.com.sg. **$$$$**

Maxwell Road
Hawker Center
Maxwell Rd. at Neil Rd.

Restaurant André
41 Bukit Pasoh Rd.; 65/6534-8880; restaurantandre.com. **$$$$$**

Singapore Food Trail
30 Raffles Ave.

Singapura Seafood
Restaurant
01-31 Selegie Rd.; 65/6336-3255; singapuraseafood.com. **$**

Sin Huat Eating House
659 Geylang Rd.; 65/6744-9755. **$$**

Tippling Club
8D Dempsey Rd.; 65/6475-2217; tipplingclub.com. **$$$$**

Wild Rocket
Hangout Hotel, 10A Upper Wilkie Rd.; 65/6339-9448; wildrocket.com.sg. **$$$**

PANGLAO, PHILIPPINES

A secret beach for intrepid travelers

IT TAKES A BIT OF EFFORT to reach Panglao, a blissful speck off the southwestern corner of Bohol Island (one of more than 7,000 in the Philippine archipelago). The payoff, however, is worth the journey—an hourlong flight from Manila and a 25-minute drive to the Ananyana Beach Resort & Spa. Along a mile of sugary sand, the 12 luxe thatched-roof huts are set in a tropical garden threaded with stone paths. Local artisans crafted most of the furnishings, including abaca chairs and bamboo-framed beds. The open-air restaurant puts a Mediterranean twist on traditional Filipino dishes (order the penne with pork adobo).

Tempting as it is to lie on the beach all day, outsize adventures await. A trip to the Chocolate Hills—a surreal geological wonder of more than 1,000 domelike mounds—lives up to every expectation. Hop a resort boat to spot dolphins and dive with barracudas, or bring a packed lunch for a beach picnic on deserted Puntod Island. Nearby, the restaurant at the Bohol Bee Farm serves traditional dishes with organic ingredients grown on site. End your meal as a local would: by ordering the house-made *ube* (purple yam) ice cream, a concoction every bit as exotic as your surroundings.

The palm-fringed pool area at Ananyana Beach Resort & Spa.

GUIDE

STAY
Ananyana Beach
Resort & Spa
Doljo Beach; 63-38/502-8101; ananyana.com. **$$**

DO
Bohol Bee Farm
Dao, Dauis; 63-38/502-2288; boholbeefarm.com. **$$**

AUSTRALIA+ NEW ZEALAND+ ANTARCTICA

Lifeguards calling in the surf report at Bondi Beach, in Sydney.

The dinner rush at Garagistes, in Hobart.

TASMANIA, AUSTRALIA

The next great epicurean destination

Stackings at Peppermint Bay's poached hapuku fillet. Below: The entrance to the Source Restaurant.

K

NOWN FOR ITS WILD BEAUTY, Australia's southernmost state supplies some of the country's finest ingredients—from apples to abalone. Recently, however, the remote and rugged island has also become a playground for young, food-mad chefs from Sydney and Melbourne, who are striving to keep the remarkable bounty closer to home by heading up kitchens in and around Hobart, Tasmania's capital. The result? This rough-around-the-edges city with a real pioneer vibe is suddenly brimming with good things to eat.

THE ALL-DAY CAFÉ

Breakfast at the Pigeon Hole Café—an adorable bolt-hole stuffed with flea-market furniture, fresh-baked bread, and pristine produce—means crusty sourdough, baked eggs with *jamón serrano*, fresh spinach, and a *macchiato* as expertly made as any in Rome. Although it's set on a quiet residential stretch in West Hobart, the café attracts a young, rakish crowd who spend hours lost in thick books and laptops, fueled on caffeine and sweet treats. Jay Patey, a transplant from Queensland who founded the café with barista Emma Choraziak, might pop out of the tiny kitchen to examine a neighbor's stash of fruit—peaches, lemons, and plums—which he'll turn into jam or filling for the impossibly flaky *crostate*. His famous hazelnut meringues are only available on Saturdays. Arrive early—they sell out fast.

THE CULTURAL TABLE

The Museum of Old & New Art may be the big news out of Tassie these days, but the Source Restaurant—housed in MONA's glass-wrapped upstairs pavilion—is making headlines of its own. Chef Philippe Leban, who was born in Brittany and raised in Sydney, draws on locavore-friendly ingredients to create the region's most refined dishes (roasted duck in coffee sauce; oysters from

Adams Bay served with spanner crab meat, foie gras, and Pedro Ximénez sherry gelée), all set against a stunning Derwent River backdrop. He also grows his own herbs and produce in the restaurant's garden. On your way out, pick up a few bottles of Moorilla wine, made on site by Canadian vintner Conor van der Reest. The winery, one of Tasmania's oldest, produces dynamic cuvées with art-themed labels on every bottle. Then retire to one of the geometric, glass-and-steel guest rooms located on MONA's grounds.

THE DESSERT EMPORIUM

If there's one vexing problem with Alistair Wise's diminutive spot, Sweet Envy, it's the "What do I order?" paralysis it inspires as you walk in the door. Before you can decide between the salted caramels, French nougat, chocolate bonbons, and *tuiles,* a young salesgirl may dare you to take the "cupcake challenge"—devour it in 60 seconds

or less, and the frosted concoction is free (it doesn't seem particularly difficult until you hear about the "no-hands" stipulation). Wise, a Tasmanian native who worked as a pastry chef at Gordon Ramsay at the London, in New York City, uses fresh fruit to concoct Willy Wonka–esque ice cream flavors such as Guinness with blackberry and white beer with peach. On the go? Keep an eye out for Wise's soon-to-launch ice cream truck, a 1964 Commer Karrier named Big Bessie that he personally restored.

THE DESTINATION LUNCH SPOT

Don't bother renting a car. In just one hour, a 75-foot catamaran (courtesy of the restaurant) takes you down the coast from Hobart to Stackings at Peppermint Bay, a soaring metal-and-glass gastro-temple. Chef David Moyle—a recent arrival from Byron Bay's Beach Hotel—enthusiastically embraces the foraging zeitgeist

Above, from left: Pigeon Hole Café's eggs *en cocotte;* **a view of the sea from a patio at Stackings at Peppermint Bay.**

with three- and five-course lunch menus that are improvised daily, highlighting whatever is at its peak: sea lettuce that Moyle plucked from the shoreline, tart Kentish Red cherries from the trees of a friend, or wild garlic gathered along country roads.

THE GASTROPUB

Crowded with a rotating cast of regulars nursing their pints, the New Sydney Hotel is a working-class pub in Hobart that dates from 1835. But across from the beer signs and dinged license plates is a blackboard that reveals 21st-century offerings. Chef John Wiseman stocks his menu with dishes of Spanish-style blood sausage accompanied by a red-onion aioli and crisp goat shoulder with chickpeas, pumpkin, and watercress, and lamb breast with almonds and mint. Sometimes you'll find local game (possum and wallaby) and, in winter, bowls of risotto with shaved Tasmanian truffles. Try one of the restaurant's infused beers, such as the spiced porter with ginger and chiles made using the region's first "hopinator," an oddball brewing contraption.

THE HAUTE FARMSTAND

If there's a poster child for Tasmania's new food pilgrims, Matthew Evans is it. In 2005, he retired from his position as a restaurant critic for the *Sydney Morning Herald* and moved to the island, determined to learn farming. His *Green Acres*–style experiment, chronicled in books and on the Australian reality show *Gourmet Farmer*, gave rise to A Common Ground, a tiny shop near Hobart's waterfront. Every square inch of shelf and floor space is devoted to made-in-Tasmania products—pickled walnuts, bespoke chocolate bars, truffled honey, and saffron. Handmade sausages and rillettes (some from pigs Evans reared himself) sit alongside cheeses created by Nick Haddow, a partner in the store and owner of the Bruny Island Cheese Company; ask for a sample of the intense Raw Milk C2. In keeping with the local focus, the shop hosts long-table lunches in the countryside—in a paddock, say, or a potato field—where diners are often joined by the farmers who grew their food.

THE URBAN WINE BAR

Judging by its black-clad kitchen brigade and industrial-loft vibe, Garagistes could be a burgeoning hot spot in New York or London. A haunch of ham and other artisanal salumi hang in a showcase cooler; the modern wooden furniture is handmade by area craftsmen. The perennially packed restaurant takes its name from its setting: an airy converted Volkswagen garage with scuffed brick, exposed beams, and an open kitchen that overlooks rows of communal tables in the dining room. Here, chef Luke Burgess, a former food and travel photographer, prepares small plates that are complex and obsessively local. The house-cured Wagyu brisket—which melts on the tongue—comes from cattle grass-fed on a small island off Tassie's northwestern coast. If you can't snag a seat right away (the case more often than not), wait it out at Sidecar, a cozy annex bar that Burgess and his partners opened to help ease the restaurant's nightly bottleneck.

Adapted from "Homegrown Australia," by Jay Cheshes.

GUIDE

STAY

MONA Pavilions
Museum of Old & New Art, 655 Main Rd., Berriedale; 61-3/6277-9900; mona.net.au. **$$$$$**

EAT

A Common Ground
Shop 3, Salamanca Arts Centre, 77 Salamanca Place, Hobart; 61-4/2937-0192; acommonground.com.au.

Garagistes
103 Murray St., Hobart; 61-3/6231-0558; garagistes.com.au. **$$$**

New Sydney Hotel
87 Bathurst St., Hobart; 61-3/6234-4516; newsydneyhotel.com.au. **$$$**

Pigeon Hole Café
93 Goulburn St., West Hobart; 61-3/6236-9306; pigeonholecafe.com.au. **$$**

Source Restaurant
Museum of Old & New Art, 655 Main Rd., Berriedale; 61-3/6277-9904; mona.net.au. **$$$$**

Stackings at Peppermint Bay
3435 Channel Hwy., Woodbridge; 61-3/6267-4088; peppermintbay.com.au. **$$$**

Sweet Envy
341 Elizabeth St., North Hobart; 61-3/6234-8805; sweetenvy.com. **$$**

MELBOURNE

Shop-hopping on an up-and-coming block

Once merely an off-the-beaten-path strip in the Northcote neighborhood, High Street has become a new hub for Melbourne's creative crowd, with a mix of bohemian-cool businesses. You'll find one-of-a-kind fashion boutiques, live music venues, and a destination restaurant—all of which make this eclectic block well worth the four-mile trip from the city center.

At the bar inside Northcote Social Club.

Estelle Bar & Kitchen

This kitschy-chic restaurant-bar might be the buzziest dinner spot in town. Chefs Ryan Flaherty—a disciple of Heston Blumenthal and Ferran Adrià— and Scott Pickett, who trained under British toque Phil Howard, turn out experimental dishes such as coffee-cured raw salmon and cauliflower sausage with cumin-infused mousse. The classic cocktail menu (grapefruit-flavored gin fizz, anyone?) is the ideal prelude to the adventurous three- to nine-course tasting menus, which feature house-smoked meats (don't miss the pork-and-carrot terrine) and kangaroo fillets.
243 High St.; 61-3/9489-4609; estellebarkitchen.com.au. **$$$**

Flashback Fabric & Wallpaper

In-the-know stylists rave about Flashback Fabric & Wallpaper, the go-to source for vintage materials and wall coverings of every stripe. Among the merchandise: cotton paisley dress fabric from the 1960's; Miró-inspired wallpaper; and bold disco-era velvet upholstery. Retro lampshades and A-line

skirts emblazoned with acoustic guitars reinforce the groovier-than-thou atmosphere.
79 High St.; 61-3/9482-1899; flashbackfabric.com.au.

Hummingbird 60

Nature-themed murals by Melbourne artist Belinda Suzette add a feminine touch to Hummingbird 60's light-filled space, stocked with hard-to-find labels like Sadie and Piper Lane. Run by sisters Penelope Tsoukalis and Kathy Panopoulos, the boutique carries quirky limited-edition jewelry, flouncy dresses, and Aussie children's brands, plus the Scandinavian clogs that have become de rigueur footwear for the city's fashion set.
244 High St.; 61-3/9486-6778; hummingbird60.com.au.

I Dream a Highway

Hand-printed totes and knit hats—plus other crafty accessories such as earrings made from comic-book pages—are the stock-in-trade at the diminutive I Dream a Highway. Women cull from clothing by funky Australian designers Nancy Bird and Surface Art; men drop by for the store's signature

brand of checkered western shirts and Status Anxiety wallets. The music collection, however, is equal opportunity. Don't leave without sifting the racks for local bands like alt-rockers Downhills Home.
259 High St.; 61-3/9481-8858; idreamahighway.com.au.

Northcote Social Club

This no-frills performance venue showcases emerging indie acts and underground musicians playing everything from melodic surf pop to banjo- and-mandolin folk rock. Between sets, head to the outdoor beer garden for such

satisfying pub grub as kangaroo burgers and fish-and-chips.
301 High St.; 61-3/9489-3917; northcotesocialclub.com. **$$**

Retro Active

Midcentury Modern furnishings (think Danish oak chairs with woven-cord seats and 1950's sea-themed wall lamps from Italy) and accessories are the draw at Retro Active; there's also an emphasis on homegrown talent with pieces from designer Fred Lowen's Fler & Tessa line and Australian brands like Parker and Summertone.
307 High St.; 61-3/9489-4566; retroactive.net.au.

Pimm's Cup cocktails at Estelle Bar & Kitchen. Left: A street view of the restaurant.

Women's fashions at Hummingbird 60. Right: Flashback Fabric & Wallpaper's vibrant prints.

Kicking
back at the
waterfront
Pinetrees
Lodge.

272

LORD HOWE ISLAND, AUSTRALIA

An overlooked sliver of sun and sand

A CLOSE-KEPT SECRET among the cognoscenti, this tiny Pacific Ocean isle—where tourists are capped at 400, streetlights are a rarity, and most people get around on bicycles—is an easy two-hour flight from Sydney. (It's also a favored vacation spot for Aussie-bred film star Eric Bana.) Brooding basalt-stack mountains plunge directly into the sea, the remnants of a volcanic eruption 7 million years ago that gave rise to the entire archipelago. For jaw-dropping views, follow guide Jack Shick of Sea to Summit Expeditions through banyan and palm forests on a challenging 10-hour hike up 2,870-foot Mount Gower. Down below, snorkelers have the run of a long and vibrant coral reef tucked into a brilliant blue lagoon.

But you didn't come to the so-called "last paradise on earth" simply to exert yourself. Book a stay at the chic Capella Lodge, which sits atop Lovers Bay on the island's southern end. The nine-room retreat—owned by James and Hayley Baillie, whose other property is Kangaroo Island's celebrated Southern Ocean Lodge—is known for its spa. (Aching from the rigorous ascent? Opt for the Gower's Foot Therapy, which features a cooling wrap of Tasmanian kelp and native pepper berry.) Or check in to the low-key Pinetrees Lodge, which has been run by the same family since 1848. It's the kind of place where the chef hangs ten during his lunch break.

GUIDE

STAY

Capella Lodge
*61-2/9918-4355;
lordhowe.com;
all-inclusive.* **$$$$**

Pinetrees Lodge
*61-2/9262-6585;
pinetrees.com.au;
all-inclusive.* **$$$**

DO

Sea to Summit
Expeditions
*61-2/6563-2218;
lordhoweislandtours.net;
daylong hike $50.*

AUSTRALIAN BEACHES

Have bathing suit, will travel

In a country bounded by some 31,000 miles of coastline, beaches take pride of place. From far-flung hideaways to see-and-be-seen hot spots, here are six of Oz's ultimate stretches.

The morning scene on Sydney's Bondi Beach.

Bells Beach, Torquay

Two hours southwest of Melbourne along the Great Ocean Road, expert surfers ride huge breaks against a backdrop of craggy cliffs. Once a year, international wave chasers make the pilgrimage to Torquay for the Rip Curl Pro, the longest-running surfing competition in the world. You can learn from the best at Torquay Surf Academy *(34A Bell St., Torquay; 61-3/ 5261-2022; torquaysurf.com.au; lessons from $120)*. If sticking to shore is more your speed, head here from June through August, when southern right whales migrate through these waters.

Bondi Beach, Sydney

Just 20 minutes from downtown Sydney, this half-mile crescent is the fulcrum around which the city—with its enviable work-life ratio and dominant beach culture—revolves. Australia's most famous golden swath bustles with surfers, families, and scenesters jockeying for position among the open-air cafés. If the ocean gets too crowded, opt for a dip in the seawater pool at Bondi Icebergs *(1 Notts Ave., Sydney; 61-2/9130-3120; icebergs.com. au)*, the venerable swimming club on a cliff overlooking the ocean.

Cable Beach, Broome

Adventurous types take the 2½-hour flight from Perth to Western Australia's exotic pearl-farming port for this 13-mile sweep of white shore. From March to October, watch for the natural phenomenon known as Staircase to the Moon—small waves rippling over mudflats to create the illusion of silver steps ascending to the sky. Hole up at the Cable Beach Club *(1 Cable Beach Rd., Cable Beach; 61-8/ 9192-0400; cablebeachclub.com; $$)*, a garden retreat with Bali-inspired décor. Staff can arrange for you to view fossilized dinosaur footprints or join a 15-camel sunset caravan with Ships of the Desert *(61-419/954-022; shipsofthedesert.com.au; 30-minute tours $31 per person)*.

Four Mile Beach, Port Douglas

This pristine arc of coastline along Queensland's Great Barrier Reef is the getaway of choice for the stealth-wealth set. The white-on-white Peppers Beach Club *(20-22 Davidson St., Port Douglas; 61-7/4087-1000; peppers.com.au; $$)* makes a perfect base on steamy summer days, with its lagoon-style swimming pool, deep soaking tubs, and spa with specially designed Vichy water treatments. Craving an adrenaline rush? Cruise through crocodile-laden rivers in nearby Daintree National Park, or soar in a hot-air balloon over the rain forest.

Watego's Beach, Byron Bay

Hippies and artists used to run this former whaling town, located a two-hour drive from Brisbane and known for its gentle, dolphin-filled surf. But Byron Bay has evolved into a sybaritic getaway, thanks to an influx of fashion-industry players who love the calm breaks and yoga devotees who practice on the hard-packed sand. Byron at Byron's 92 spacious rooms *(77-97 Broken Head Rd., Suffolk Park; 61-2/6639-2000; thebyronatbyron.com.au; $$$)* are connected by a series of wooden boardwalks that cut through 45 acres of jungle.

Wineglass Bay, Tasmania

Nature lovers flock to this flawless beach on the island's eastern end to view wallabies and Tasmanian devils in their true habitat. There's just one place to stay, but it's a stunner: the glass-and-steel Saffire Freycinet *(2352 Coles Bay Rd., Coles Bay; 61-3/6256-7888; saffire-freycinet.com.au; $$$$$)*, a 20-villa architectural jewel in a eucalyptus forest fringing Great Oyster Bay. The hotel's epicurean focus makes for memorable guide-led excursions, including harvesting oysters on a working marine farm and observing a cooking demonstration by chef Hugh Whitehouse.

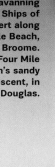

Overlooking the pool at Bondi Icebergs, on Bondi Beach. Left: Catching a wave off Bells Beach, in Torquay.

Caravanning with Ships of the Desert along Cable Beach, in Broome. Left: Four Mile Beach's sandy crescent, in Port Douglas.

A view of
Wairau Valley
vineyards, in
Marlborough.

MARLBOROUGH, NEW ZEALAND

South Island's secret wine enclave

OTHERWORLDLY LAKES, ALPINE GLACIERS, and snowcapped mountains have established New Zealand as the go-to destination for extreme-sports enthusiasts. But a new group of travelers is making inroads into South Island's sunny Marlborough province, quietly renowned for its crisp Sauvignon Blancs and fruit-forward Pinot Noirs.

The town of Blenheim, in the Wairau Valley, is a good jumping-off point into the area, with plentiful restaurants, wine bars, and hotels. Drop your bags at the stylish 11-room Hotel d'Urville, within the 1920's Art Deco Public Trust building, then set out for the vineyards, which stretch for miles to the mountains. Two of the region's best assets lie across the road from each other: Allan Scott—where standouts include a citrusy 2009 Riesling and a subtle Prestige Chardonnay from 2011—and Cloudy Bay, the first winery in Marlborough to export Sauvignon Blanc. Now owned by Moët Hennessy, the latter is increasingly known for its celebrated selection of Riesling, Chardonnay, Pinot Noir, and sparkling wine.

From there, it's a short but steep ride to Highfield Estate, off State Highway 6 and up a narrow farm road flanked by hundreds of vine tresses. Highfield is more than a winery—it's also a restaurant and a one-room B&B. Savor a glass of the 2011 Sauvignon Blanc with a hearty seafood-and-saffron chowder on the terrace. After lunch, climb up to the estate's Tuscan-style tower for panoramic views of the grapes you've just tasted.

GUIDE

STAY
Hotel d'Urville
52 Queen St., Blenheim;
64-3/577-9945;
durville.com. **$$**

Highfield Estate
Brookby Rd., Blenheim;
64-3/572-9244;
highfield.co.nz.

TASTE
Allan Scott
Jacksons Rd., Blenheim;
64-3/572-9054;
allanscott.com.

Cloudy Bay
Jacksons Rd., Blenheim;
64-3/520-9140;
cloudybay.co.nz.

ANTARCTICA

The world's most epic adventure

INTREPID GLOBE-TROTTERS ARE ALWAYS one-upping each other with tales of their latest travel conquests. But a journey to the ends of the earth—that is, Antarctica—is guaranteed to put you ahead of the pack.

Such a once-in-a-lifetime experience can be made in luxury thanks to White Desert, a company that leads treks through the Antarctic interior. From Cape Town, a private plane jets you across the Southern Ocean to Whichaway Camp, a solar-and-wind–powered base of six fiberglass sleeping pods and three living-and-dining tents connected by sheltered passageways. The trip caters to a variety of interests and activity levels: Founder and modern-day explorer Patrick Woodhead (who first made the voyage a century after Ernest Shackleton's ill-fated 1904 attempt) will guide you through all manner of exploits, from kite skiing and ice climbing to visiting the 6,000 emperor penguins that colonize the nearby Ekström Ice Shelf. One couple recently spent their time photographing ice waves, massive breakers frozen in a permanent swirl. Still, there's no shame in simply curling up in the camp's pods, which are snugly outfitted with cowhide rugs and heaters trimmed in leather and brass. Just don't forget to bring your sleep mask: during the months the trip is offered (November through January), the sun shines 24 hours a day.

GUIDE

STAY
White Desert
*Three days from $33,685
per person, all-inclusive;
white-desert.com.*

AUSTRALIA + NEW ZEALAND + ANTARCTICA

279

A cold-weather take
on sunbathing outside
Whichaway Camp.

TRIPS DIRECTORY

INDEX

Cocktail hour
at the Colony
Palms Hotel,
in Palm Springs,
California.

CONTRIBUTORS

Christine Ajudua

Richard Alleman

Tom Austin

Aimee Lee Ball

Colin Barraclough

Raul Barreneche

Grace Bastidas

Thomas Beller

Kate Betts

Vinita Bharadwaj

Laura Begley Bloom

Anya von Bremzen

Alysha Brown

Dominique Browning

Stacey Brugeman

Karen Burshtein

Jennifer Chen

Colleen Clark

Rebecca Dalzell

Lara Day

Jonathan Durbin

Nina Fedrizzi

Michael Frank

Alice Gordon

Sue Gough Henly

Timothy Hornyak

Matthew Hranek

Karrie Jacobs

Howie Kahn

David Kaufman

David A. Keeps

Matt Lee

Ted Lee

Peter Jon Lindberg

Mimi Lombardo

Heather Smith MacIsaac

Andrew McCarthy

Daniel Mendelsohn

Karryn Miller

Heidi Mitchell

Shane Mitchell

Niloufar Motamed

Reggie Nadelson

Kathryn O'Shea-Evans

Brooke Porter

Mariana Rapoport

Mark Robinson

Karina Rodríguez

Douglas Rogers

Frank Rose

Adam Sachs

Bruce Schoenfeld

Maria Shollenbarger

Gary Shteyngart

Emma Sloley

Andrew Solomon

Guy Trebay

Brooke Le Poer Trench

Stephen Wallis

Valerie Waterhouse

Jane Wooldridge

Lynn Yaeger

Nora Zelevansky

A fashionable
young local in
Ho Chi Minh City,
Vietnam.

PHOTOGRAPHERS

Keepsakes from an island vacation at St. Lucia's Hotel Chocolat.